DOGS &
DOG CARE

FEEDING, GROOMING, BREEDING, TRAINING, HEALTH CARE AND FIRST AID

DOGS &
DOG CARE

A directory of 175 breeds and practical advice on choosing the right pet

DR PETER LARKIN

WITH MIKE STOCKMAN

LORENZ BOOKS

Contents

Introduction

The dog is our oldest companion. Humans and dogs came together thousands of years ago for mutual comfort, and slowly developed the interdependence seen today – caring for the dog in return for continuing companionship and a great variety of working functions.

The gradual recognition of the many different ways in which the dog could contribute to the association with mankind has led to the development of an enormous variety of dog types. All varieties of dog are members of a single species; it is the most varied of any species known, ranging from the tiny Chihuahua to the massive Irish Wolfhound or English Mastiff.

So close has the association of dog and human become that there are now probably only two breeds of truly wild dogs left – the Cape Hunting Dog and the Australian Dingo. Many countries, of course, have roaming packs of wild dogs that lead an independent existence, but these are invariably domestic dogs that have 'gone wild' for one of any number of reasons.

To a remarkable extent, a dog of any breed can mate with another of any other breed and produce fertile offspring. This fact has led to even more varieties developing over the centuries, as new functions and fashions were conceived. The Kennel Club currently cites 222 recognized pedigree breeds, whereas the American Kennel Club lists 199 and the World Canine Organisation recognizes about 350. The precise figure is impossible to determine, because previously unrecognized breeds continue to emerge, and types of the same breed are recognized as distinct; or conversely, varieties previously considered as separate can become combined as one breed.

As part of this continuing evolutionary process, some breeds have also died out; several have disappeared even in the last 100 years, possibly due to reduced fertility or the particular type ceasing to be fashionable. Loss of the traditional function of a breed may be another reason, but more often the breed has changed

▲ ▼ *All dogs are members of a single species,* Canis lupus familiaris, *from the tiniest 15cm (6in) Chihuahua (above) to the massive 79cm (31in) Irish Wolfhound (below). Despite their differences in size, any breed can mate with any other breed and produce new varieties of dogs.*

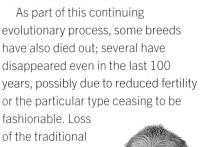

▲ *The bond between dog and human can be very strong and rewarding for both parties.*

in conformation to such an extent as to be almost unrecognizable as the original breed. The war dogs of old, for instance, have developed into the civilized mastiff types.

Although every breed of dog, in the Western World at least, is expected to be domesticated, certain type characteristics tend to persist through many generations, and these are not just characteristics of conformation. Everyone realizes that if you buy a Great Dane puppy, for instance, small though it may be at eight weeks old, it will grow into a very large dog. If you buy a terrier of any breed, it will have terrier behaviour characteristics, inherited from its working ancestors.

If you have decided to buy a dog, look into all the breed characteristics, and consider them carefully before you decide which type of dog you want to live with. A dog may live for 10–20 years; it is yours to care for over a significant portion of your life.

▲ Putting in the time to train your dog is essential for safety reasons, and must be considered before purchase.

IN THIS BOOK

This book is organized into four main sections. The first part includes Getting Started – which gives advice on how to choose the right dog for your lifestyle, as well as practical information about equipment and safety; Nutrition and Feeding; Grooming; and Breeding – which covers everything from things to consider beforehand through to the mating process, pregnancy, whelping and rearing puppies.

Training Your Dog provides step-by-step instructions for how to turn a new puppy or untrained animal into a well-behaved member of the family. All the most important commands are covered, including 'sit', 'down', 'leave it', 'stay', 'wait' and 'settle down', as well as walking nicely on a lead, coming back when called, and dealing with issues such as digging, jumping up and biting.

Health Care explains how to keep your pet in the best condition possible. There is veterinary advice on first aid, neutering, spaying and breeding, as well as holistic approaches such as hydrotherapy and homeopathy.

▶ The Cavachon hybrid is believed to have been first produced in the United States in the mid-1990s. It can have a curly coat like a Bichon, or a flatter coat similar to a Cavalier. It is impossible to tell which kind you will get when they are small puppies.

▲ Play brings great pleasure to both dog and owner, so it is worth training your dog to play nicely.

Finally, The Breeds is an illustrated directory of more than 175 of the main dog breeds of the world, including hounds, gundogs, terriers, utility, working and herding dogs and toy breeds, and also a few of the most popular unrecognized breeds and hybrids. For every type of dog, a 'Breed box' panel summarizes the animal's size, grooming and feeding requirements, exercise needs and general temperament.

GETTING STARTED

A great deal of thought and discussion should precede
your decision to get a puppy. It is important to choose
a breed that will fit in with your lifestyle; for example,
it would be foolhardy to acquire a dog that needs an
excessive amount of exercise if you lead a sedentary
lifestyle. You need to decide if you can put up with the
amount of hair some breeds shed; if not, you should look
for a non-moulting breed. Whittle down your long list to
a few select breeds, and try not to go for looks alone.
Ask around vet surgeries and other pet owners to find the
best breeder you can. It is also important to take into
consideration the costs of your puppy — not just the
purchase price, but the cost of vaccinations, health
checks, food and equipment. Good puppy classes are
an added expense. Owning a dog is not cheap, but
well worth the love and affection that you get in return.

◄ *Before getting a dog, such as this Norfolk terrier, it is important to ensure that
you can provide it with the environment it needs.*

What type of dog?

Dogs are companions. If you want one just as a guard, buy a burglar alarm. Dogs are usually effective burglar deterrents, whatever their breed, but their first function in a home must be as a friend – and there is no better friend. They don't criticize you (or not too unkindly), they don't sulk (or not for too long), and they are always there to comfort you and love you.

Choosing the right breed is an intensely personal matter, but there are broad guidelines.

The size of the fully grown dog is important, but perhaps not quite so critical as it may seem. Very large dogs need a lot of exercise, and once you have decided that there is room in your house for a large dog, exercise is the most important consideration. Most people, however, want a dog that fits reasonably into the home environment. A couple of Wolfhounds may be your ideal, but their bulk may make a small living space uninhabitable.

◄ Dogs enjoy the companionship of other dogs, with some surprising friendships emerging. Adult size is an important consideration when deciding which breed is right for you.

The Labrador Retriever, if not overweight, weighs about 30kg (66lb) when mature, and according to kennel club statistics it is the most popular dog in both the UK and the USA. Second in the USA is the German Shepherd Dog, and third the Golden Retriever. In Britain, the Cocker Spaniel is second,

with the French Bulldog being the third most popular breed. These statistics can only be tracked by applications for kennel club registrations and take no account of the numbers of hybrids or unrecognized breeds, both of which have seen a dramatic increase in popularity in recent years.

▲ The Labrador Retriever belongs to the Gundog Group and loves long walks and splashing in water.

▲ Terriers come in a range of sizes, but most tend to be rather 'sharp' and are not afraid to give a warning nip.

▲ Many dogs in the Toy Group, such as this Cavalier King Charles Spaniel, are active and not just lap dogs.

◄ *Most dogs love chasing toys. This is helpful in exercising highly active breeds from the Working and Herding Groups.*

Looking at past statistics, there appears to be a gradual swing in the UK from owning large dogs to owning those of a smaller size. There is no clear reason for this, but it may be influenced by house size.

Breed or type behaviour is probably more important in choosing a dog than any other characteristic. It pays to ask

not just dedicated owners, but also knowledgeable people outside the breed – your veterinary surgeon sees a wide variety of dogs every day.

Typically, the terrier types are lively, not easy to train, but very responsive dogs. If they are properly trained, they are good with children.

Toy dogs are usually better companions for owners who do not have young children. The dogs may be upset by what they perceive as large, noisy humans rushing around. Their fear may make them snappy, with unhappy results. All toy dogs will enjoy as much exercise as you can give them, but they may be equally content with only a moderate amount.

Hounds need as much exercise as possible. If this condition is met, they make very good house dogs who love their comfort. Breeds in the other groups vary, but, in general, the working breeds are all better with an occupation that keeps them out of mischief.

The gundog (sporting) breeds are generally easy to train, and settle into the human environment without difficulty. They need exercise – and lack of exercise shows!

Certain animals of the herding breeds, typified by the Border Collie, are, or should be regarded as, specialist working dogs. They demand more attention than other breeds if they are not to become neurotic pets. Outside their traditional working function, they have become the outstanding type in obedience work of all sorts. Provided you are able to give sufficient attention to them to keep their very active minds occupied, they are among the most rewarding of pets. But if you don't, they will find something to occupy themselves, and it will be trouble.

With so many breeds to choose from, as well as crossbreeds and mongrels, there really isn't a typical household pet these days.

▲ *The Otterhound will follow an interesting scent regardless of the owner's entreaties to come back.*

► *This charming Bernese puppy will make a beautiful house pet, but it will grow to 70cm (27½in) at the shoulder when fully mature.*

The cost of keeping a dog

Can you afford it? Buying a dog is just the start. Very few puppies can be acquired for nothing. Almost everyone will want to sell the litter they have reared, even if only to try to recoup the cost of feeding the puppies to weaning.

The cost of good pedigree puppies varies from country to country. In the United Kingdom, depending on breed, a puppy may cost from around £500, although probably the average cost of a well-bred puppy of most breeds is between £600 and £1,000. In the United States, asking prices are usually somewhat higher, from about $1,600 upwards. Australian prices are similar to those in the UK. Imported puppies in any country may cost a great deal more.

The initial examination by the veterinary surgeon, and the puppy's primary inoculations, will be around another £65, perhaps $95 in the USA, and you can spend as much as you wish on toys and other equipment.

A substantial part of the price of keeping a dog may be the cost of veterinary treatment. These days, veterinary surgeons are capable of sophisticated treatments of illness or injury, but they have no subsidy for the costs. If your dog ever needs complicated or prolonged veterinary treatment, the cost may be high.

There are many pet insurance companies catering for veterinary treatments; each has its own approach, and dog owners would be well advised to study what each company offers before deciding which policy to buy.

The premium-grade policies offer sums for the death of your dog, and for rewards to be offered if the dog is lost. They may include kennelling fees

▲ *A fair return for the cost of keeping a dog may be the exercise it encourages its owner to take.*

in case of your own illness, and even holiday cancellation costs. The level of veterinary fees covered is variable on most schemes, and it may be worth discussing this with your veterinary surgeon before you choose a policy. All additions cost money.

▼ *Puppies need vaccinations and annual boosters, and this cost is not covered under any insurance scheme.*

◄ *When considering a puppy, the price of good training and socializing classes should be factored into the overall cost.*

Some companies offer a basic veterinary fee insurance as an alternative to the premium schemes. It will be up to you to decide which of the various forms of insurance best fits your own needs.

Most insurers offer a puppy scheme, sometimes with an incentive to transfer to the adult scheme when it expires. Many breeders will offer puppy insurance to buyers, either as part of or as an extra cost to the purchase price of the puppy.

Feeding costs vary greatly. In theory, the smaller the dog, the less expensive it is to feed, but this is frequently offset by choosing more specialized, and therefore more expensive, foods for the very small pet. It is possible to feed a 14kg (31lb) dog very adequately for about £5.00 ($6.00) a week, provided that it is a healthy adult.

▼ *A large dog such as this Great Dane will cost at least £1.50 ($1.80) per day to feed. As well as the cost of food, if you don't have a local safe place to exercise your dog, daily travel costs can also quickly mount up.*

▼ *Older dogs benefit from regular veterinary check-ups and may be prescribed ongoing medication.*

▼ *Buying budget food is not a saving if your dog won't eat it. Household scraps are not a healthy option.*

▼ *The superb grooming of this Maltese may be achieved by a professional at considerable cost.*

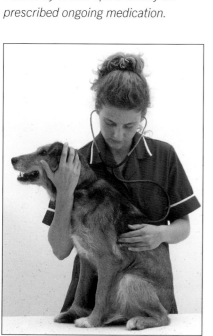

Pedigree or non-pedigree

Crossbred dogs, the most identifiable of which is the Lurcher, are usually not expensive to buy, which is an obvious advantage. They have their own 'mutt' charm, and their apparent type may be just what you are looking for. But remember that the tiny puppy may become an enormous adult. The best way to judge is to see both parents, but in the nature of things the father is likely to be 'away on business' when the puppies are ready to leave.

It is not necessarily true that crossbred dogs are healthier than purebreds, as many people believe. Every veterinary surgeon can tell you about crossbreds or mongrels suffering from recognizable, inherited diseases.

The advantage of choosing a purebred dog is that you know what you are getting. From a reputable

◄ *If you choose a pedigree dog, you must still look for a strain in that breed that fits your lifestyle. Gundogs, such as this Irish Red and White Setter, can come from a 'working' or a 'show' strain.*

breeder, a Cocker Spaniel puppy will grow up into a Cocker Spaniel dog, of a size and weight that is within the breed norm, and with potential behaviour characteristics typical of the breed. There is, or should be,

advice available to deal with whatever problems may arise as a particular feature of the breed.

There is no doubt that many breeds have inherited problems associated with that breed, although these have often been exaggerated in the press. It is up to the potential owner to enquire about these problems, and to take independent advice on their significance. It is worth bearing in mind that no species of animal, including human beings, is free from inheritable disease. Dogs may actually be less afflicted than most.

◄ *A lovable mongrel. Did its owners know how it was going to turn out, and have they got the time to give that coat the attention it demands?*

▶ *Crossbred dogs are often the basis for new working types. A cross between two recognized breeds is likely to have characteristics somewhere between the two.*

Dog or bitch

▼ *Unless you are planning to breed a litter, it is wise to have a bitch spayed.*

Choosing whether to have a male or female — a dog or a bitch — is one of the earliest decisions you will make.

Dogs tend to have a more 'macho' outlook on life than bitches, and if that attracts you, the male of the species will be your choice. Dogs are possibly more outgoing, certainly on average a little harder to train, but often more responsive once trained.

They do not, of course, come into season twice a year, with the attendant bother of oestrous discharges, and the attraction of all the dogs in the neighbourhood. But don't forget that it is the male dogs that are attracted, and if you have a male, it could be yours that has to be dragged home each night from his wanderings.

▼ *In general, a male dog — such as this Airedale Terrier — is broader, heavier and more muscular, and therefore stronger, than a bitch.*

On balance, if there is such a thing in this particular choice, the female is likely to make a better family pet. She is less likely to be aggressive, although dominance is as much a breed characteristic as it is related to the gender of the dog. Bitches are much less likely to try to wander for most of the year, and they are inclined to be more loving to their human family.

▼ *Both dogs and bitches can be equally aggressive if not trained and socialized correctly. Bitches are more focused on their owners, which can make the training process easier.*

▼ *Neutering a male dog is cheaper than spaying a bitch, because the former operation is less intrusive.*

Buying a puppy

Let us assume that you know more or less the type of dog you feel you can best live with. The next step is to look for the right breeder — not necessarily the top one in the breed, who would expect a premium price for puppies of show standard. Many dogs are still sold through so-called 'puppy farms' and pet shops. Neither is a suitable place to find a puppy. Take your time, and be prepared to wait to get the dog you really want. Above all, visit the kennels and make sure you see the dam with the puppies in the litter (and other litters), and, if possible, the sire.

There is some argument about the right age to buy a puppy, although the general consensus seems to be that about eight weeks is right. Much before that may be too early to remove the puppy from the nest, while leaving it later can give rise to socialization problems, with the time between six and eight weeks regarded by behaviourists as a critical period in the puppy's development. Certainly, if the puppy is much older than eight weeks, you need to be satisfied that it has been exposed to a sensible social environment and not simply left in its rearing kennel to make its own way.

Be honest with the breeder. If you are looking for a dog that you may later want to show, don't pretend that you are only looking for a pet puppy, in the hope that the price might be lower. Explain truthfully the life that the puppy will lead, especially its home environment. Never expect a guarantee that your puppy will be a show winner. Even though it comes from the very best show stock, with a pedigree as long as your arm, no one can pick a 'cert' at eight weeks.

The breeder should provide you with the puppy's pedigree and a receipt for its purchase. If the breeder has already taken the puppies for their first inoculation, this may be included in the quoted price or regarded as an extra. You should ask.

You may be asked to sign a contract setting out the limitations of the breeder's liability in the event of the

▲ A 'pedigree puppy' should always come with a kennel club registration certificate, but this is not a guarantee of its health or temperament.

puppy later developing an inheritable condition. This is likely to consist of a statement drawing your attention to the known inheritable diseases of the breed, so you can't claim ignorance.

The breeder should provide you with a feeding chart for the next stage of rearing your puppy. It is worth taking this to discuss with the veterinary surgeon when you take your puppy for its first visit. Many breeders give the new owner some sample feed to start the puppy off in its new home.

You should expect a healthy puppy, which has been wormed adequately, probably twice, and is free from skin parasites such as fleas or lice.

Pet insurance companies have short-term cover schemes, available to breeders for issue to new owners. Ask the breeder if they have such cover. If not, arrange your own as soon as you have bought the puppy. Puppies are at their most vulnerable during the first few weeks in their new home.

◄ Retrievers tend to have very large litters, often ten or more. Weaning can start as early as three weeks with suitable supplements.

Choosing a puppy

Never accept excuses about a puppy's condition or behaviour, and never buy a puppy because it's the last one left and you feel sorry for it.

It is often said that puppies choose their new owners rather than the other way around, and there is much truth to this claim. An overly shy puppy may have socialization problems later, and the puppy that comes forward from the nest, asking to be chosen, is probably the right one.

The puppy must be alert and have bright, clean eyes. Its nose must be clean (but forgive a little crust of food), its ears must be free of wax, and its coat must be clean and pleasant to handle and smell. There must be no sign of sores or grittiness on the skin and coat. Black 'coal dust' is usually flea dirt — fleas themselves are more difficult to spot. Examine all the puppies briefly to ensure that they have been well cared for.

▲ Make sure there is no discharge from the eyes. Forgive a scratch or two on the face — puppies in the nest don't always agree.

▲ The membranes of the nose must be clear and free of discharge. There must be no sign of a runny nose. Check the puppy is not coughing or wheezing.

▲ The inside of the ears must look pink and shiny, without inflammation or dark-coloured wax. The area should not look sore.

▲ Soreness or inflammation of the rims of the eyes, or eyes that are not completely clear, may be serious signs of present or potential disease.

▲ The puppy's coat and skin should feel loose and soft. The skin should be free of sores. There should be no baldness or patches of hair loss.

▲ Sturdy, strong limbs are a must for any breed, although if you fancy an Italian Greyhound, don't expect it to be this sturdy.

▲ Puppies should have a clean bottom. Signs of diarrhoea are obvious from a quick examination behind. The whole litter should be examined.

Settling in

Bringing home a new puppy or even an older dog is an important family occasion. Everyone wants to touch, hold and stroke the new member of the family, especially the children. But you should take things slowly.

In the case of a puppy, this will be its first time away from the only environment it has ever known, and away from its mother and litter mates. The world is huge and frightening. For an older dog, there is still a lot of adjusting for it to do.

Bring it home when there are not too many people around, and introduce it to its new environment in as relaxed a manner as possible. Let it look and sniff around, offer it a little something to eat, which it probably won't accept, and allow it to have a run around the garden. Bring your family and friends to meet the dog one or two at a time, and give it time to make friends before introducing anyone else.

▶ *Puppies hate to be left alone until they are confident that you will quickly return.*

▶ *Puppies' curiosity about new toys helps to overcome their awe of strange surroundings.*

At some stage, you have to cause a little more trauma by taking the dog to the veterinary surgeon for a health check. If at all possible, take it to the vet on the way home from the breeder or kennels. If there should be a problem that necessitates returning the dog to the seller (fortunately, a very rare occurrence), it is going to be much easier if the family haven't met and already fallen in love with it.

Once the settling-in process has begun, interrupt the dog's established routine as little as possible. For a puppy, follow the breeder's feeding regime, giving the same number of feeds at the same time each day. To start with, give the food the dog is used to – the seller might have provided a 'starter pack' – even if you have decided eventually to use a different type of food. Make any dietary changes gradually.

Clean water should always be available; show the dog where it is. Make sure that not only is the water bowl always full, but that it is washed regularly – dogs are messy drinkers, and the bowl soon gets dirty. Most dogs, some breeds more than others, are also very splashy drinkers, spilling more water around the bowl than they

Safety guidelines on toys for dogs

The jaws and teeth of nearly all dogs are much stronger than you think, so toys should be very tough. Fluffy dolls will be torn to pieces, so if you must provide them, make sure that they do not have parts that can be detached and swallowed.

Balls are popular toys for dogs because the owners can throw them and join in the game. Fine, but make sure the ball is large enough not even to be half-swallowed by the dog. A dog being rushed to the vet choking on a tennis ball that is stuck in its throat is a common emergency.

The use of a bone as a toy is controversial. Most veterinary surgeons advise against it, unless the bone is so big that the dog cannot break pieces off and swallow them. There is no doubt that a good chew at a bone is a dog's delight.

▲ *Toys should be solid enough not to risk pieces being chewed off and swallowed.*

swallow. So, it is important to choose the site for your water bowl carefully.

The ideal water bowl may be made of ceramic or non-rust metal, but it must be non-spill, and preferably too heavy for the dog to pick up and carry around. If you start with a heavy bowl, the puppy will soon get the idea that this is not a toy to be picked up and carted around, and it will look for something else to play with.

Feed bowls may be much the same as water bowls, with the same idea: the dog should not regard the bowl as a toy. Apart from anything else, if the bowl gets carried around, you can never find it when you want to feed the dog at mealtimes!

The new dog's bed is also very important – the bed is the dog's own special place. It is important to introduce the dog to its bed as soon as it arrives, and to insist that the bed is where it sleeps. This may be difficult, but if you give in and let it

▼ *Puppies take great comfort from a hot-water bottle, but beware leaks from chewing. A ticking clock seems to soothe them at night.*

sleep on your bed 'just until it settles in', you have lost the battle – and probably the war!

To make sure the dog uses its bed, the best way is to shut it into a 'bedroom' on the first night with nothing else to choose for a comfortable sleep but the bed. Make sure it is sited away from any draughts. Young puppies will miss their litter mates and perhaps their dam. A useful tip if the puppy doesn't settle – that is, if it is crying

◄ *Hygiene is important for feed bowls. Never add another meal without first thoroughly cleaning the bowl.*

▼ *Rawhide chews are usually an excellent substitute for bones.*

pitifully just as you are getting to sleep – is to provide it with comforters. Traditionally, these are a hot-water bottle and a ticking clock, and like many traditions, they often work well.

Toys are important, whatever the age of the dog, but particularly for a young puppy. There is an enormous range on sale, from fluffy dolls that amuse the owner but soon become unrecognizable once the puppy has had a chance to tear them apart, to specifically designed training aids.

Some dogs are obsessive about a particular toy – this occurs more in the terrier breeds than in other types – but mostly dogs have a rather short attention span, dropping one object for another after a short spell of play. Each dog has a different fancy, but do provide choice for a puppy, bearing all safety guidelines in mind.

Beds and bedding

The dog must have a bed of its own. From the owner's point of view, washability is the priority. Plastic beds made for this purpose are not expensive and easily cleaned, but they must have soft bedding for comfort.

Providing a mobile cage as a bed and a private place for your puppy has several advantages, not least of which is that there is somewhere to put the puppy when non-doggy friends, who may not appreciate dog hairs all over their clothes, arrive.

Cages may be the completely collapsible type, useful for folding and taking with you when you are travelling with the dog, or, probably better in the long run, the 'sky kennel' type, which is fastened by nuts and bolts around the middle. This enables the cage to be divided in half for travelling, but provides a more permanent kennel for the dog to use at home.

There are plenty of choices of bedding. The most satisfactory from the hygiene point of view, as well as for comfort and warmth, are veterinary

◄ Flexible dog beds seem to pass the comfort test. They are usually insulated against cold floors and are easily cleaned. They may be destructible by determined dogs, and can be quite expensive.

brand names, made of synthetic fur backed by a strong woven base. These veterinary beds may be machine-washed, they stay dry because moisture goes straight through them, they are long-lasting, and they are resistant (but not if the

dog is really determined!) to being chewed up. They can be bought or cut to any size, and using the principle of 'one on, one in the wash', you can easily keep the bed clean and free from doggy odours. Wash on a 30°C (85°F) cycle.

▼ Left to right: An old blanket is best in a bed rather than just on the floor; synthetic veterinary bedding is probably more hygienic than any other soft bedding; the bean

bag is supremely comfortable and warmly insulating; a plastic basket is easily cleaned, but it does need a comfortable lining to be given the dog's personal accolade.

◄ Dogs all appreciate a warm covering to lie on, wherever they choose to sleep. Ideally, this should be in a quiet spot away from traffic, but where the dog can still keep an eye on its family. Every dog needs a place to call its own.

Behaviour tip

Dogs will often accept your displeasure if it means you are paying attention to them rather than ignoring them. To ignore your dog is the most severe punishment you can inflict. So for peaceful nights for you and your dog, make it sleep elsewhere.

▼ *A dog's bed should be a place of safety and comfort, not somewhere to be sent to as a punishment.*

Cushions filled with a memory foam or orthopaedic pad are possibly the most comfortable beds. Those filled with polystyrene granules are popular but difficult to wash. Some dogs enjoy chewing their bed, and this results in a myriad little polystyrene balls rolling around the floor, which are almost impossible to sweep up.

Still probably more used than anything else is a square of old blanket or a blanket off-cut. There

▼ *An outside kennel must always be dry, warm and of an adequate size to ensure your dog's comfort.*

is nothing wrong with them, provided you have enough so that you can wash them regularly, bearing in mind that they leave a fluffy deposit that needs to be removed from the washing machine, and they take forever to dry.

WHERE TO SLEEP

The kitchen or a warm utility room are the best places for a dog to sleep. The kitchen floor often has non-absorbent flooring, useful for a puppy before it is able to avoid accidents. Once it has become accustomed to the kitchen, if it remains convenient to you, this is possibly the best place for the dog to stay. The kitchen tends to be one of the warm places in the house, and dogs like warmth.

Most dogs are not kennelled outdoors. There is no particular reason why they should not be, and if that is your intention, it must be instituted from the start. Use plenty of warm bedding and pay attention to draughts and waterproofing.

One problem with outside kennels, however, is that it becomes too easy to ignore the dog. Few owners would indulge in the outright cruelty of neglecting to feed their dog, but if the weather doesn't look too good, plenty would put off the walk until another day. If a dog is to be confined in a kennel, you must ask yourself if you really want a dog. At worst, the kennel must provide an adequate exercise area, as well as the essentials mentioned here.

▼ *A basket containing a cushion and a washable fleece makes a comfortable and practical bed.*

Equipment

Pet shops and online sites sell a wide array of basic equipment, and it is essential that you have done your homework in advance, knowing the most suitable collars and the best types of lead to buy. Under UK law, your dog will need to wear a flat collar with an identification disc containing your name and address, and without these details you could be fined £5,000. Even if your dog has been microchipped, it will still need a collar and disc. Microchipping of all dogs became compulsory in the UK in 2016. In many European countries, dogs need to be microchipped and/or tattooed An identification tag is required in the USA, while some states also require that your dog has a licence.

FLAT COLLARS

A flat collar with a buckle or clip fastening is by far the best piece of equipment for training your dog.

▼ *A flat collar with either a buckle or clip fastening is suitable for training.*

◀ There is a vast array of basic dog control equipment on the market, such as flat collars, head collars and body harnesses. If possible, try before you buy.

When your dog is fully grown, it is a good idea to buy the best you can afford. A leather collar is the most hard-wearing and is kind on your hands and the dog's neck. Puppies tend to grow quickly, so an ajustable collar for them is a wise buy.

If you buy a collar with a clip fastening, regularly check that it doesn't become loose and that you cannot pull it apart, because if your dog pulls away and the clip fastening comes undone, your dog could end up in the road, causing an accident.

HEAD COLLARS

These are devised to work in the same way as reins on many large animals such as horses, bulls and camels: they steer the animal from the head instead of the strongest part of the body – the neck and shoulders. There are varous types and designs of head collar available, and it is worth trying several to find the one that your dog feels most comfortable in.

▼ *A body harness has thick straps, but may encourage your dog to pull more.*

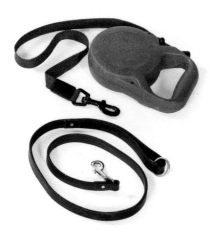

▼ *Retractable leads are popular, but a leather lead is better for training.*

All head collars must be correctly fitted and be the right size for the dog.

There are positive and negative sides to head collars, and they can take some getting used to. It is worth putting one on your dog before giving it a treat, so that it associates it with pleasure, then take it off. Gradually let your dog get used to it. Some dogs scratch their faces along the floor, trying to get the head collar off, or rub themselves up and down your legs because they do not like the feel of it. The problem is it can be hard for the dog to concentrate on what you want it to do if it is uncomfortable wearing a head collar. If it keeps pulling on it while being trained, it could end up walking sideways, which can damage its neck.

Head collars are often mistaken for muzzles, and so other dog walkers may give you a wide berth when out walking. On the other hand, a head collar is useful for stopping an aggressive dog from staring at other dogs. A head collar should not be left on an unattended dog, as it might get caught up on something, causing the dog stress or injury. If your dog really does not like a head collar, then you could consider using a body harness instead.

BODY HARNESSES

There is a wide choice of body harnesses on the market, but choose wisely. The best kinds have a front and back or side attachment, and need a double-ended lead, which means that your dog cannot pull you from its strongest point – its shoulders. The weight is evenly distributed by the lead being attached to the front and side or back of the harness. The harness stays away from the dog's neck area and won't interfere with its natural body language when approaching another dog.

Avoid those with very thin harness straps, because they can chafe under the dog's legs and cause pain and discomfort. Look for a body harness with wide straps and padding.

Most basic harnesses are unsuitable for training your dog to stop pulling, and you only have to watch a team of huskies to understand how the harness lets them pull. A fixed harness without the use of a double-ended lead can only encourage your dog to pull, the lead being attached to the back and front of the harness in the middle of the chest. Specialist harnesses are available to help stop a dog pulling while on the lead, but these are not generally available in smaller pet shops.

LEADS

Always buy the best you can afford. Avoid chain leads, as these can hurt your hands. A range of materials is available, from leather through to braided fabric; they should be soft and pliable while still retaining strength. Always check that the clip that attaches to the collar is both strong and of good quality.

Retractable leads are very popular but are not suitable for training, because they can actually encourage dogs to pull, since they allow the animal to go to the end of the lead. In some situations they can be dangerous, with the lead getting tangled around your legs or another dog's feet, which could lead to a fight. Your dog could also run out into the road if you are not quick enough to put on the lock, and the lock mechanism could fail, resulting in a car accident.

Retractable leads are made in differing breaking strain, so check that the one you intend to use is suitable for the weight of your dog. A retractable lead should only be put on your dog when you have arrived at the location where it is going to be walked.

CRATES

A crate is absolutely essential for the puppy owner. It is an invaluable aid to house-training, because you can contain your puppy when you cannot watch it – puppies dislike messing the

▼ *A crate is useful for house-training and for taking your dog in the car.*

area that they sleep in, and so will cry to be let out to go to the toilet.

A crate also provides a safe place for times when you cannot supervise your dog. It makes a snug sleeping space and an area of safety in the car. However, never keep your dog locked up in a crate for hours, and don't use it as punishment. Get a crate that is large enough for when your dog becomes an adult, and in which it will be able to stand up and move around.

Light-weight fabric crates are ideal for travel but are not as easily cleaned as the folding metal type. They are not suitable for a dog that is not used to being crated, as they can turn over if the dog makes any energetic moves inside. They are also not the best option for puppies or for dogs that are likely to chew the fabric.

FOOD AND WATER BOWLS
There are many types of bowls on the market. The best are the stainless-steel bowls that are hard-wearing and tough. Cheaper plastic bowls should be avoided – they can be easily chewed, and splinters could cut your dog's mouth or be swallowed.

Some dogs benefit from specialist bowls. Spaniel bowls have a wide base, narrower top and sloping sides that cause their long ears to fall outside of the bowl and not get covered with the contents. Some food bowls have plastic ridges or knobbles at the bottom, which make it harder for a greedy dog to bolt its food. Stands are available to raise the bowl to a comfortable level. This is helpful for the veteran dog that may have back ache or a stiff neck. Many vets recommend the use of raised bowls for all dogs.

TREAT BAGS AND WASTE BAGS
Any small bag that can hang around your waist can be used to carry treats. Waste bags should also be carried at all times. Eco-friendly biodegradable waste bags are available at most pet shops. Nappy (diaper) bags are an economical alternative.

▲ *Groom your dog every week. Its coat will benefit, and it will enjoy the attention and get used to being held.*

BRUSHES AND COMBS
Even if you have a short-haired dog, it is a good idea to brush it once a week to keep its coat in good condition and to stimulate the skin and circulation.

▼ *Match the size of the food bowl you choose to the size of your dog.*

▼ *There are many types of food bowls, including stainless steel and ceramic. Both of these are strong, long-lasting and easy to keep clean.*

▼ *Single or double raised bowl stands are available in different heights and diameters to accommodate the particular needs of your dog.*

▼ *A huge range of toys and equipment are available that allow the owner and dog to interact together. These can be used as rewards when training.*

▼ *Some toys allow the dog to self-reward, by making a noise when they are played with. These are fun for the dog, but can become annoying for the owner.*

CLICKERS, WHISTLES AND TOYS

Useful training aids such as clickers and whistles are available from most pet shops, and there are more toys on the market for dogs now than ever before. There are tug toys, interactive toys, educational toys, home-alone toys, teething toys, training toys and ball-on-a-rope toys. There are squeaky toys for terriers, fetch toys for retrievers, and balls for collies.

One of the best-selling dog toys is the Kong, an interactive stuffable toy that can keep any dog quiet for hours. Stuffing it with some of your dog's daily diet will teach it that it is rewarding to be left home alone. It can also be used to reward your dog for being calm when you have visitors, and will keep it busy if it has to be shut in its crate for any amount of time.

It is neither wise nor economical to buy cheap plastic toys, especially for puppies. Cheap toys are easily ripped apart by sharp teeth, and they are usually made of hard plastic that can lodge in the puppy's tummy and cause an expensive trip to the vet.

Do not throw sticks for dogs – these can puncture the skin, damage the mouth, and even prove to be fatal.

CLOTHING

From the bizarre to the practical, there is an almost unlimited choice of dog clothing. For dogs that live in centrally heated homes, protection against the cold and rain is an important issue. Duvet-style coats come in all shapes and sizes, and will keep your dog warm on even the coldest winter day. Older dogs and those with arthritis will benefit from the additional warmth. Heat-reflecting or cool coats stop your canine companion from over-heating on hot summer days.

Waterproof apparel serves two purposes: the dog is comfortable, and the home is not spoiled by wet mud. Water-resistant fleece jumpers are very popular and easy to clean after a country walk. Boots are available to prevent or to protect sore feet.

Designer products command high prices, but as long as the clothing is comfortable to wear, easy to clean and fit for purpose, your dog will not mind what name is on the label.

▼ *The range of dog clothing is enormous and includes everything from heat-reflective coats to faux fur jackets.*

Home, garden and car safety

Of immediate interest to most new dog owners is the need to make the home and garden dog-proof. This may prove to be difficult and costly.

INSIDE THE HOME

Prior to bringing a puppy or dog into your house, look around and try to eliminate some of the dangers. All electrical flexes should be tidied away or clipped neatly to the wall. Fitting safety covers to unused floor-level power sockets is a good idea.

Some houseplants are toxic to dogs, including African violets, calla lilies, hyacinth bulbs, mother-in-law's tongue and poinsettia. The Internet is a useful source of information, and any suspect plants should be removed or placed out of reach.

Puppies are no respecters of your ornaments, and these also need to be placed out of reach. Not only can they get broken, but the resulting shards of china or glass can cause injury to you and your dog.

Cleaning solutions are poisonous to humans and animals alike. They are often stored in low-level cupboards that are not lockable, for example under the kitchen sink. It is possible to buy childproof catches for kitchen cupboards. If your dog manages to get hold of any of these items and pierces the container, there is a strong likelihood that they may have inhaled, swallowed or got splashed with corrosive chemicals. Prompt veterinary advice should be sought. Remember to take the container with you if you have to visit the vet, so that they know what they are dealing with.

Childproof locks should be used on the refrigerator or freezer if the door opens at or just above floor level. We

▶ A childproof gate designed for children also works well for puppies.

store many foods that are potentially lethal to dogs. Chocolate, blue cheese, grapes and any food containing raisins can, at best, cause sickness and diarrhoea, and at worst, death. Food waste needs to be stored safely. Dogs quickly learn how to operate a pedal or swing bin. Gorging on the contents may be fun at the time, but the resulting stomach problems from eating plastic, sharp bones and food that is well past its best are not so pleasant, and can be life-threatening.

Internal glass or patio doors may not seen by an excited puppy, who may run into them. Most doors of this type contain safety glass, but it is worth checking. Dogs must be trained to be calm in the house and not to charge through doors in front of their owner.

Prescribed human medication is often left lying around. Place all medicines in a drawer or high cabinet. If you drop a tablet, look for it straight away – do not leave it.

Small children have a habit of not putting their toys away. These brightly coloured objects are irresistible to child and dog alike, and are a choking hazard. Keep small toys in a safe place.

Keeping your home safe for your dog takes a little time, lots of common sense and some financial investment, but it will be a cheap price to pay for peace of mind.

FENCING

You have a responsibility in law to keep your dog under control. This means that your garden must be fenced in such a way as to prevent the dog escaping. As the puppies of almost any breed other than the very smallest grow, so does their ability to jump over fences. There can be no hard and fast rule for the height needed to prevent this; even within the same breed, one will be a jumper and another may never learn the skill. However, the minimum height for any dog-proof fence for anything but toy breeds will be 1m (3ft 3in). Often, for dogs from the smaller terrier breeds, such as Jack Russells, and the more agile larger breeds, this will not be sufficient. Plenty of dogs can scale a 2m (6ft 6in) fence. A fence this high starts to make the garden look like Fort Knox, and the usual compromise is a fence of about 1.5m (5ft). If it is a wire fence, it must be tightly strung. Many gardens are close-fenced to this height, and close fencing has advantages as a dog fence. Being unable to see the world outside often removes the temptation to investigate it.

There are two ways through a fence, even if it is in good repair. One way is over the top, and the other is underneath. Dogs enjoy digging. You need to be sure that there is no way under. Wire fencing is particularly vulnerable to the tunnelling dog, unless it is firmly attached to some sort of hard, impenetrable base.

Plants that are toxic to dogs

- African violet
- Amaryllis
- Asparagus fern
- Azalea
- Calla lily
- Cyclamen
- Daffodil
- Day lily
- Delphinium
- Foxglove
- Hyacinth
- Mother-in-law's tongue
- Poinsettia

GARDEN SAFETY

Even if you feel that the garden is securely fenced, it still contains other dangers. Young puppies can drown in the shallowest of ponds, and so these should either be covered with a mesh frame or fenced off.

Garage and shed doors need to be kept shut, and items such as pesticides, antifreeze, fertilizers and herbicides stored on a high shelf. Make sure your dog cannot access areas treated with weed killer.

There are many commonly grown plants that are poisonous to dogs. Even the best-trained dog may nibble at leaves and flowers, or dig up roots and bulbs. Websites, or your vet, give a comprehensive list of dangerous plants in your country. Daffodils, day lilies, foxgloves, delphiniums, azalea, amaryllis and asparagus fern are just a few examples of plants that are harmful to dogs, and should either be removed or carefully fenced off.

It is wise to shut your dog indoors when using electric or power tools in the garden. The electric flex of a lawnmower snaking across the grass may prove irresistible to the curious puppy or playful dog. Sadly, many dogs are electrocuted each year by biting live power cables.

Preventing the dog from escaping from the house is usually a matter of care rather than built-in precautions. The 'perfectly trained' dog will not push past its owner when the front door is opened unless required to do so, but in real life plenty of dogs try to. The family has to learn to keep the dog shut in the kitchen when anyone answers the door – one reason for not restraining the dog's barking when someone knocks at the front door; at least the dog is reminding you to shut it away. Downstairs windows, and occasionally upstairs windows, may attract the dog. It is a matter of vigilance unless you are prepared to barricade yourself in.

DOGS IN CARS

The idea of travelling with a dog in the car is very appealing, but in the event it sometimes becomes a nightmare. Part of the very earliest training for the puppy must be to learn to travel in a safe and socially acceptable way in the car. For the smaller breeds, a collapsible cage is ideal.

If your car is a hatchback, a dog guard is an obvious and sensible investment. It needs to be well fitting and strong enough to prevent a determined dog from climbing through it into the front of the car. There are dozens of dog guards designed specifically for each make and model of car. They are advertised in dog magazines and are available from most of the larger dog shows.

Unrestrained dogs in cars cause accidents and in the UK, and other

▶ *In the event of an accident, an unrestrained dog could be thrown forwards through the windscreen.*

▶ *Dogs may escape despite all precautions you take. Identity discs for collars should have at least one contact telephone number as well as your name and home address.*

countries, restraining your dog is a legal requirement. Harnesses, designed to clip to the rear seat belt fastening, are a way to keep the dog on the back seat if you must travel that way, but it is much better for them to be in the boot of the car, either in a crate or behind a dog guard. If using the latter, it is sensible to also use a harness, to stop the dog moving around too much. Take care nothing can fall on the dog and harm it.

Some dogs become 'barkers' when in the car. This is dangerous and distracting, and steps to remedy it must be taken before the behaviour becomes totally engrained. Specialist advice may be necessary, but the first step is to restrain the dog with a short lead below the window level of the car.

NUTRITION AND FEEDING

The diets of yesteryear, of home-mixed meat and biscuits, have long gone. Nowadays, professional nutritionists produce feeds of a variety and quality that should satisfy any dog, packaged in forms convenient enough to suit any owner. Nutrition is a complex subject, and there is a simple question: do you know more about the nutrition of the dog than the experts? Teams of nutritionists form part of a booming industry involving science, marketing and, most importantly, competition between feed companies. For modern dogs, palatability is considered to be of great importance, and the professional feed laboratories spend a great deal of time getting the flavour just right. Commercially produced food is carefully balanced to provide the correct level of components to aid and support the dog through the various stages of life. Breed-specific diets are also available, and even kibble size is variable to suit the needs of large or small dogs.

◀ *It is important to provide your dog, such as these Labrador Retriever puppies, with a nutritious diet that is appropriate for its age and activity level.*

Types of food

Dogs are carnivores. Their digestive system, from the mouth through their intestines, is designed to cope with a meat diet. The dog's teeth are adapted to tear food into swallowable-sized chunks rather than to grind the food in the mouth, and their stomachs can digest food in this state.

Dogs have probably evolved from animals that mostly lived on a diet of other animals. However, as with the fox in modern times, meat was not always available to them, and the dog is also able to digest and survive on a diet that is mostly vegetable; but a complete absence of meat is likely to lead to nutritional deficiencies.

Foods, whether for dogs or humans, have to supply energy, from which, as well as being the means of movement, the animal's body derives heat, materials for growth and repair, and substances that support these activities. For dogs, this involves a satisfactory mixture of the major nutrients – carbohydrates, fats and proteins – in proportions similar to those required for a healthy human diet. In addition, they must also have a sufficient intake of minor nutrients – vitamins and minerals – in proportions that do differ significantly from the needs of humans.

Dog foods may be divided into several broad categories. For many years, the so-called 'moist' diets held the major part of the market. They are the tinned foods seen on every supermarket shelf.

Over the past few years, other types of food have infiltrated the market. Complete dry feeds are becoming increasingly popular. They need minimal preparation – if desired, they can simply be poured into a dog bowl and given to the dog. It is only very slightly more demanding to pour hot water on to moisten the feed.

Semi-moist diets are not intended to provide a balanced diet on their own. They hold a small but significant place in the market, largely, in all probability, because they involve some degree of preparation before feeding. It is still fairly minimal, involving the addition of carbohydrate supplements as a mixer, often some form of biscuit, to balance the nutritional quality of the food. This is a psychologically important exercise for the owner, who likes to think that they are doing something for the dog, as previous generations did when they mixed a bowl of table scraps with some meat and gravy. The one thing to remember is that too much mixing of modern foods can result in nutritional problems. What happens too often is that the concerned owner adds not just a carbohydrate mixer, but high-protein feed as well, resulting in a diet that is unbalanced, with too much

▶ If a dog is hungry and healthy, it will eat. If it is healthy but won't eat, it isn't hungry, so take the food away and let it miss a meal.

Nutrients

The major nutrients, required in substantial quantities by every animal include the following:
- Carbohydrates, which provide the body with energy, and in surplus, will be converted into body fat.
- Fats, which are the most concentrated form of energy, producing more than twice as much energy, weight for weight, than carbohydrates, and which will also convert to body fats if supplied in excess.
- Proteins, which essentially provide the body-building elements in the diet.

The minor nutrients include the vitamins, minerals and trace elements, which, although critical to the animal's health, are required in comparatively small amounts. The vitamins are usually divided into two groups:
- Fat-soluble: vitamins A, D, E and K.
- Water-soluble: the B complex vitamins and vitamin C.

▼ *Puppies should be introduced to solid food from about three weeks. This food needs to be soaked and mushy.*

▼ *Each dog should have its own bowl, although the food is often more interesting on the other dog's plate.*

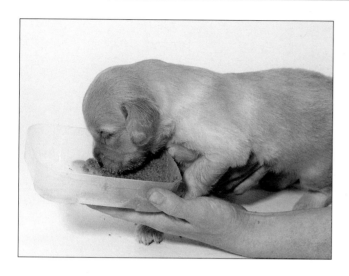

protein. There is usually no harm; animals, like humans, can deal with an astonishing variety of diet, but too high levels of protein can occasionally exacerbate an existing metabolic problem. There is an old adage, 'When all else fails, follow the instructions.' It is worth bearing this in mind when feeding your dog.

One feature of all modern compound dog foods is that they will contain adequate minor nutrients, which did not always happen in the meat and

biscuit days. The outcome is that there is rarely any need for the proprietary feed supplements that are still widely advertised. Calcium, for instance, may have been lacking in some traditional diets, and a bonemeal supplement often used to be recommended. Today, such a supplement may do harm in certain circumstances, such as pregnancy in the bitch.

Special diets have been developed over the years. These are generally of two types: first, those that target

healthy dogs with special requirements – puppies, for instance, with special growth needs, especially active dogs and older dogs; and second, those designed as supportive diets for various illnesses. There are kidney diets, for instance, which control the amount and type of protein the dog is given. These latter special diets are dispensed strictly under the control of a veterinary surgeon, many of whom are trained specifically in the use of such diets.

◄ *Canned food must be used within 24 hours of opening and kept refrigerated. Cover open cans with plastic lids, and reserve an opener and fork just for dog food.*

▶ *Dogs love bones, but vets don't because of the risks of bowel stoppages or choking. Very large bones minimize such risk. Never give a dog a chop or chicken bone.*

Food requirements

Dogs are adaptable creatures. They can, for instance, utilize protein foods for energy if their intake of carbohydrates is deficient. They must, however, be provided with a minimum level of each of around 30 nutrients, including the vitamins and minerals, if they are to stay healthy. All the modern prepared foods, and the great majority of home-mixed diets, will provide an adequate supply of essential nutrients.

Some animal protein is essential to maintain a dog's health. A vegetarian diet for dogs can be devised but requires skill, although there is no doubt that dogs do not need the level of animal protein in their diet that is commonly provided.

Some fats are also vital in the dog's diet, providing certain essential fatty acids, and acting as carriers for the fat-soluble vitamins.

Carbohydrates form the bulk of most diets, including normal dog foods, whether commercially compounded or home-mixed.

Provided your dog's diet has a reasonable balance of the major nutrients, and the foods are not themselves wildly out of the ordinary, the owner's concern need only be with the actual quantity given to the dog, and the total calorie provision.

▲ Butcher's scraps, canned or fresh, is not a complete feed.

▲ Canned chicken must be balanced with other foods.

▲ Cooked chicken is a cheap way of providing meat protein for small dogs.

▲ Commercial canned food may be a complete feed or mixed.

▲ Rice is a source of carbohydrates for home-mixing.

▲ Dry complete feeds have become very popular in recent years.

▲ Semi-moist feeds must be kept in sealed packets to keep them fresh.

▲ The traditional, old-fashioned dog feed of biscuits with gravy.

▲ Wholemeal biscuits are not adequate on their own as a dog's only food.

Average calorie requirements for 24 hours

Growing puppies	6 weeks	3 months	6 months
Terriers, mature weight 10kg (22lb)	330	530	700
German Shepherds, mature weight 30kg (66lb)	1,200	1,800	2,600
Giant breeds, mature weight 50kg (110lb)	1,950	2,500	4,000

Adult dogs	Maintenance
Terriers	400
German Shepherds	1,600
Giant breeds	2,400

At first sight, the figures in the table here suggest that the obvious and cheapest way to feed a dog is to give it biscuits alone. Dog biscuits offer the highest calorie content, weight for weight, of any food except pure fat, and they are cheaper to buy than canned foods. But this is misleading – a diet consisting solely of dog biscuits would be seriously deficient in protein, as well as fats, vitamins and minerals.

The table gives average amounts and should be regarded as a guide only. Take account of whether the mature dog on this level of food intake is gaining or losing weight. Puppies should gain weight steadily, without becoming too fat.

▲ *Meaty treats make excellent rewards when training your dog.*

▲ *Most dogs enjoy bone-shaped biscuits, and hard-baked (safer) bones.*

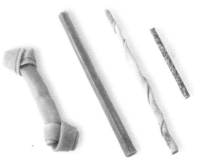

▲ *Raw or processed hide chews are a safe substitute for bones.*

▲ *Give only special-formula dog drops (see panel for chocolate warnings).*

▲ *Some biscuits include a charcoal variety, to help digestive problems.*

Chocolate and canines

Experts agree that certain chemicals in chocolate can be toxic to dogs, especially in large quantities. The chemical theobromine, found especially in dark (bittersweet) and baker's chocolate, can cause a toxic reaction, while caffeine may also lead to digestive problems.

Reactions will vary according to dog weight and sensitivity, and although most owners report few or no ill effects where only small amounts have been consumed, it is safest to avoid giving your dog any chocolate at all.

Calorie content of common food per 100g (3½oz)

- Dog biscuits used as mixer feeds — 300–360
- Fresh meat — 140
- Soft, moist, complete feeds — 320
- Dry complete feeds — 270

Manufacturer's declared calorie content per 100g (3½oz) in their canned foods (Hill's Science Diet)

- Canine Growth — 136
- Canine Maintenance — 126
- Canine Performance — 140
- Canine Maintenance Light — 87
- Canine Senior — 117

SPECIAL DIETS

Quality of feed is particularly
important during puppyhood, to
provide nutrients for the rapidly
growing animal. Similarly, an in-whelp
bitch needs high-quality food if she is
to produce healthy puppies without
putting undue strain on her own bodily
resources. Pregnant animals will
deplete their own tissues to provide
sufficient nutrients for their puppies,
both in the uterus and afterwards
when they are suckling. A bitch with
a litter of several puppies will almost
inevitably lose some weight; her
condition needs to be watched
carefully. However, there is no point
in over-feeding the bitch while she
is pregnant.

◄ *Regular veterinary
examination of older
dogs will reveal the
possible existence
of nutritionally
controllable diseases.*

There may be specific demands
for particularly active adult dogs, for
the older dog, and for the overweight
dog. Scientifically formulated diets are
designed to provide for these various
special requirements.

Several pet food manufacturers
provide prescription diets that, used
under veterinary supervision, aid
in the management of a number of
diseases. They are only obtainable
through a veterinary surgeon.

The range is wide and includes
products that may either contain
greater proportions of certain
nutrients than usual – one is a high-
fibre diet, for instance, which may be
of benefit in cases of diabetes, and in
fibre-responsive intestinal problems –
or smaller elements of the normal diet.
Low-protein diets assist in the control
of chronic kidney disease; low-sodium
diets are used in the management of
congestive heart failure.

► *If puppies share
a bowl of food, it is
difficult to be sure they
both get a fair share.*

OBESITY

One of the commonest afflictions in the dog is simple obesity. Owners will frequently not see it and, once acknowledged, it may still be extremely difficult for them to understand that reducing the dog's food intake is not cruel. The obesity diet has its part to play by enabling the owner to feed a low-calorie diet to the dog, which will satisfy the hunger pangs while reducing its intake of nutrients.

The table here indicates a suitable intake of calories for an overweight dog, with a target weight indicated in the first column. The diet needs to be balanced by sensible variations of other nutrients. Cooked green vegetables can be added to provide bulk to the ration.

Daily calorie requirement for the overweight dog

Target weight	Scale 1	Scale 2
2.5kg (5½lb)	120	90
5kg (11lb)	200	160
7kg (15½lb)	275	220
10kg (22lb)	350	270
12kg (26½lb)	400	320
15kg (33lb)	470	375
20kg (44lb)	600	470
25kg (55lb)	700	550
30kg (66lb)	800	650
40kg (88lb)	1,000	800

You can see from this just how few calories, and consequently how little food, a dog really needs if it is to lose weight at a satisfactory rate. Scale 1 will cause reduction in body weight at a fairly slow rate, and even with ordinary foodstuffs the dog should not be too drastically hungry. Scale 2 is necessary when a more rapid reduction in weight is called for. It is still not a drastic diet regime.

As an example, if you wished to reduce your dog's weight to 20kg (44lb), using the slower scale you would need to feed not more than 600 calories a day. Without resorting to a special diet, this could be achieved by a total daily feed of 115g (about 4oz) of meat and 130g (4½oz) of biscuit mixer. This is not a lot of food on a large dog's plate, and it explains why special reducing diets, which provide bulk to fill the dog's stomach, are popular.

▼ *Obesity is best controlled by careful attention to diet before the dog's weight gets out of hand.*

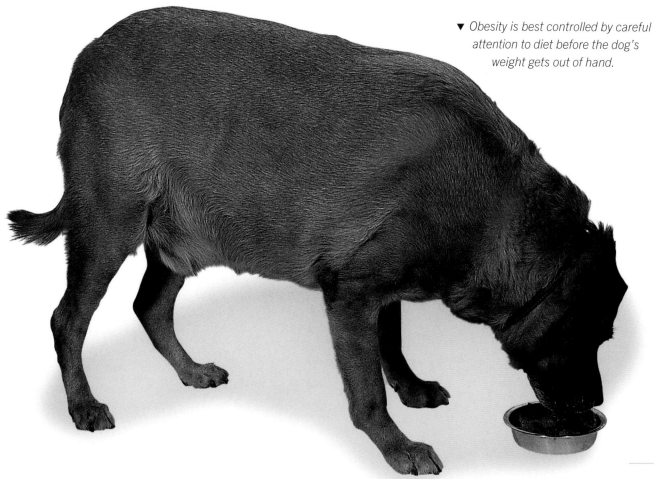

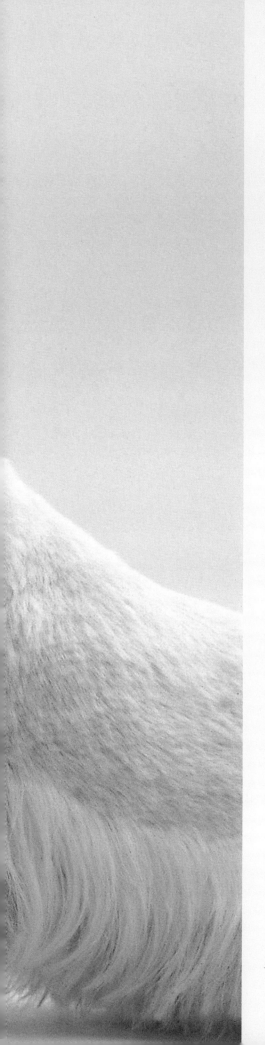

GROOMING

Grooming your dog performs two functions. The obvious one is to keep it looking, and smelling, acceptable to you and to other people. The second function is just as important: grooming between dogs establishes and maintains the relative status of each animal, so by daily grooming you are telling the dog, in the most gentle terms, that you are in charge. The whole ritual of insisting that your dog stands while you brush and comb it emphasizes that when push comes to shove, what you say goes. Regular grooming sessions also provide the opportunity to go over your dog's body thoroughly and check for any potential health problems. Sore or flaky patches of skin and the presence of parasites, such as fleas or ticks, are easily detected while brushing the coat. Regular inspection of the teeth, ears and eyes will reveal any abnormalities, and unusual lumps and bumps will be felt when handling the dog's body. All of these problems, if found at an early stage, can be treated straight away before they become too serious.

◀ *Grooming should be an enjoyable interaction between dog and owner. This West Highland White Terrier is clearly used to having its body handled.*

Handling and grooming

From an owner's, a vet's and a groomer's point of view, being able to handle your pet is vital. It makes it easy for everyone to do their job, so that the dog doesn't have to be pinned down (which is alarming for both pet and owner), and ensures that the dog is relaxed. If your dog feels nervous and threatened, on the other hand, it might bite.

BENEFITS OF HANDLING AND GROOMING

About 20 per cent of dog bites are directed at the owner's hand when they are trying to grasp their dog's collar, while many children have their faces bitten when they try to give their dog a hug. Research has shown that dogs that have been handled by many different people when they are puppies become much better socialized and are rarely aggressive

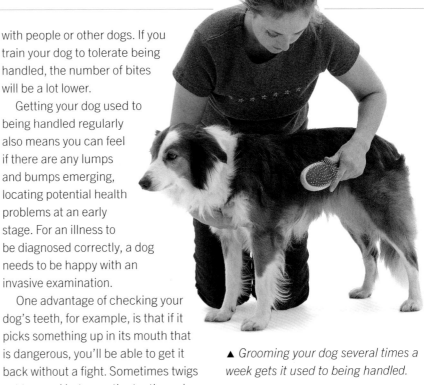

▲ *Grooming your dog several times a week gets it used to being handled.*

with people or other dogs. If you train your dog to tolerate being handled, the number of bites will be a lot lower.

Getting your dog used to being handled regularly also means you can feel if there are any lumps and bumps emerging, locating potential health problems at an early stage. For an illness to be diagnosed correctly, a dog needs to be happy with an invasive examination.

One advantage of checking your dog's teeth, for example, is that if it picks something up in its mouth that is dangerous, you'll be able to get it back without a fight. Sometimes twigs get trapped between the teeth, and you should be able to get these out without too much fuss. Likewise, if you need to give your dog medication or handle it when it's in pain, it shouldn't see that as a threat.

Similarly, getting your dog used to grooming means that you'll be able to wipe the mud from its feet and comb

▼ *If your dog is used to being handled, vet visits will not be so traumatic.*

out tangled knots without any fuss. It is equally as important to groom a short-haired dog as a long-haired one, to get rid of any dead hair.

Regular grooming will help eliminate fleas or ticks that might cause health problems, but this should not be limited to giving your dog a quick going-over with a brush. Get it accustomed to having its teeth, ears, eyes, paws and the area under the tail examined, so that when it has to go to the vet to get its temperature taken, this will not be such a shock.

BE GENTLE

Not all dogs are instinctively happy at being examined closely. Some like having their ears and tummy stroked, but draw the line at having their feet or teeth examined. Don't make this a battle, forcing the dog's mouth open, because you'll alarm and possibly even hurt it. It also means that next

▲ *It is important to be able to regularly clip your dog's claws without stress.*

time you go near your dog, it will know what's coming and try to warn you off with a snarl and maybe even a bite. Be gentle, rewarding your dog at each stage. Let it realize that nothing awful is happening. Build up its confidence. It doesn't matter if it takes several sessions before it lets you check its teeth. There's no rush.

HOW TO BEGIN

The best way to get your dog used to being handled closely is to begin by stroking it gently, letting it get used to the feel of you. With a young puppy that tries to bite, wait until it is tired. While you are stroking it, play around with its ears and have a look inside them. Stroke it down the front legs and gently feel between its toes. If it pulls its foot away, it needs to be desensitized to your touch. If it doesn't

▶ *Build up your dog's confidence by praising it while gently handling its paws.*

like you looking at its teeth — and not many dogs do to begin with — again you need to desensitize it to your handling. Let it lick a piece of cheese held between your thumb and finger, and lift its lip up to look at its teeth while it is busy.

You could also try smearing some soft cheese on the refrigerator door or, if you have a tiled floor, squash some cheese on to the surface so that while your puppy is busy licking it off, you can examine it thoroughly, including its back, belly and under its tail. When it is happy to let you handle it, get your friends to give it a once-over. If you have children, you can supervise them, but make sure they are gentle. If your puppy complains or pulls away from any area being handled, reward it well when it lets you touch it there. Be especially gentle around its mouth while it is a puppy, because its gums may hurt when it is losing its puppy teeth and the adult teeth are coming through.

▲ *Get your dog used to you handling its mouth, so you can look at its teeth.*

▲ *Reward your dog with a tasty treat when it lets you check it all over.*

▼ *Once your dog is used to being handled, it should enjoy being towel-dried after it gets muddy.*

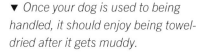

Grooming for different coats

Short-coated dogs may need less attention than other types, and usually require no professional care at all. The downside to owning a short-coated dog, however, is that they moult all the time, sometimes more than long-coated dogs. Dedicated owners of the short-coated breeds, especially those with white coats like Bull Terriers, will tell you that there is no colour or type of clothing that you can wear that does not get covered in dog hairs.

Daily grooming helps. A brush with stiff but not harsh bristles is all that is required, and it takes about ten minutes. Be careful to avoid the eyes, but otherwise brush the entire body.

Rough-coated dogs may need more attention. Some rough coats do not moult in the way that short coats do, but they 'cast', which is a more substantial moult, every 6 months or so. When they cast, hair is lost in mats, especially if the dog has not been regularly groomed throughout the rest of the year.

Regular, daily brushing and combing will prevent the coat from matting. Again, a stiff brush is the main piece of equipment, but a comb is also useful. It is essential to brush or comb right through the thickness of the coat. Just skimming over the top is of very little use.

Some rough-coated breeds need occasional attention from a professional groomer, particularly if you are intending to try your hand in the show ring. All those artfully dishevelled creatures you see at major shows are the result of hours of attention by their dedicated owners.

The silky-coated breeds – such as Cocker Spaniels and Irish Setters – need exactly the same attention as

SHORT COAT

1 A short-bristled brush is being used to clean the coat of this Brittany.

2 A wire-bristled glove makes easy work for short-haired breeds that need minimal attention.

ROUGH COAT

1 Rough-coated terriers need more attention to their coats than might sometimes be realized.

2 Regular, daily brushing out is essential. This dog looks about ready for a professional trim.

SILKY COAT

1 Dogs with long, silky coats demand much grooming. Their coat should never be clipped.

2 Careful grooming right through the coat with a not-too-stiff brush should be a daily task.

▶ *A Standard Poodle in perfect show trim, called the 'lion trim'.*

▼ *No breed is more difficult to keep in trim than the Old English Sheepdog.*

Trimming a Poodle

The Poodle is generally thought of as a trimmed dog, and the prospective owner usually realizes what is likely to be required. Daily attention is necessary, and a monthly visit to the dog parlour may become a welcome ritual.

The exaggerated trim, derived from a working cut of long ago (the Poodle was originally a gundog), is not essential to these breeds, and a version of the puppy trim can be carried on throughout the dog's life. This is simply a closer trim all over without the topiary of the show dog. Many owners feel it still keeps the essential nature of the breed. It takes less grooming than a show trim, but nevertheless needs daily attention. It also still needs regular attention from a professional to keep it in shape. The coats of ungroomed Poodles quickly get into an appalling state. It is wise to bear this in mind.

the skin to keep it socially acceptable. A beautifully groomed dog is seen on television advertisements and the family all cry, 'That is the dog we want!' But none of them has the time or the inclination to spend a long time every day, brushing and combing and cleaning up their new dog; and still less after the novelty has worn off.

So if you must have a dog that needs a lot of daily work, be sure you are going to be happy to spend time on it. Before you make up your mind, go and see the breeder to find out exactly what is involved.

Expert owners and breeders will usually trim their own dogs, but if you are getting one of the trimmed breeds as a family pet, it is sensible to contact your local grooming parlour with your puppy as soon as it is allowed out. The groomer will give you advice on daily care of the puppy's coat, discuss with you when to start trimming, and suggest what you can best do to keep the dog's coat in good shape between professional visits.

◀ *The coat of the Afghan is long and very fine-textured. Gentle but thorough grooming is necessary to maintain this breed's condition.*

rough-coated dogs. Some tend to grow rather heavy coats and need to be trimmed regularly.

The breeds that demand really skilled attention are, of course, the long-coated ones – Poodles of all sizes, Old English Sheepdogs and the trimmed terriers.

Question one, therefore, is, 'Do you want the expense and the trouble of professional grooming for your dog every four weeks?' This is the question that many prospective dog owners fail to ask themselves. Sadly, the typical result is the Old English Sheepdog that has its coat trimmed to

Bathing a dog

Dog owners in temperate climates are generally reluctant to bathe their dogs, remembering all sorts of old wives' tales regarding the adverse effects of doing so. These are probably the same arguments that people used in the Middle Ages about their own personal hygiene.

Some dogs may not need to be bathed, especially the short-coated breeds that tend to shrug off dirt; but the smell may remain.

There are, in fact, very few breeds of dog in which regular bathing causes any ill effects, although these are sometimes cited by breeders whose dogs' coats are less than ideal for the breed. 'The new owner must have over-bathed or over-groomed the puppy' can be a convenient excuse. Some breeds should never, according

BATHING TIPS

1 Early training makes the task of bathing a dog easier, but few of them actually enjoy it. In time, the dog will learn to accept the procedure.

to the breeders, be bathed. These are the dogs that veterinary surgeons can smell through the door when the dog is brought to the surgery!

2 A double-drainer sink is suitable for small breeds, while the family bath can be pressed into service for larger dogs. A non-slip bath mat is helpful.

In many tropical or sub-tropical countries, dogs must be bathed weekly, without fail, if certain tick-borne diseases are to be avoided. There is no evidence of poor coats in show dogs in these countries.

There are three types of dog shampoo: cleansing or coat-enhancing shampoo; the anti-parasitic variety of shampoo; and specialized veterinary shampoos that may be prescribed for particular skin conditions. If a dog is prone to allergies, any of these may precipitate one, but rarely. In all cases, it is extremely important that any shampoo residue is carefully rinsed from the coat. Shampoos from a reputable source will minimize such problems. Information can be obtained from the Internet or other dog owners.

◄ *Nail-clipping is a regular necessity for many dogs. If you are not confident of your skill, ask a professional to do it – if you clip into the quick of the nail, you will never be able to persuade the dog to submit to the task again.*

3 A tiny dog may fit in a basin. Choose shampoo with care, and ensure all residue is rinsed out of the coat.

4 Rubbing the dog semi-dry will prevent some of the water splashing all around the room when the dog shakes itself.

5 A good shake should be followed by some vigorous exercise to complete the drying-out process.

6 Avoid getting water into the eyes during bathing, and wipe around them once the dog is out of the bath.

7 Grooming while the coat is still slightly damp, but not wet, will help make the job of removing tangles much easier.

8 (right) Clean and sweet-smelling, until some more horse manure is found!

BREEDING

There are tens of thousands of four-legged reasons for not breeding from your pet. Dogs occupy hundreds of welfare and rescue kennels, so consider very carefully indeed whether you are at risk of adding to the large number of unwanted dogs. If you decide to go ahead, breeding is a most rewarding experience, however never decide to breed in the expectation that you will make money. This is almost certainly not true – the appetites of eight unsold 12-week-old puppies are devastating – and you would be breeding for all the wrong reasons. The cost of worming, vaccinations, health care and screening, registrations plus advertising must be factored into the overall cost. Introduction to noise and household activity is also an important and time-consuming activity that must not be neglected. Time also needs be given to interviewing potential purchasers to ensure they can offer the puppy a suitable home forever. All of that is before taking into account the hours wasted in waiting for people who make an appointment but never turn up.

◄ *Breeding from your dog can be satisfying, and many breeds, such as these Golden Retrievers, are in high demand. However, it does entail a lot of hard work.*

To breed or not to breed

When considering whether to breed from your pet, the first thing to acknowledge is that you cannot expect a crossbred dog or bitch to produce puppies in its own image. If you own a crossbred, and your reason for breeding is that friends have said that they want one 'just like her', remember that the chances of a litter producing even one puppy that is just like its mother are small to very small.

Crossbred dogs, by reason of their own breeding, have a wider genetic pool than purebred animals. Any selection of the characteristics of either parent is a matter of chance, and the greater the variety of characteristics for nature to select from, the greater will be the differences between puppies in the litter, and the greater the difference between the puppies and their parents.

▶ *The Standard Schnauzer, the middle size of the Schnauzer breeds, is not very common in English-speaking countries, but is a delightful dog.*

▼ *Looking after a litter of puppies is very demanding work for bitch and owner alike. For both, it may easily involve many 24-hour days.*

If you breed from parents of mixed ancestry, you will produce puppies that may not even remotely resemble the dog or bitch that your friends were looking for. Potential buyers may well melt away.

But it is not only with crossbred dogs that the phenomenon of the melting buyer exists. Many litters of purebred dogs are bred on the apparent promise that several friends are anxious to have a puppy of that breed, just like yours. From the time of your bitch coming into season there will be about two weeks before she is mated, nine weeks before the litter arrives, and another eight weeks before the puppies are ready to go to their new homes. That's 19 weeks since the friends made their remarks — over four months for the enthusiasm to wane, for their circumstances to change, or for them to become really keen and buy a puppy from elsewhere. If you think this is a cynical attitude, try asking for a small deposit.

There are, however, good and sensible reasons for breeding. The dog or bitch should be purebred. One or other should either be of a good working strain — and have shown itself to be a good working dog in the field — or be a sufficiently good show dog for the breeder or an expert to recommend that you should breed

◄ *The Airedale Terrier is an old-fashioned breed. It is less spoiled than most, but has the terrier temperament.*

▼ *In every healthy litter, the puppies are looking for mischief as soon as they are able to run around.*

from it. The most straightforward way to determine the animal's show quality is to exhibit at shows with success.

The reason for restricting breeding to these two groups of animals is that there is much less likelihood of your being left with puppies on your

hands, or worse, running the risk of sending them to unsuitable homes. No reputable breeder would ever do this. Remember that buyers of purebred puppies want the very best, which means that both parents have shown their quality.

A litter of puppies is great fun. But after seven or eight weeks the fun may become an expensive and exhausting chore. Being left with six or more 14-week old crossbred puppies that are starting to reveal that they had Great Dane in their ancestry is not as amusing as it sounds.

The same applies whether you own the dog or bitch. There may not be the same imperatives if you own the dog and the bitch belongs to someone down the road, but you both have the same responsibility for the outcome.

There is no truth in the commonly held belief that siring a litter will settle a dog down. Neither is there any truth that a bitch needs to have a litter. There is no medical reason for either belief. The reverse may very well be true as far as the male is concerned.

▶ *The pregnant bitch needs special care and feeding, but should continue exercising regularly until the day she whelps.*

▼ *Cleanliness in the litter box is, as they say, 'next to dogliness'.*

Choosing mating partners

Stud dogs are always selected from the best. This may mean nothing more than being currently the most fashionable, but to be among the fashionable always means that the dog has sufficient merit, either as a working dog or as a show dog, to have attracted widespread attention.

It would be unusual for someone's pet dog to become a stud dog, but if a number of fellow enthusiasts ask if they can use your dog, take advice from someone you trust in the breed. Handling matings is a skilled job. If you want to learn, become an apprentice to an expert.

The better, or more fashionable, the stud dog, the higher will be the fee payable for its services. As a guide, the stud fee is likely to be somewhat lower than the price you might expect to get for a puppy. Special arrangements such as 'pick of litter' are by no means uncommon. This means the stud dog owner has the right to pick whichever they regard as the best puppy from the litter, either in lieu of the fee, or as a consideration for a reduced fee.

However, it is not necessary or even desirable to go to the most fashionable stud dog for your bitch's mating. An experienced breeder will advise on which dog to choose, using the physical appearance and pedigree of your bitch and the available dogs as a guide. Some breeders take more notice of pedigree, others of conformation. Learn about the breed, and decide how close to your ideal each breeder's stock is.

PEDIGREES AND CHAMPIONS

In the UK, the Kennel Club (KC) has sole responsibility for registration of pedigree dogs. National clubs have the same responsibility in their own

▶ *This outstanding Rough Collie may be the ideal stud dog.*

countries throughout the world. The American Kennel Club, although not the only registration authority in the United States, reciprocates its registrations with the Kennel Club and the international Fédération Cynologique Internationale (FCI), to which the Australian Kennel Control is federated.

Most kennel clubs have reciprocal arrangements, and dogs registered in one country can be re-registered in another if the dog is imported. Official pedigrees are derived from the registration particulars of all purebred dogs that are themselves registered with the kennel club. Unless a dog is itself registered, its offspring cannot in turn be registered, except in certain special circumstances. Pedigree records are held for at least four generations, although some breeders will be able to show you much longer ones than that.

Different countries have different criteria for awarding the title of Champion. In the UK, the title is awarded to show dogs and working dogs. Some aspire to, and some achieve, both titles.

▼ *The Boxer is a very popular breed. There should be no difficulty in finding a dog to suit your bitch.*

▲ *Careful noting of pedigree and breeding records is essential if you are serious about breeding.*

▶ *All breeding programmes start from small beginnings, but may end with a Champion like this Yorkshire Terrier.*

To become a Champion in the UK, a show dog must have been awarded three Challenge Certificates under different judges, with at least one of the certificates being awarded after the dog has reached the age of 12 months. Challenge Certificates are awarded to the best dog and bitch in each breed at specified Championship Shows. The term 'Challenge Certificate' derives from the fact that the judge may invite any or all unbeaten dogs from earlier classes to challenge the winner of the open class for the certificate.

The Australian system is identical to that of the UK, but in the United States, Championships are gained under a points system with points awarded in different fields: breed, obedience, field and herding.

The qualifications for Champions in working dogs take account of the dog's success in the working trials.

Finding homes for puppies

There is no point in breeding from a bitch unless you can expect to sell the puppies. Your best bet is to produce a litter that will be acceptable to enthusiasts, unless you have firm orders that ensure the sale of your puppies. The breeder of your bitch may be able to help.

▲ *At three weeks old, all puppies are delightful, but this pair is likely to get into mischief next week.*

In many breeds, good puppies are at a premium. Reputable breeders will be asked regularly when or where there is a litter due. Your bitch's breeder may be happy to pass on applicants to you, and to explain to them about the breeding of your bitch.

▼ *A 'rough-and-tumble' is a vital part of puppies' learning process.*

Mating, conception and pregnancy

Male dogs become sexually mature at about six months of age. From that time onwards, their sexual behaviour is not cyclical, and they are capable of mating at any time and almost any place!

The bitch usually comes into season for the first time when she is aged about nine months, and fairly regularly every six months thereafter. It is not unusual, nor is it in any way abnormal, for the first season to be earlier, even as young as six months, or for it to be postponed until the bitch is over a year old. Neither is it unusual

▼ *Dogs will be interested in the bitch from day one of her season, but she will usually refuse to mate until she is in full oestrus.*

or abnormal for the interval between seasons to be longer than six months. If the interval between one season and another is very much less than six months, and particularly if it has become irregular in this respect, there may be some abnormality, and advice should be sought from your veterinary surgeon.

A bitch's season lasts for about three weeks. She will show some swelling of her vulva shortly before presenting a blood-stained discharge. The discharge is usually very bloody at the start of her season, becoming paler after about ten days.

Although no risks should be taken from the first signs of season, the bitch will normally not accept a dog until about halfway through the season,

at which time she will become fertile (i.e. capable of conceiving). There is normally no odour detectable to a human from a bitch in season, but there is a very powerful one detectable by dogs a considerable distance away. Do not assume that because you live a long way from the nearest male dog, your bitch will not be mated.

Do not assume, either, that a dog that lives together with a bitch, even although they may be brother and sister, will not be interested.

True oestrus begins at about 12 days from the first signs of the bitch coming into season. From that time, she will accept the male's attempts to mate her, and will be fertile for about five to seven days. Ovulation – the release of eggs into the uterus – takes

▼ *Mating takes place when the bitch has ovulated. Ejaculation occurs quickly, and the tie is not necessary for conception. A mating without a tie is called a slip mating.*

▼ *Although not essential, the tie – when the male dog climbs off the female and faces the other way – has a physiological function in helping the sperm to move up the genital tract.*

place during this period. The timing is variable, and the dog and bitch are the best practical arbiters of the bitch's fertile period, although laboratory tests are available to help timing if the bitch fails to conceive.

The mating act may be prolonged. Once the dog has ejaculated, the bitch continues to grip his penis in her vagina, by means of a ring muscle, for up to about 20 minutes. The dog

may climb off the bitch's back and turn to face the other way, but both stand 'tied'. The tie is not actually essential for a successful mating, although all breeders prefer to see it if possible.

Pregnancy lasts for about 63 days from mating. The normal variation is about 60–67 days. Outside this range, veterinary attention should be sought, although it does not necessarily indicate

a problem and may simply be an extension of normal variation. Bitches should not be bred from until they are physically mature. The ideal age for a first litter is about two years old.

▼ *The bitch should be introduced to her whelping box at least a week before whelping is due, in order to give her time to become comfortable with the surroundings.*

▲ *Bitches should continue with normal exercise throughout pregnancy, although they are likely to become increasingly placid for its duration.*

Whelping

Giving birth, known as 'whelping', is a natural event. Nine times out of ten there is no need for interference; in 99 cases out of 100, interference takes place before it is necessary.

Be prepared. Let your veterinary surgeon know well in advance. They may have confirmed that the bitch is in whelp, but ask the vet to note the expected date on the calendar.

Make sure that you have decided where the bitch is to whelp, and that she has agreed with you. If it is to be in a special place and in a special bed, introduce her to it a week or two in advance, and teach her that it is now her bed. The ideal place is a quiet corner without passing traffic, and away from where children might play. Bear in mind that you, or the vet, may have to attend to her at some stage. Under the stairs may not be a good idea, for this reason.

She should have a whelping box. It needs to be large enough to accommodate the bitch and a litter, which may number as many as 12 puppies. Most breeders will show you a suitable box with a rail around the edge to prevent the bitch from lying on her puppies and squashing them – some bitches are very clumsy.

Bedding for the box needs to be disposable – whelpings are accompanied by a great deal of mess. Almost universally, the basic bedding for a whelping box is newspaper in large quantities, so start saving these some weeks in advance. You can always do the crossword while you are waiting for the puppies to arrive!

Most bitches give warning of imminent whelping by going off their food. If you have a thermometer, you may use it at this stage. A dog's normal temperature is approximately 38.5°C (101.5°F). A drop in temperature of two or three degrees nearly always indicates that the bitch will start to whelp within 24 hours.

For several days before whelping, many bitches will start to make a nest somewhere, usually somewhere inappropriate. Most bitches become very restless a few hours before they start to whelp.

Right up to the point of producing her first puppy, a family pet that in the nature of things is used to human company will probably want the comfort of human attention, but once she starts to strain for the first puppy, the great majority of bitches will become uninterested in the people around them and just get on with the job of producing their litter.

It may take several hours from the time the bitch starts to strain until the first puppy is delivered. Provided she is continuing to strain, there is no panic. If, after serious effort for an hour or more, she stops trying, ask your veterinary surgeon for advice.

The first sign that a puppy is due is the appearance of the water bag. This is an apt description for the foetal membranes; they look just like a small bag of water, which appears through

GIVING BIRTH

1 Bitches do not normally need human assistance to produce their puppies, although whelping may be a somewhat prolonged business.

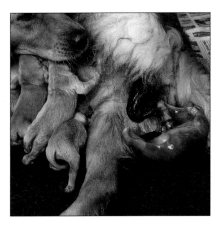

2 The bitch breaks the puppy out of the foetal membranes and often eats the membranes. It is not usually necessary to tie off the cord.

3 The puppy needs plenty of stimulation by licking from the bitch or, if necessary, by rubbing in a towel, to be sure that it is breathing satisfactorily.

▼ *New-born puppies spend virtually all their time drinking or sleeping. If the litter is restless, urgent attention should be sought. It is always better to be safe than sorry.*

the vagina. Do not attempt to remove it; it has the function of enlarging the birth canal to permit the following puppy to pass through.

The puppy may be born either head or tail first. Each is as common as the other, and the appearance of the tail first does not indicate a breach birth.

The first puppy may take some time to be born after you get first sight of it, and it may often seem to disappear back up the canal. The time for concern is when the puppy is obviously stuck fast with no movement up or down despite continued straining, or when the bitch appears to have given up straining and is lying exhausted. If this happens, veterinary attention is needed urgently.

CAESAREAN OPERATIONS
Veterinary assistance at a whelping is as likely to involve a caesarean operation as not. The bitch is usually too small to allow very much manipulation if she has problems producing her puppies. In earlier

times, assisted whelping involved the use of instruments inserted into her vagina, but this has largely been discontinued in favour of surgery.

Caesareans are now more popular, partly for humane reasons, but mainly because of the existence of low-risk anaesthetics coupled with surgical techniques that have improved so

much over the years that a successful outcome of the operation can usually be anticipated.

To produce live puppies and a healthily recovering bitch, the operation must be carried out earlier

▼ *With a large litter, you should make sure all the puppies get their share.*

▲ *Any puppies that do not get their share may be bottle-fed successfully with a suitable bitch-milk substitute.*

rather than later. The subject should be discussed with the veterinary surgeon well before the whelping is due, so that both parties know the other's feeling about the operation. The vet must be called in before the bitch has become exhausted from straining unsuccessfully to produce her puppies.

Sadly, some breeds have such a poor reputation for natural whelping that caesarean operations are carried out routinely, without waiting for indications of failure by the bitch.

Breeders of these breeds must reconsider their whole outlook on dog breeding if their breeds are to continue to be popular.

Other than in these special circumstances, caesarean operations are usually carried out as a matter of emergency. Most veterinary surgeons will ask you to bring the bitch to the surgery if there are whelping difficulties, rather than visit the house, so that operating facilities are at hand.

The otherwise healthy bitch and her puppies will thrive best back in her home environment, and the veterinary surgeon will release them as soon as possible. Once home, the dam may need a little coaxing to accept and feed her puppies; as far as she is concerned, they just appeared while she was asleep. Careful introductions almost always work, but she may need some help initially to attach the puppies to the teats. Once they are sucking normally, the bitch will realize what she is supposed to do.

After the first day or two, a bitch who has had a caesarean may be treated the same as a bitch who has produced the puppies naturally.

AFTER WHELPING
The puppies must be cleaned behind every time they feed. This stimulates the passage of urine and faeces; without this stimulation they will not pass excreta, and may become fatally constipated. This is one of the bitch's jobs. If she has been under anaesthetic, she may not realize this. Holding the puppy tail first to her will quickly teach her the routine.

Normally, the bitch remains with her puppies constantly for at least the first couple of weeks. There may be difficulty in persuading her to leave them even for her own natural functions. If this is the case, don't worry. She will go eventually. Let her do it in her own time.

A healthy bitch with puppies quickly develops a large appetite. For the first few days it may be necessary to feed her in or very close to her bed, but you should make sure there is plenty of food available, and particularly plenty of fluids. She may prefer milk. Forget the usual once-a-day feeding routine; let her have food whenever she wants it. She has an enormous task in feeding all those pups.

▲ *A puppy that is not nesting with its littermates needs watching because it could be sick or too hot.*

▲ *The whelping box needs to be high enough to stop puppies escaping, but low enough for the dam to get out.*

▲ *Puppies' claws need trimming weekly to prevent them from making the bitch sore when they are feeding.*

Rearing puppies

The first two weeks are the easiest, when the puppies are relatively inert. They will wriggle around the bed a great deal but are incapable of recovering the nest if they accidentally fall out. Most whelping boxes have high fronts for this reason.

At this stage, the puppies need no supplementary feeding, just their mother's milk, and should spend most of their time sleeping quietly. If they do not, seek help urgently.

Puppies open their eyes at about ten days old, though some breeds are notoriously lazy about this.

By about three weeks old, the puppies are moving around much more; they will mostly have fallen out

▲ At three days old, the puppy's eyes are still closed, and its only active movement is likely to be towards its dam for feeding.

▲ By three weeks old, the puppy will be trying to get out of the nest box.

▶ Five-week-old puppies are active and alert, and learning lessons about the world.

of the box several times, indicating that it is time to add another layer to the barrier at the front. It may also be time to start supplementing their diet. This is done by hand-feeding.

Although most people think of the puppies' first hand-feeding as an occasion for something delicate and perhaps milky, just try putting a little raw beef on your fingers. You will be lucky to have a finger left!

The main reason for starting to wean puppies at three weeks is to spare the bitch. With a large litter,

▶ By eight weeks, it is time for the puppies to leave home, usually to the relief of their dam and often their owner as well.

there is a tremendous physical demand on her, and she will certainly lose a lot of weight during the course of rearing a litter. By starting to wean the puppies relatively early, she will be spared some of this load. Puppies do, in any case, start to look for more solid food at this age, if given the opportunity.

At three weeks of age, the litter must have its first worming dose. Take advice on this. Modern wormers cause no side effects.

From three weeks to about five weeks, a gradually increasing proportion of the puppies' diet should be supplied from sources other than their dam. By six weeks, they should be completely weaned, although the dam may take some convincing of this, and may keep trying to feed the pups. The action of sucking by the puppies prolongs the production of milk by the dam, and after six weeks this should be discouraged.

At six weeks, the puppies should be feeding on a puppy food of your choice. It is also time for a second worming dose to be given.

TRAINING YOUR DOG

Every dog is capable of learning a great deal more than is generally recognized. Although it may take a special type of dog and a special type of owner to create a canine film star, home helper or agility champion, there is no reason why every dog should not achieve the essential basics of obedience and well-socialized behaviour. A well-trained dog is less likely to develop unwanted behaviour patterns, partly because dogs often adopt bad habits when they are bored. Dogs enjoy the stimulation of training, and most love to please their owners, too. Trained dogs are able to become full members of the family and take part in many aspects of home life. It pays to keep this in mind, for there will be many times during the first few months of owning a puppy when you might wonder if you have taken on more than you can cope with. Biting, chewing, digging, stealing and attention-seeking behaviour can stretch your patience to the limit. However, with training, kindness, understanding and consistency, and occasionally the help of experts, most problems can be solved.

◄ *Spending time training your dog will reap its own rewards. This Border Collie is waiting quietly for the next command from its owner, relaxed and eager to please. A trained dog is a joy to behold.*

House-training

The most crucial task with a new puppy is house-training. Hopefully the breeder will have begun taking the puppies into the garden to get them used to going to the toilet outside. What you shouldn't do is encourage your puppy to go inside, even on newspaper. You must also be alert to its signals, understanding when it needs to go, because when a puppy is desperate, it can't wait.

HOW OFTEN?

The frequency with which your puppy will need to go to the toilet depends on several factors. First, its diet. If you use dried food, it will drink more water than when eating wet food, prompting more visits outside. Second, if you buy cheaper dog food with cheaper ingredients, it usually makes a great deal more waste and so, again, your puppy will need to go to the toilet more often. Third, the size of your puppy influences the number of visits to the toilet, with a small breed needing to go more often than a large dog, because the former has a smaller bladder.

◄ *Reward your puppy for being quiet in its crate – feed it small food treats for good behaviour. It is helpful if it learns to sleep in a crate, as it is unlikely to foul its sleeping place.*

HOUSE-TRAINING METHODS

Training your puppy not to go to the toilet in the house takes time, and there are bound to be some accidents along the way. It helps to get your puppy to sleep in a crate, because it won't want to foul its sleeping place. Introduce your puppy to the crate by feeding it in the crate, giving it treats there and lying it down in it when it's sleepy. Make sure that the moment it starts whining, you take it outside.

If your puppy does have an accident inside, do not punish it, because that will make it wary of going to the toilet in front of you, and house-training will then become very difficult. It will probably end up going where you can't see it – even in a handbag.

To begin with, take your puppy out soon after it has woken up, after it has eaten, after playtime, when it's excited and every 45 minutes. Make sure it knows which is its toilet area in the garden, especially if you have young children; you don't want your children wading through piles of faeces on the lawn. Fence off a small toilet area and take your puppy

HOUSE-TRAINING USING A FENCED-OFF AREA

1 Take your puppy on its lead to an area designated as its toilet – ideally a fenced-off area of the garden.

2 Reward it with a small food treat as soon as it goes. It's important to do this the moment it has finished.

▲ *Buy a special cleaner from a pet shop for cleaning up after your puppy when it has toilet accidents.*

there on the lead, rewarding it enthusiastically when it does what's expected. Give it a small treat, but remember that it is crucial that you get the timing right: reward it the moment it has finished going to the toilet.

Some puppies give signs that they are about to go, and they may begin sniffing the carpet or floor, circling or squatting. When this happens, clap your hands to get your puppy's attention, and encourage it to follow you out the door. If it really is about to go, pick it up and take it outside very quickly.

CLEANING UP

If your puppy does have an accident, treat the site with a cleaner that is specifically designed for the job. This will remove the scent of urine. If the odour is left, your puppy will think that's its toilet, and will be attracted there by the smell in future. Note that household cleaners and disinfectants

don't usually remove the scent, they just mask it, so you do need to use a special cleaner available from good pet shops.

OTHER OPTIONS

If for some reason you need to leave your puppy alone for long periods of time, you won't have any option but to use puppy pads, which are specifically designed to soak up urine, or sheets of newspaper on the floor, but at least make sure that the puppy understands what the pads or paper are for. As with house-training, every time the puppy shows any inclination to go to the toilet, put it on the pads or newspaper. Dog flaps are not suitable because young puppies don't understand the concept of going out to the toilet and in any case, they should not be unattended outside.

You could also teach your puppy to try to go on command, which is very useful if you are taking it out for the day or visiting friends, but you must use the command just as it's going to the toilet, so that it makes the correct association between the two events.

RINGING A BELL

If your puppy isn't very good at asking to go out, you can teach it to ring a bell. It's an easy little trick. All you need is a small, light bell. Hang it on a piece of string so that it is dangling at about nose height for your puppy. When you walk it to the door to let it out, ring the bell immediately before you open the door. It willl associate the door opening with the ringing bell. In future, the puppy should ring the bell if it wants to go. When you go on holiday, take the bell with you.

TRAINING A PUPPY TO RING A BELL

1 Attach a bell to a piece of string and hang it from the back door, making sure it is at nose height for your puppy.

2 Ring the bell before you open the door to let your puppy out. In time, it should ring it itself when it wants to go.

Socialization and habituation

Puppies need to be socialized so that they are happy meeting other puppies and adult dogs, people of both sexes, children, babies in pushchairs, older people and people in wheelchairs. The list is endless. It is important to note that the socialization window is only open for a short time – up to the age of 14 weeks – so you need to make the most of it to ensure your puppy doesn't have problems when it's an adult. Make all such encounters enjoyable, asking adults who are new to it to toss it a few treats.

SOCIALIZATION
Your breeder should already have begun the socialization process, with the puppy being handled regularly on a daily basis. If you have a busy household, your puppy will already have become used to household appliances, visitors and the hustle and bustle of day-to-day noise. If you have a quieter home, you will have to put more time and effort into exposing it to different experiences.

BEFORE 12 WEEKS
There are several things your puppy should be introduced to before it's 12 weeks old. First, when it has settled down, invite visitors of all ages to meet it. Keep it quiet when they arrive so that it learns to be calm when people are around. If you don't have children, ask friends who do have them to visit, but make sure they are well briefed to be gentle and don't get your puppy too overexcited.

Put something tasty in your puppy's food dish so that it gets used to people being around when it eats.

Groom and handle your puppy every day. Look in its ears, at its teeth and between its paw pads. Also get other people to handle your puppy, so that when it has to visit the vet, it isn't frightened. It needs to get used to wearing its collar, too.

▲ *Children should be taught how to care for their dog's needs by grooming and handling them. Start the process before your puppy is 12 weeks old.*

HABITUATION
This is the name given to a natural process of learning by repetitive exposure to a stimulus. For example, a puppy may be frightened of the noise of a washing machine, but each time the machine is turned on, its reaction will diminish. Eventually, it will show no reaction to the noise at all, and it has become 'habituated' to it. Habituation to a wide range of items and experiences is vital for the young puppy, and the process will continue throughout its lifetime.

◄ *Cats and dogs can live in harmony, especially if they grow up together.*

▲ *Stay with your puppy when it is eating; it will get used to people around its food bowl.*

▲ *Giving your puppy a weekly health check will prepare it for its first visits to the vet or the groomer.*

▲ *Carrying your puppy everywhere you go will habituate it to the environment in which you live.*

Habituation can also be used as a training tool. If your puppy becomes overexcited when you pick up its lead, this is because it expects to go for a walk. But if you take the lead with you every time you leave the house, the puppy will soon come to realize that the act of picking up the lead is not a signal for walk time.

TOWN AND COUNTRY

Carry your puppy out to meet the postman, so that it won't bark at them. If you live in a town, try to take your puppy into the countryside, but keep it under strict control so that it learns to leave wildlife and livestock alone. Reward it for obeying your commands and staying with you. Never let it off the lead when around livestock. Remember that a farmer has the right to shoot your dog for worrying their animals, especially

▶ *If your puppy gets used to horses early, it will behave well around them.*

sheep around lambing time. If you live in the countryside, it is imperative that you carry your puppy around the nearest town to get it used to all the sights and sounds. Initially go when it is quiet, gradually building up to busier periods. Before its vaccinations, before it is around 12 weeks of age,

it is important that you don't let your puppy walk outside in parks and fields that are visited by other dogs – your puppy might get a fatal disease. However, you can carry it with you everywhere you go, and it can visit friends' houses whose dogs have been vaccinated.

Sit

▶ *Teaching your puppy to 'sit' when it is off the lead is important.*

Teaching a dog to sit is relatively easy. Have a handful of small treats. Hold one in front of your dog's nose, and slowly move it upward and slightly backward towards its tail. You'll quickly see that as its head moves up, its bottom will go down. As soon as its bottom hits the floor, reward it and say 'good boy' or 'good girl'. If your dog begins jumping up at your hand, you are holding the treat too far away from the front of its nose; put your hand behind your back until it settles down. When you start again, make sure the treat is right at the end of its nose.

Repeat this three or four times with a small treat, then let it have a rest. This stage needs to be repeated three or four times a day. The second time you try teaching a sit, if your dog's bottom hits the floor consistently, keep the treat in your hand behind your back and use your other hand to give the signals, moving it upward and backward. Say 'good boy/girl' as its bottom hits the floor and reward it with the treat from your other hand.

The next stage is to make sure you say the word 'sit' as it is going into the sitting position – not a second before. Follow this up by checking that it understands what you are asking it. Hide the treat behind your back and tell it to sit. Does it do it the first time? If it stands looking at you, it doesn't understand, in which case you should go back to saying 'sit' as it's going into the sitting position. Only proceed to the next stage when it sits immediately every time, on command.

You'll soon note that once you've said 'good boy/girl' or given it a treat, it stands up again. To get it to stay in the sitting position, initially withhold the treat for a couple of seconds, gradually making this period longer.

The final stage is getting your dog to sit by the roadside. If it ever hesitates, do not push down on its back – you may damage its developing bone structure; plus the dog will usually push back, which causes you to push harder every time you want it to obey.

Down

▶ *Once your dog has learned to sit, it is easy to train it to lie 'down'.*

Teaching your dog to lie down on cue is another essential command. First, get your dog to sit in front of you, then hold a treat under its nose and move it in a straight line from under its nose to its paws on the floor. As soon as the dog's chest hits the floor, reward and praise it. Only practise this about four or five times in each session, to keep it interested.

If you have a terrier, who finds it easier to go straight down from the standing position, again have the treat right under its nose and lure it down and slightly backward. If it goes down with its nose and front legs but leaves its rear in the air, don't push down on its bottom. Just hold the treat on the floor between your finger and thumb and wait, and it will eventually lie down or get up and walk away. If it does walk away, repeat the exercise but reward it for each stage that it completes. So, if you reward your dog for putting its front end down first, it may well put its front end down and its chest, and before long it will be lying down.

If you have a small dog or puppy that is having real trouble lying down, sit on the floor with your legs outstretched in front of you, bend one leg up and lure your dog under the crook of your knee. This works particularly well with terriers.

The time to introduce the word 'down' is just as your dog is going into the correct position. Gradually increase the amount of time before you reward it. After that, try getting it to lie down where there are minor distractions, for example in the back garden. The rule to apply is that the harder the task, the better the reward.

Never use force; this will get you into a wrestling match, or alternatively your dog will become suspicious and will immediately shy away from you.

Leave it

▶ *'Leave it' is an essential command if you want your dog to ignore an object.*

There will be many times in your dog's life when you'll want it to leave something or someone alone. When teaching a 'leave it' command, let your dog decide what position it wants to go in. You shouldn't suddenly ask it to obey two commands at once, for example 'leave it' followed by 'down'.

Get five or six high-value treats and put them to one side. Put a dog biscuit in the palm of your hand, show it to your dog, close your hand and hold it under its nose. Let your dog sniff, paw and lick your hand, but don't say anything. Your dog will eventually back off, confused, but as soon as it moves its face away from your hand, say 'leave it' and give it one of the treats. You're teaching your dog that it won't get the object you've told it

to leave. At the end of the exercise, put the dog biscuit away and don't give it to it. As you teach the 'leave it' command, your dog should begin to back off faster and sit patiently. You can then hold your hand open for a couple of seconds before you praise and reward it.

When the dog is consistently leaving treats in the palm of your hand, start making the exercise more difficult. Try higher-value rewards for the dog to leave, and roll a biscuit along the floor, being prepared to put your hand over it to begin with until the dog understands it has to leave it.

When it has mastered all these 'leave it' commands, put your dog on the lead and let it see you put some food away. Tether it to something or

ask someone to hold it while you do this. The food should be about 3m (10ft) away from you. Walk towards it and, as soon as your dog begins to pull towards the treat, walk backward until your dog stops pulling towards the treat and looks at you. Then reward and praise it for looking at you.

Once your dog has realized that looking at you gets it a reward, it should be easier to get it closer and closer to the treat on the floor, until it will eventually walk past.

Stay

▶ *Teaching your dog the 'stay' cue will help to keep it out of danger.*

The 'stay' command means 'stay where you are until I get back to you'. So, if your dog escapes and runs across a road, tell it to 'stay' until you can get to it. Your dog will also need to master the 'stay' command if you want it to enter dog competitions.

There are two aspects of the exercise to work on: duration and distance. Gradually increase the amount of time your dog stays, while you move further away. It needs to have the confidence to stay where it is. In fact, this is much harder for a dog than you realize, so never get angry if it can't stay for long. After all, the training you have done with it previously has been right in front

of it, with a reward just seconds away. If you do get angry, the dog will get stressed, which will make it even more likely to get up and follow you. If it does break a 'stay', take it back to where it was, put it back in position and go back a few steps so that it understands what you want.

First, tell it to 'sit' but don't move away yet. Say 'stay' while holding up the flat of your hand (this visual command will reinforce the verbal cue). Then count to five and reward it. When it can sit and stay for 1 minute, you can begin to move away from it. Do this very slowly, taking one step back, then move back and reward and praise your dog.

The next time you do this, take two steps before going back to it with a reward, and so on. If it gets up to follow you when you move back, it does not understand what you want. Go back a few stages, then continue to slowly increase the duration and distance.

When you are confident that your dog understands the word 'stay' and you can move a few steps away, start to train in a safe area with distractions.

Wait

▶ *Teaching your dog to 'wait' will help it with patience and good manners.*

There is a subtle difference between 'stay' and 'wait' commands. 'Stay' means 'stay where you are until I get back to you' and is usually used when it is essential that a dog doesn't move. In contrast, 'wait' means 'we are going to do something else' and is more a case of good manners when you want your dog to keep quiet and behave. You could also ask your dog to wait while you open the front door, so that it learns to leave the house in an orderly fashion, instead of barging past you in its hurry to get to the park. Similarly, asking your dog to wait while you open the car door is a good habit to get into.

To teach a dog to wait, take a small treat and hold your dog by the collar. Roll the treat away from you, just out of reach of your dog. Don't say anything to it yet, but let it pull towards the treat while you hold on to its collar. It will eventually relax, sit and possibly look at you. Say 'wait' and then let it get the treat.

Next, teach your dog to wait at the front door. Put it on a lead, get it to sit next to you and ask it to wait. Open the front door a bit and, if it gets up to charge out, close it immediately, making sure you don't trap its nose. Drop the lead, walk away, wait a few seconds, then try again. It may take six or seven attempts before your dog sits nicely while you open the door, and don't forget to reward it on each occasion. Teaching it this self-control will make going out for a walk a much calmer experience.

When in the park, practise asking your dog to wait while on a flexi-lead or long line first — not when your dog is running, which is too dangerous. Wait until there are other dogs or people around. Let your dog get slightly ahead of you, then ask it to wait. Put the brake on the flexi-lead or hold on to the line and, when it stops to look at you, praise and reward it.

Eye contact

▶ *A dog should enjoy eye contact. It will improve a shy dog's confidence.*

Teaching your dog to make eye contact with you should be one of the most rewarding things you do with it. Once learned, it's a good exercise that you can use, for example when you want to keep your dog's attention so that it doesn't go dashing off after a group of dogs in the park. It's also useful if you have a shy dog. Teaching it eye contact is a good game, and will help build its confidence.

It used to be thought that you should never look a dog in the eye. However, this only applies to staring a dog down when it's wrong, in which case it will associate eye contact with punishment. Because children are about head-height with dogs, they will almost always look dogs in the eye. If a pet has not been trained to make eye contact, there is a risk of being bitten in the face by an apprehensive pet. By teaching a dog that eye contact is a rewarding experience, it will not fear being looked at.

Start in a room without any distractions, holding treats, with your dog off the lead. Show it the treats, then close your hand and hold it out to the side. The dog will try to jump up to get the treats, but if you wait, it will sit down and glance at you. Tell it it's a good dog as soon as it looks you in the eye, and reward it by tossing the treat away from you to encourage it to move away. What you are hoping is that it will come back and sit in front of you again, offering more eye contact. After five or six attempts, your dog should sit in front of you and look at you when you hold out your hand. When it is looking you in the eye consistently, you can begin to say 'watch me' so that it understands the command.

If your dog is shy, it may find it hard to make eye contact, but persevere, rewarding even a glance at you.

Settle down

▶ *Your dog should be able to 'settle down' quietly and happily when asked.*

Having a dog that is able to settle down means that it won't be a pest when you are trying to eat a meal, that it will lie beside you when you have visitors, and that it will curl up next to you when you are reading. In many households, there's already enough noise and confusion. You don't need to add to it by having an agitated dog that you have to shut away. The command 'settle down' will allow calm to reign over the chaos.

When your dog is lying down of its own accord, reward it with a treat, tell it it's a good dog and stress the word 'settle'. The more you reward a dog's natural behaviour, the more it will be able to do it. The delight of this command is that it doesn't involve one fixed position. The dog can flop over on its side, curl up, roll or stretch, as long as it is settled. Unfortunately, we often ignore dogs when they are quiet, not realizing that such behaviour should be actively encouraged. The more you reward a particular behaviour, the more often your dog will do it.

When you teach your dog to settle, make sure it is tired, for example after an evening meal or its walk. Put it on a long, loose lead so that it can sit, lie or stand. Ignore it, and while it may find this (and being tethered) rather odd and get restless, it will eventually settle down. Don't say anything (no 'down' or 'sit' cues); just wait it out until it settles. The hardest part is getting it to settle down for the first time, and thereafter your dog should find this easier. Don't go overboard with praise, because this will just make the dog jump straight back up again. Gently stroke its head, slip it a treat and say 'settle down'.

Drop it

▶ *Teaching your dog to drop an object will make games of fetch fun.*

There will be times when your pet picks up something it shouldn't, and teaching your dog to 'drop it' means you can retrieve your possessions without it becoming a battle of wills. From a safety point of view, it is important that your dog is able to give things up willingly on command.

Teach this is in stages. Use a favourite toy that can be used for tug, and some tasty treats. Offer your dog the toy and initiate a game of tug. Soon after, put a treat right under the dog's nose, at which point it should drop the toy and take the treat. The crucial point is to say 'drop it' at the moment it drops the toy. Then show it the toy again and have another game.

Play this game of tug a few times each day, always putting a treat under its nose and saying 'drop it' at the appropriate moment. After a few days, try saying 'drop it' before you offer the treat and, if the dog drops the toy, give it a handful of treats as the jackpot.

Your dog should learn to give things up as a young puppy, and whenever you take something away from it, always swap it with something equally rewarding. Don't take bones and other prized objects away from your dog just because you think you should, because this is the fastest way to teach a dog to guard its possessions. If it does tend to guard, get specialist help from a behaviour counsellor.

When your dog has mastered the 'drop it' command, this will open up the possibility of playing a whole range of interactive games. Most dogs love fetching a ball, but nothing can be more frustrating for an owner than having to hunt all over the house for a dropped toy. Because your dog has learned that it can exchange a toy for a treat, it will now bring the ball back to you to gain its reward. You could also try hiding a toy and getting your dog to seek it out and return it to you.

Some formal obedience tests involve retrieving and returning an item, and dogs working to the gun must seek and return fallen birds. For all of these, a well-taught 'drop it' command is a good basis on which to build.

Recalling your dog

▲ *Once your dog is trained to come to you, it will be free to play off the lead.*

Of all the commands that you will teach your dog, a recall is one of the most important. If your dog does not come back when called, it will always have to be kept on a lead. This will reduce its social skills with other dogs and people, as it will not be free to interact. Being on the lead all the time would also mean that it couldn't have as much fun following weird and wonderful scents, snuffling away through the undergrowth.

There are many reasons why a dog does not come back when called, the most obvious being that it has never been trained. Owners can be lulled into a false sense of security when their dogs are puppies, because they rarely go off, instead tending to stay by their side. However, a dog may suddenly realize it's not so bad being away from its owner, and when you shout 'come back', you might as well be yodelling in another language.

Some dog owners think that just calling a dog by its name when it's off playing with other dogs will get an instant result. It won't. Calling like this

means that when you use its name in future, it will associate that with the end of its fun and the end of the walk, making it less likely to return.

So it's important when training your dog to come back that you use a suitable reward – one that compensates it well for being told to stop chasing other dogs. Ordinary dog biscuits will not be enough. Instead, try a high-value treat such as cooked chicken or a piece of cheese. With recall training it is important to put a firm foundation down before you move on to the next level. Always set your dog up for success.

The secret to getting your dog to obey is time, work and plenty of patience. Once your dog has learned to return to you, you can safely let it off the lead so that it can have some fun on its own. Training a recall is all about conditioning your dog so that when it hears the 'come' command, it will automatically turn and come charging back to you.

SIMPLE RECALL

Start teaching your dog in a place where there are no distractions. Carry a handful of treats and your dog's

favourite toy. Feed it a few treats from your hand to get its attention, then toss a small treat away from you. If necessary, show it where the treat has gone and, just as it is eating the treat, back away a few steps from the dog and call its name. When it looks towards you, praise it just for looking up and paying attention. As it comes back to you, get really excited that it is coming in your direction – give it a round of applause. Dog owners can be reticent about praising their dogs, but getting a recall is a situation in which you should go overboard with praise. Make its tail wag with happiness.

When your dog gets back to you, give it a treat immediately and let it play with its favourite toy. Don't tell it to sit before giving it the reward; this would incorrectly reward the sit rather than the recall.

Then toss another treat out and, again, just when the dog has eaten the treat, call it by name. As it is coming towards you, say 'come'. Only do this five or six times, then finish. If you carry out short training sessions four or five times a day, your dog will stay alert and happy. You can practise recalls in the kitchen when the kettle is boiling, tossing treats up and down the room when the advertisements are on the television – in fact, during any spare couple of minutes that you have.

▼ *Be enthusiastic and reward your dog keenly when it comes to you.*

◄ *Use extra-tasty treats for rewarding recalls in places with distractions.*

RECALLING WITH DISTRACTIONS

The next stage is to try this training in the garden, where there are plenty of distractions. Use a highly visible reward such as a chunk of red cheese that can be seen in the grass (this will give hunting breeds plenty of stimulation). Let your dog use its sense of smell to hunt down the treat. To create even more excitement, throw the cheese behind you when your dog is running towards you, so that it has to fly past you to get the reward. This makes recall a really exciting game for your dog.

After about a week of this training, choose a time when your dog is in the garden and you are indoors, watching it through the window. Call your dog by name and give the cue 'come'. If it comes charging into the house, give it a really high-value reward and praise it until it wags its tail. It now understands what 'come' means.

Having achieved this result, take your training to the next level. This requires a willing volunteer, some boring dog biscuits and a handful of really tasty treats. Place your dog by the volunteer and tell them to hold an ordinary dog biscuit right under the dog's nose. Stand about 3.6m (12ft) away, then call your dog. Repeat the command until it comes. Initially,

you'll have to call it five or six times but, eventually, it will respond more quickly. Always give it a special reward so that it knows it's worth responding. Give it better treats for better responses, until you eventually give it a handful of chicken.

If you practise a little and often, you will quickly reach this stage. The secret is to add the command 'come' after you call your dog's name and it runs towards you. This ensures that it's second nature for the dog to come whenever you ask it to.

For the final stage, you need a volunteer who knows your dog. Stand about 12m (40ft) away from your volunteer, get them to call your dog and, as it obeys and goes off, call it back when it is halfway there. Then try calling it back from playing with a friend's dog and even from strange dogs. Never forget how good it has been to obey you — make sure it gets an excellent treat for every recall. Having a good recall is the most important command that you teach your dog. A life on the lead is not good and, with that in mind, never stop rewarding successful recalls.

WHISTLE RECALLS

There are a number of benefits to teaching your dog to respond to a

whistle, not least because a whistle is much louder than your voice and can easily cut through a blasting winter wind. If you have a quiet voice and don't like shouting, a whistle is ideal.

Another advantage is that the sound is always the same, whether you walk the dog yourself, use dog walkers or if different members of your family walk the dog. It is a clear, distinct sound that will cut through any distractions or the sound of people talking. It is used for one command only — 'come here' — and should not be confused with anything else.

There are many different whistles on the market, and a loud one is best. The range includes specialist gundog whistles and a referee's whistle, and you might also like to try a silent dog whistle. It doesn't matter which one you use, provided you stick to it.

Like recall training, whistle training is all about repetition, so that the dog instinctively associates the sound with the command 'come here'. When training your dog, carry out the above procedure but exchange the 'come' command for a blow on the whistle. You can also make the association between the whistle and good news at meal times: hold a bowl of food, blow the whistle, then give your dog its dinner. If you do that for a week at every meal when it is a puppy (three times a day), it will make the connection. If your dog will retrieve a ball, try blowing the whistle as it comes towards you. This will strengthen the association between the whistle and the 'come' command. Finally, if you take your dog on a walk with a friend, practise whistle recalls between the two of you, increasing the distance as its reliability increases.

Lead-walking

▶ Reward your dog when it obeys your command to 'walk close'.

Teaching your dog to walk on a loose lead is one of the hardest things you'll have to do. Roads and parks are full of fascinating smells, the scents of other dogs and the aroma of dropped food, all of which entice your dog to pull away and investigate. When it becomes an adolescent, the urge to scent-mark over those smells will be very strong, and there'll be an extra need to pull you in all kinds of directions. In addition, most dogs quickly realize that if they pull when they are keen to get to the park, their owner tends to walk faster.

Most dog owners do not want obedience-style heelwork; all they want is to keep their arm in its socket and to have a pleasant walk! Dog-training classes often teach you to walk a dog on your left, simply because obedience competitions demand it, but for the average dog owner it really doesn't matter which side it walks on. If you are walking along a main road, it is usually safest to have your dog walking on the inside, away from the traffic.

Lead-walking can be difficult in terms of being consistent. If you are pushed for time and have to get home to leave for work after the morning walk, there isn't always time to stop every time your dog pulls. If so, unfortunately your dog's pulling behaviour will be reinforced.

There are many training aids to facilitate lead-walking. If you have a strong dog, a harness is a great help, and a head collar will give you more control, provided your dog will accept wearing one over its nose. Try out a few different ones to see which type your dog is most comfortable with.

Start by training your dog to walk by your side without its lead on. If your dog cannot do this without being distracted, it will not be able to walk on a loose lead. Begin by sitting it by your side, feeding it a few treats to get its attention. Pat the side of your leg as you step off to signal where you would like it to be, then reward it after a couple of steps. In fact, you cannot reward your dog too much in the early stages of teaching it to walk on a lead. Every couple of steps, offer another reward. Eventually, however, you'll want it to learn to walk calmly by your side with its head up, taking in a wide range of sights and smells; it would

▼ If your dog likes to pull hard, a harness will give you more control.

be unnatural for it to trot along while fixated on your hands and a possible reward. Until it reaches this more advanced stage, reward it when it's walking by your side, but don't stop to make it sit for its reward, otherwise it will think it's being rewarded for the act of sitting.

If your dog pulls ahead, resist the urge to yank it back on the lead – this is a sure way to damage its neck and hurt your shoulder. Instead, stop walking and take a couple of steps back until your dog is by your side. Get it to sit, gain its attention, then start again. Do not praise and reward your dog for just being by your side; save that for when it's walking calmly by your side on a loose lead.

Continue using vocal praise when the dog is positioned exactly where you want it to be, and always use the words 'walk close' when it is in the right position – not when it is pulling. Also reward your dog when it obeys you, especially when it stays by your side while walking past a distraction. The more encouragement you give it, the more it will learn not to pull and try to investigate everything. When it consistently and automatically responds to your commands, you can dispense with the food treats.

Phasing out the reward

The ultimate aim of training your dog is to get it to obey your commands whether you provide a reward or not. When your dog is a puppy, you need to reward and bribe it, but that state shouldn't exist forever. You can't keep stashing away rewards that will excite it (which soon becomes a practical problem), just to make sure it's obedient. The use of food becomes bad psychologically: there's a very real danger that your dog will become too reliant on rewards and bribes, and will never obey a command without food. In addition, rewards can become boring over time, and the behaviour you want to encourage will gradually diminish. But at what point should you start phasing out food treats? The answer is as soon as your dog understands a command and can respond correctly with a treat.

Put your treats somewhere that you can reach them but your puppy cannot, such as in your pocket or in a treat bag. Using the same hand movement that you used with the food lure, ask your dog to 'sit'. When it does, praise it profusely. Repeat the request several times, sometimes giving your dog a treat when it sits and sometimes not. There may be some confusion on your puppy's part when you first dispense with the food lure, but bear with it. You may need to ask it twice to begin with.

When your puppy manages to sit successfully without the food in your hand, you can now go on to rewarding the best responses. Make the rewards intermittent, only rewarding the very best responses and ignoring those that aren't as good. Use different rewards, such as a game of tug or throwing a ball, combined with verbal praise.

Improving training is all about getting the best out of your dog, so now is the time to ask more of it. Ask your dog to follow a few commands before you praise it – maybe a 'sit' and then a 'down'. Next, ask it to 'sit', walk ten paces away from it, then return and praise it. Then try asking it to 'sit', 'lie down' and 'sit' again, and then reward it. Don't be too predictable with your training; ask for cues in different combinations and reward your dog at different times.

Delay the time your dog follows a cue and gets its reward. Ask it to 'sit', count to ten, then reward it. Next time, ask it to 'lie down', count to five and then give it its reward. You will get the best out of your dog if you keep it guessing. If your training is boring and predictable, the dog will also find it boring and predictable, and you won't get the behaviour you deserve for all your hard work.

▲ *Eventually, praise, strokes and games can replace food rewards.*

When you begin asking more of your dog, it may break its positions – the dog is used to being rewarded immediately, but you are changing the conditions. Don't panic; just put the dog back in position and try an easier task. If you were trying for a ten-second sit and your dog gets up, put it back calmly and count to five instead. In time it will get it right, and its confidence will grow accordingly.

PHASING OUT FOOD REWARDS

1 Hide some treats in a bag. Ask your dog to 'sit', using the hand movements you used before, but without any food.

2 When the dog sits, praise it. On some occasions, give it a food treat; at other times, reward it with a game.

Biting

▶ *Biting is natural puppy behaviour, but don't encourage rough games.*

Like a baby, a puppy explores texture and taste by taking objects into its mouth and biting on them. However, a puppy learns from a very young age that its teeth can hurt, and that its biting behaviour has negative consequences. For example, when it begins hurting its mother while suckling, she will get up and walk away, thus initiating weaning it on to solid food. It also learns that its siblings have teeth that can hurt, usually ending in a fight or one puppy refusing to play.

Unfortunately, a puppy can be persistent in its biting, and if it bites children, their cries could send it into a biting frenzy. The more noise, the more biting; and the more you push the dog away, the more it throws itself back at you. Such puppies are usually overstimulated or over-tired, or

terriers, and the best way to respond is by calmly getting up and ending the game. If the puppy comes after you to bite your trouser leg, then put it behind a baby gate for a 'time out' period, and you will usually find that it lies down and falls asleep. If you respond with your own freneticism, you'll simply encourage more of the same. Don't forget that dogs only have one form of defence when it comes to self-preservation, and that is their teeth. This does not make them bad – they're just being dogs.

To help your puppy learn to have a 'soft mouth', and ultimately never to use its teeth on human skin, you have to act like its litter mate. If you receive a nip from your puppy, give a high-pitched squeal and turn your back on it. It should back off, possibly returning to lick you. Also make sure that you

give it acceptable items to chew, including raggers, rawhide chews and cardboard tubes from kitchen rolls.

Note that this method becomes less effective over time. An older dog is more likely to come at you with renewed vigour when you squeal. To avoid this, finish the game, get up and move away. If your dog follows you, put it calmly behind a baby gate. It is vital that everyone in the house responds in the same way, discouraging rough games. Remember: children should be supervised at all times when playing with a puppy.

Chewing

▶ *Provide your puppy with a good selection of chew toys.*

An activity that all puppies and adolescent dogs enjoy, chewing usually begins during the teething stages: 4 months old for puppies, and about 8 months old for adolescents. During the teething phase, puppies explore everything with their mouth. It is up to you to teach your puppy which objects are acceptable for it to chew.

To a dog, all of your possessions can seem like a stream of chew toys. Some items are obviously dangerous, such as electric and telephone cables, television remote controls, mobile phones and poisonous plants (including many bulbs, which dogs

can easily dig up). Discarded shoes and clothing can be tempting for your dog, as can children's toys. Maybe this is a good time to train everyone in your household to put their belongings away! Check that cupboard doors close correctly.

You can never eradicate a puppy's natural need to chew, but you can make sure that it chews safely. There are many types of virtually indestructible chew toys. Note that you should never give your dog plastic toys. These are dangerous because they can easily be broken into small pieces that get stuck in a dog's throat

or stomach, sometimes causing tearing when the dog passes a stool.

When teething, a knotted dish towel soaked in water and frozen will ease your puppy's sore gums. Some stores stock puppy teething toys that can be either frozen or chilled in the refrigerator. These are clean, dry and safe to use, even on a carpeted floor.

Digging

▶ *Digging is second nature to a dog, so it needs its own area in the garden.*

Do you have large craters on the lawn? Are your flowerbeds shredded? You have a puppy! Most dogs will do some digging at some time, whether they're burying a toy or just for the fun of it.

The best way to control this tendency is not by trying to eradicate it, but by fencing it off – literally. Trellis off part of the garden so that there is a clearly defined area where your dog can dig. Hide a few of your dog's favourite toys or biscuits under the soil. Teach it that this is its special digging place by allowing it to dig them up, and let it enjoy itself in its area.

If your dog is digging in another part of the garden, don't chase it away or you will simply teach it a new game –

next time it wants to play, it will start digging so that you come running after it. If you don't want it to dig in any part of the garden, buy it a child's sandpit, fill it with builder's sand and bury toys or biscuits in it. Cover the sandpit at night so that cats don't use it as a toilet.

Some dogs will try to dig under the garden fence in an attempt to escape. This will be dangerous if they succeed, so immediate action must be taken. Placing large rocks or boulders in the area where your dog is digging will put it off, but it may just move its tunnelling activities to another part of the boundary. In the short term, the best course of action is to fix strong wire mesh to the bottom of the fence

and to bury it at least 60cm (2ft) under the ground. Ensure that there are no sharp edges to the fencing.

In the long term, try to work out why your dog feels the need to escape. Does it have enough exercise, or could it be bored? Is there anything in the garden that it is afraid of? Increasing exercise, providing mental stimulation and ensuring the dog is not left alone for long periods will all help.

Jumping up

▶ *Jumping up is a nuisance and can become a dangerous habit.*

Particularly if you have a large breed of dog, jumping up can be a problem. It can be downright dangerous when a dog jumps up on children or the elderly, and although smaller dogs are not as dangerous, they can be a nuisance. The problem is that when puppies are young, we inadvertently teach them to jump up to say hello so that we don't have to bend down to reach them. But a puppy's growth rate is so fast that within 3 months you will have created a problem.

Training your dog not to jump up at people is important, as this problem can have very serious consequences. A stranger may mistake an over-enthusiastic greeting for an attack and be frightened. This could result in an

official complaint against your dog, and pleading a lack of training is not a very good defence! It's always your responsibility to control your dog.

To convert jumping up to sitting down for a greeting, ask your friends and family to help. Put your puppy on a lead and ask someone to approach it, but they must stop as soon as the dog strains on the lead to jump up. Ignore the puppy until it calms down, then reward it with a treat and get your friend to back off and approach again. It should only take four or five attempts to get your dog to understand that sitting for a greeting is the acceptable way to act. Practise on all family members, especially children. You, the owner, should always be the

one to reward the dog, otherwise it will assume that everyone carries treats around, making its jumping-up behaviour even worse.

If your dog jumps up on you at other times – not just when you have visitors or when you open the front door – this is probably attention-seeking behaviour. If so, you need to walk away from it as soon as the unwanted behaviour begins. It may take time and patience to re-model the jumping-up behaviour, but persevere.

71

Barking

▶ Once you have determined the cause of barking, it can be controlled.

It is natural for dogs to bark, but persistent barking can be a big problem, bringing trouble from neighbours and the authorities. If your dog barks when left alone, there could be several reasons for this. It could be bored, it could be guarding its home, or it might be suffering from separation anxiety. Puppies often feel anxious when their owners go out, and rescue dogs in particular can suffer from separation anxiety – and when anxious, they bark. But it's possible to overcome the problem.

First, you need to find out what the problem is. Perhaps your dog is being left alone for too long without adequate exercise and a chance to go to the toilet (dogs hate going inside the house). If this is the case, employ a dog walker. Also try taking your dog for a walk before you go to work, and leave it a good selection of toys to play with while you're out. If it barks when people walk past the window, close the door to that room so that it can't see out. It may be that your dog is alarm-barking because it can hear your next-door neighbours or noise from outside the home. If you think this is the case, try leaving a radio on when you go out. This will help to muffle any noise and make your dog feel more secure, so that it is less likely to feel it has to be on guard duty. Some dogs will also bark at cats or birds in the garden, in which case closing the curtains may help.

It is up to you to find out why your dog is barking – observe what is happening when it barks, make a checklist, and then do something to change the situation.

Stealing food and begging at the table

Understandably, dogs can be a nuisance when there's food about. Some dog owners advocate the use of punishment and setting up booby traps, but the reward of food is usually so good that most dogs are prepared to take the risk. It's actually very simple to stop a dog from stealing food: never leave it unattended where your dog can reach it.

Similarly, if raiding the bin is becoming a nightmare, keep it out of reach. As much as anything else, this is important for health reasons. There may well be dangerous items in the rubbish bin, such as broken glass or sharp chicken bones, which can cause your dog a bad injury, or even poisonous items. Don't risk it. Some dogs are very clever and can open refrigerator doors. Remedy this by fitting a child-proof catch.

It is also important that you are not taken in by those imploring, pleading, 'feed-me' eyes when your dog is looking up at you while you're eating at the table. If you give in and feed your dog a juicy sausage, it will begin a lifetime of hoping that you'll do it again next time. Eventually the pleading will become more animated, and it will begin to paw at you, whine and bark at every mealtime.

Be aware that dogs are very good at manipulating young children and are more than happy to act as dustbins for any food the child dislikes. It does not take long for a dog to learn to steal from a small child, whether the child wants to feed the dog or not. So it is important that children, too, understand the reasons why their pet should never be fed at the dinner table.

▲ A begging dog can become a problem, and should not be indulged.

If you do want to give your dog a treat, give it some food out of its own bowl. While you are eating, keep your dog happy by giving it a hide chew on its bed or in its crate.

Jumping on the sofa

You might never want your dog to jump on the sofa, you might want to move it out of the way when you sit down because it takes up so much room, or you might not want it leaving muddy marks on the furniture. What can you do? What you must *not* do is react with haste, grabbing your dog by the collar and yanking it off the sofa, accompanied by shouting at it. If you do this, the next time the dog is asked to get off the sofa, it may become defensive and give a warning growl. Further, the dog may have an ear infection, in which case grabbing the collar will also hurt it. So, it is best not to do it in the first place.

Instead, the best way to get your dog off the sofa is by using a training game, first teaching it to get on – yes, ON – the sofa. With a handful of treats, encourage the dog to jump on the sofa. You may want to cover the surface with an old sheet of blanket first. Reward the dog when it jumps up, then hold a treat near the floor to encourage it to jump off. Just as it is getting down, say 'off' (this is preferable to 'down', which can be confused with 'lie down'). Go through the process several times. Once your dog has learned the command, you should be able to get it to jump down whenever you want it off the sofa.

▲ *To train your dog to stay off the sofa, you must first teach it to jump on the sofa. Then, reward it for jumping off.*

If you let your dog into the bedroom, you can use the same 'off' command to teach it to get off the bed. The 'jump up' command can also be used to train it to jump into the car.

Problem behaviour in the older dog

If you have an older dog displaying problems that have not been covered in this book, it is best to get specialist help. In particular, aggression towards people or other dogs really needs professional help. Other problems might have an underlying medical cause that can be picked up by a vet or qualified behaviour counsellor.

Think about your dog's genetic history, training, diet and the circumstances that provoke or are associated with its bad behaviour. Observe and keep a diary, noting down what it does, when, for how long, and what external factors might have been the cause, then consult a vet. If you try to guess why problems occur and to cure them in a haphazard way yourself, you might exacerbate the bad behaviour, with the dog eventually ending up in a rescue centre.

If you need specialist help, don't be afraid to seek it. Ask your vet or dog-owning friends to recommend a good dog trainer and/or behaviour counsellor. If your vet refers you directly to a behaviourist, it is worth looking at the small print in your insurance documents to see whether you are covered for this and could make a claim. Specialist help can be costly, but it is nearly always well worth the expense if a satisfactory outcome can be achieved.

Take the diary that you have written regarding your dog's behaviour when you have your first appointment with the chosen trainer/behaviourist, as it will help them to get a clear picture of the problem. They will be able to advise you of any changes that you should make in your dog's lifestyle and help you put a remedial training

▲ *Older dogs may have problems that take a long time to sort out. Do not be afraid to seek specialist help from a professional, especially for aggression.*

programme in place. Do not expect an instant fix, but with patience and consistency most issues can usually be dealt with or, at the very least, the severity of the problem lessened.

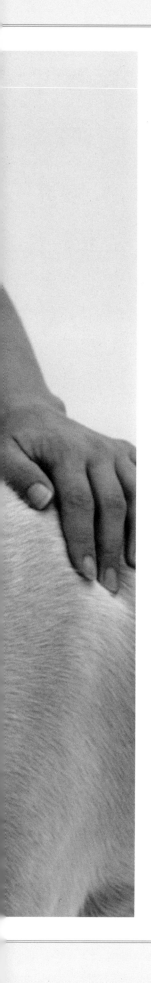

HEALTH CARE

The responsibility for a dog's welfare rests with the owner. This includes first aid, veterinary attention, pain relief and, sometimes, holistic medicine, which treats symptoms and looks for underlying causes. All dogs should be registered with a veterinary practice before they become ill. First aid cannot be considered a substitute for veterinary attention, but can be vital in stabilizing an injured or sick dog prior to transporting it to a veterinary clinic. It is also useful in treating minor injuries such as stings and small wounds.

All dog owners need to be aware of the signs of good and ill health. A healthy dog is alert and lively, and takes a great interest in its environment. There should be no discharges from the eyes or nose, and the latter should be moist and shiny. The ears should be clean and free of visible wax and the coat should be shiny and free of dandruff. The skin should be free from sores or spots. The dog should move soundly, without favouring one leg over another. A healthy dog should have a good appetite.

◄ *Regular veterinary checks are important – the vet may pick up the early symptoms of illness and be able to treat it before it becomes a major problem. Going frequently also means the dog is more used to the experience, which is especially beneficial for more nervous breeds, such as this Greyhound.*

Introducing your dog to the veterinary surgeon

Ideally, if you have not previously owned an animal, you should make the acquaintance of your local veterinary surgeon before you acquire the dog. How you choose a vet is a matter of personal preference. You may be guided by friends, or the convenience of the surgery, but there is no substitute for a personal interview to get an idea of how the practice runs, its surgery times and facilities, all of which the veterinary surgeon will be pleased to discuss with you.

Within 24 hours, you and your family are going to have grown very attached to your puppy. That is just the way it happens. It is important that, if the veterinary examination discovers anything that indicates the puppy should be returned to the seller, you should know immediately before this bonding has taken place. So,

▼ *Minimum restraint is important in encouraging your dog to relax at the veterinary surgery.*

you must arrange for the puppy's vet examination to take place on the day you collect it.

The veterinary surgeon will repeat the superficial health checks that you will already have carried out before buying the dog, but will go into greater detail, with a check on the puppy's heart and lungs, its ears and skin, its legs and feet and its genito-urinary system as far as possible.

This examination should not alarm the puppy. The veterinary surgeon will spend time getting to know your new dog with a little friendly fussing to give it confidence, before making the more detailed examination.

▲ *Most dogs, if handled with confidence, will not require heavy restraint during veterinary procedures.*

Unless it has already received its first inoculation, it will be given it now. This should not alarm the puppy, and many don't even notice the injection. At worst there may be a squeak, followed by some more comforting. The whole event should be very low-key. The vet will also probably advise on worming and anti-flea regimes, and tell you how long it must be before the puppy meets other dogs in order to give the vaccine a chance to develop the dog's immunity to infections.

The inoculation regime

The dog's inoculations cover a core of four major diseases: distemper, which includes hardpad; leptospirosis, a liver and kidney infection; hepatitis, caused by a liver virus; and parvovirus. Kennel cough vaccine may also be included at a puppy's primary vaccination stage.

The first component of the vaccination course is usually given at seven to eight weeks old, although in circumstances where there has been a perceived risk in the breeder's kennels, much earlier protection may be given against certain diseases. Such very early vaccinations are usually disregarded for the purposes of routine protection.

The second injection is given at around 12 weeks of age. The interval between vaccinations is necessary to allow the puppy's immune system to react properly to the first dose of vaccine; the second dose then boosts the level of immunity to such an extent that the dog is protected for a prolonged period.

The vaccines are repeated annually, a process known as 'boosters'. Owners are inclined to be lax in their response to booster reminders as the dog gets older. Don't! Although some elements of the dog vaccination programme may confer a solid immunity for life, this cannot be relied upon, and other elements definitely need boosting annually.

LIFELONG IMMUNIZATION

Some infections in dogs are unlikely to strike the dog more than once in its lifetime. Vaccination against these diseases may confer a lifelong immunity. The virus hepatitis of the dog is one of these diseases.

BOOSTER INOCULATIONS

Unfortunately, other infections, although again unlikely to affect the dog more than once, do not confer such a solid immunity for life, although the immunity that they do confer is excellent for as long as it lasts. Typical of this group is distemper and hardpad (which is caused by the same virus). Distemper vaccinations must be boosted about every second year in order to maintain a high level of immunity in the dog.

There is a third group of infections that may recur and to which the immunity offered by vaccination is relatively short-lived. It is still worthwhile to use the vaccine because of the dangerous nature of the illness. Such a disease is leptospirosis, transmitted usually by foxes or other dogs, but occasionally, in the case of one type of the disease, by rats.

Not all diseases to which dogs are susceptible can be avoided by vaccination, but the commonest killers certainly can.

KENNEL COUGH

A particular problem for which there is no total preventive control is kennel cough, an infectious inflammation of the larynx and trachea. Kennel cough may be an unfair description. The disease is transmitted by droplets coughed into the air by dogs actively suffering from the illness. Fairly close contact between dogs is necessary for its transmission, such as a nose-to-nose greeting through the wire by dogs in kennels. At least as common a cause is dogs meeting at shows, competitions or training classes.

Kennel cough is caused by a mixture of infectious agents. The most effective vaccine is given as a nasal spray. Most kennels advise owners to make sure their dogs have had a kennel cough vaccination shortly before going into kennels. Some insist on this before accepting the dog.

▼ *Inoculations are not usually painful to dogs, particularly if the animal is relaxed.*

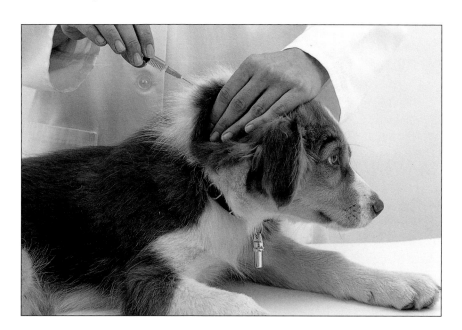

External parasites

Fleas, ticks, lice and mites are all external parasites. They affect the dog in a variety of ways. Some can cause serious skin disorders or even carry life-threatening diseases.

FLEAS

Start by assuming that your dog has fleas! They are by far the commonest external parasite of the dog, and many skin problems may be caused by fleas.

Fleas thrive in the warm and cosy environment of a centrally heated house, and there is no longer a flea season in summer followed by a flea-free winter. Treatment should be continued all through the year.

Fleas are often difficult to diagnose. They are small, move rapidly and are able to hop considerable distances. They are not very easy to see on the dog, but they never live alone. If you see one flea, it is safe to assume that there are plenty more. If you see none at all, they are probably still around.

A useful home test is to scrape hair detritus on to newspaper, and then to dampen the paper. If red smears appear, it is a certain indication that the dog does have fleas. The detritus may look like coal dust, but it is flea excreta.

Once you have convinced yourself that even your dog may have fleas, treatment is straightforward, although control is anything but. There are several effective sprays and washes available that will kill fleas safely (but some for which care is necessary), and most have some residual effect. But re-infestation is very difficult to prevent. If protection is, say, for three months, in practice the effectiveness is likely to decline well within that time. So some fleas come back.

Recent advances have been made with non-toxic preparations to be given to the dog monthly in tablet form. These do not kill adult fleas, but act by breaking the flea's breeding cycle. All flea treatments are demanding in that they must be given regularly if they are to work.

The important thing to remember is that fleas leave the host to reproduce, and that for every flea you find on

▶ *Scratching is normal, but persistent scratching demands attention. In nine out of ten cases, it will be something as simple as fleas. The most effective method to deal with the problem is to use a 'drop-on' preparation combined with a household spray. Your vet will advise on this.*

▲ *Dogs will lick and occasionally chew their paws, but if your dog does this persistently, examine its feet. Grass seeds are a common irritant.*

the dog, there are literally thousands in your dog's bed, in the nooks and crannies in the floor, in the carpets, between the cushions on the sofa, all breeding away like mad.

There are a number of preparations on the market that provide effective flea protection around the house. Thorough vacuuming of the carpets helps, but will not overcome the problem. Flea eggs, laid in their thousands, are able to survive for long periods in a warm environment. Disturbance causes the eggs to hatch, in itself a reason for regular vacuum cleaning, as the eggs in their shells are resistant to insecticides.

TICKS

These tend to be a country dog problem. The tick's usual host is the sheep. In the United States, Australia, South Africa and the tropics, ticks transmit certain rapidly fatal diseases to dogs, and the dogs are routinely dipped or sprayed against infestation, often on a weekly basis. This is not necessary in Europe, where tick-borne disease is uncommon in the dog.

Ticks engorge on the blood of their host; the engorged tick is sometimes mistaken for a wart on the dog's skin.

Dogs will occasionally pick up a solitary tick, but may sometimes be seen to have several. Adult female ticks lay groups of eggs, which hatch at more or less the same time to form a colony of young ticks attached to grass stems waiting to find a host. If a dog comes by, several of the 'seed ticks' may attach themselves to it.

The ticks are usually removed individually. Do not try to pick them off. That's rarely successful, and there are various substances that will kill them. Ear drops that are intended to destroy parasites are useful as is methylated spirit, or even gin! The tick will not fall off immediately, but it should have disappeared 12 hours

after application. Most anti-flea preparations will also kill them. In the USA, Lyme disease is transmitted by ticks that live on deer and mice, and is a serious threat to dogs. Fortunately, a vaccine is available.

LICE

Happily, lice are now uncommon parasites of the dog. They are detectable by the presence of just visible groups of eggs attached to the hair, often of the ears or head of the dog.

Lice are small and they are not mobile. They tend to occur in large numbers, but do not seem to be as itchy to the dog as fleas.

Lice are transmitted directly from dog to dog by contact. They are not transmitted to humans or to other animals. They may be controlled by the use of insecticidal shampoos.

▼ *The Elizabethan collar is extremely useful to prevent self-mutilation around the head. The cause of the inflammation must be determined.*

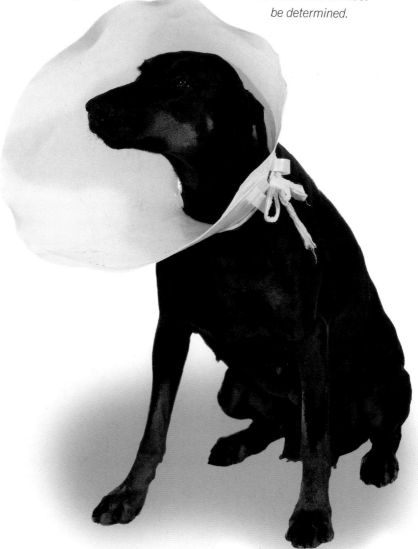

Worm control

Dogs are prone to both internal and external parasitic infestations. There are two common worms in dogs: the tapeworm and the roundworm.

TAPEWORMS

These may affect dogs at any age, although they are less common in young puppies than in older dogs. The tapeworm has a life cycle that depends on two different host species, in the case of the most frequently seen worm, the dog and the dog's fleas, although in another species they are transmitted through sheep.

Tapeworms may be recognizable as 'rice grains' in the faeces, but the dog may give you an indication by undue attention to its anal region.

Control of the tapeworm in the dog is simple; modern treatments are straightforward, requiring no fasting before dosing, and highly effective, with very little in the way of side effects (occasional vomiting).

It is a good idea to treat your dog routinely against tapeworms every six months. However, prevention of re-infection depends on control of the flea population in your house.

ROUNDWORMS

These are practically universal in puppies. They may be transmitted directly from dog to dog by faecal contamination, which is almost impossible to avoid. A high proportion of puppies are actually born infected with roundworms, transmitted via the uterus of the mother. Worms that had lain dormant in the tissues of the dam are activated by the hormones produced during pregnancy, circulate in the mother's bloodstream and pass into the unborn pups. There are

▲ *Any tablet needs to be given right to the back of the dog's mouth. Wrap it in something pleasant to distract the animal from spitting it out.*

control regimes that depend on using a safe anthelmintic early in pregnancy to destroy the maternal worm load, but this treatment is by no means universal.

A proper rearing regime includes dosing the litter when it is three or four weeks old, and perhaps again before leaving the kennels. Once home, the puppy should be treated regularly, every three to four weeks until it is six months old.

Adult dogs build up a level of immunity to the effects of roundworm infestations, and after six months do not need such regular treatment. Keep a constant look-out, although roundworms are not always easy to detect in a dog's faeces.

▶ *All dogs will lick and clean their anal region, but frequent licking is a sign that veterinary attention is needed.*

▲ *A dog will eat grass when its stomach is upset, but many dogs simply enjoy a little grazing. Some grass is an irritant and may induce vomiting.*

WORM TREATMENTS

Some drug treatments are effective against tapeworms and roundworms in one dose. The ascarid roundworm may be the cause of a very rare eye condition in children. If the dog is regularly wormed, the risk is eliminated. With this exception, the worms of dogs and of humans are not transmissible. Other species of worms, including the hookworm, may occur in dogs. Treatment is not difficult, but diagnosis may not be straightforward. Consult your veterinary surgeon. In the USA, heartworm is a common problem. A preventive medicine is given orally; treatment can be costly, and dangerous for the dog.

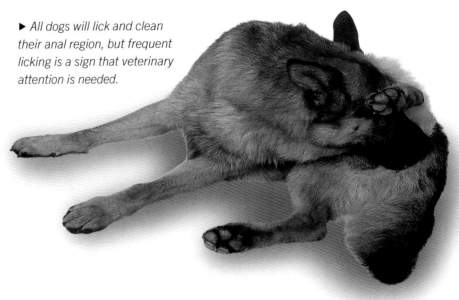

Signs of illness

One of the first signs that a dog is ill is if it refuses its food. Most fussy dogs will at least smell the food on offer, but a sick dog may have no appetite and simply not approach its food. The dog will tend to become duller than usual, although many sick dogs will still respond to their owner's enthusiasm for a game or a walk.

Signs of acute illness

Each of the following conditions needs immediate attention from your veterinary surgeon.

• Tense, swollen stomach. A drum-like swelling of the abdomen an hour or two after feeding, accompanied by obvious distress with panting and salivation may indicate that the dog has bloat. This is an emergency.

• Vomiting several times, particularly if it persists for more than 12 hours. Vomiting once or twice is common, and a normal reaction to eating something unsuitable. Some dogs eat grass, appearing to do it to make themselves sick. If this happens occasionally, there is probably nothing to worry about. However, persistent vomiting after eating grass may suggest an acute problem that needs attention.

• Diarrhoea persisting for 24 hours or longer. Diarrhoea will often accompany vomiting. If the faeces are bloodstained, treatment may be needed urgently.

• Difficulty breathing, gasping, coughing or choking.

• Loss of consciousness or fits.

• Serious uncontrollable bleeding.

▲ *The ear is an extremely sensitive organ. Any inflammation demands immediate attention from the veterinary surgeon.*

ACUTE ILLNESS

The term 'acute' does not necessarily mean a serious illness. When your veterinary surgeon refers to an acute illness, they simply mean one that has come on rapidly, whereas a 'chronic' illness is one that is long-lasting and has appeared gradually.

Young puppies are occasionally subject to fits, from which they usually recover quickly. Observe the fit carefully so that you can describe it when you get to the vet's. Did the dog just collapse silently, did it squeal or howl, did it paddle its legs, did it urinate or defecate during the fit? Once a dog has recovered from a fit, it may be very difficult for the veterinary surgeon to be precise about the cause; there may be nothing to see.

Other signs of acute illness include serious bleeding or bleeding from any orifice; obvious pain indicated by noise (squealing, crying, yelping on movement), lameness or tenderness to touch; straining to pass faeces or inability to pass urine; any obvious severe injury or swelling on the body;

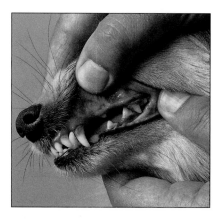

▲ *Dogs on modern diets are inclined to acquire tartar on their teeth, which needs attention if it is not to lead on to more serious problems.*

a closed eye or inflammation with excessive tears; and violent scratching or rubbing, particularly around the ears or head.

CHRONIC ILLNESS

The signs of chronic illness appear gradually and are likely to be more subtle and difficult to recognize.

Loss of weight, persisting over a period of weeks, is a common indicator of chronic disease. This may be accompanied by a normal or reduced appetite. Gradually developing swellings may indicate the growth of superficial tumours, often not cancerous but usually needing attention.

Other signs include hair loss, with or without sore skin or itching and scratching; slowly developing lameness; and excessive drinking, with or without an unpleasant odour from the mouth or body. Occasional vomiting may indicate an internal problem, although many healthy dogs may also vomit. In the normal course of events, bitches may frequently regurgitate food for their puppies.

First aid for your dog

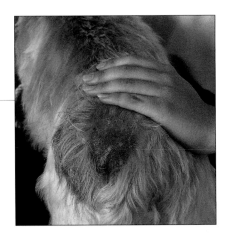

First-aid treatments may be divided into problems that you can deal with yourself, and treatments to carry out to keep the problem to a minimum before you take the dog to the vet.

SORES AND RASHES

A dog may get a sore place or a rash through chewing itself. Many dogs will chew their skin raw if there is an itch. The dog may get a rash from insect bites – typically flea bites, from skin contact with irritants such as nettles, or as an allergic response to an external or internal substance. It is often difficult to tell to what extent the sore area is caused by the irritant or is self-inflicted as a result of the irritation. The object of treatment, whether your own first aid or your veterinary surgeon's, is to eliminate the cause before attempting to cure the effect.

If a dog has been scratching itself a little more than usual, the commonest cause is the presence of fleas. Fleas never come singly. If you see a flea, there will be others. One or two may be sufficient to start the itch cycle. The answer is to treat the fleas, and the problem will usually disappear. If it doesn't, a soothing cream, such as rescue cream, will be sufficient.

CUTS AND SCRATCHES

Treatment depends on how large and how deep the cut or scratch is. A dog's skin does not usually bleed profusely, and it is easy to miss even quite a large cut because there may be very little bleeding and the dog's

▲ *Sores and rashes may develop beneath a long coat for some time before they become obvious.*

fur covers the site. If there is any sign of blood on the dog, look carefully and once you have located the cut, clip sufficient hair around it to expose the wound. If the cut looks deep, or longer than about 1cm (½in), it will need attention and probably a stitch or two at the veterinary surgery. If you decide to take the dog to the vet, do

First-aid kit

The most important item in your first-aid kit should be your veterinary surgeon's name and telephone number. Even though you may have it elsewhere, it does no harm to duplicate it.
- Absorbent cotton wool
- Adhesive and gauze bandages, 5cm (2in) and 10cm (4in)
- Gauze swabs and sterile wraps
- Cotton buds
- Sharp-pointed scissors
- Thermometer
- Medium forceps with blunt points
- Plastic syringe, 20ml (½fl oz)
- Eye drops
- Cleansing ear drops
- Antiseptic or antibiotic ointment
- Antiseptic powder and wash
- Rescue cream
- Medicinal liquid paraffin

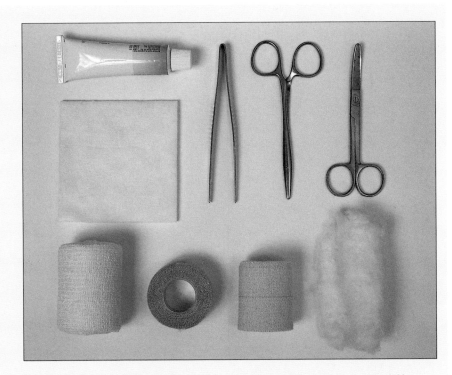

▲ *The forceps in a first-aid kit should never be used for probing around. You must always be able to see whatever it is you are attempting to remove.*

nothing with the wound, unless it is bleeding profusely. The nurse is likely to take longer cleaning your dressing off the wound than the stitching itself. A minor scratch that does not penetrate the skin will usually need very little treatment. Soothing cream will be sufficient. Similarly, a small cut needs no particular attention once you have trimmed the hair away, other than to keep the wound clean with a mild antiseptic solution, and to keep an eye out for any swelling. Swelling may indicate unfortunately that an infection has set in.

TAKING TEMPERATURE

1 First, shake the thermometer so that the level of mercury is well below the expected temperature of the dog.

2 Slide the lubricated thermometer carefully into the dog's anus and press lightly against the side of the rectum.

3 The thermometer should be held in place for at least 60 seconds before being read.

BANDAGING A PAW

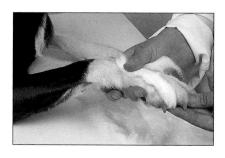

1 First, pad the leg with cotton-wool strips between the toes.

2 Place a generous amount of further padding over the end of the foot to cushion it before starting to bandage.

3 The bandage must always include the foot and be extended above the site of the wound.

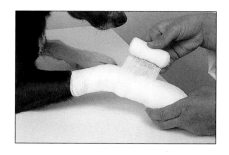

4 Bandage the leg firmly, but take care that the bandage is not so tight that circulation is restricted.

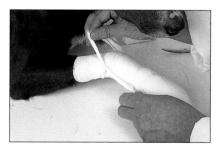

5 Tie the bandage off well above the site of the wound.

6 Cover the bandage in an adhesive dressing, firmly but not tightly, and secure it at the back of the dog's leg.

BITES

Dog bites will often become infected. This is particularly the case when the bite causes a puncture wound. Unless the wounds are multiple or very large, there is no emergency, but the dog should be taken to the veterinary surgery within 24 hours to allow the vet to assess whether antibiotic injections are needed. Prior to that, the wound may be cleansed with antiseptic lotion.

BLEEDING

Treatment will depend on how heavily the wound is bleeding. Skin wounds may only need cleansing, followed by the application of a little antiseptic cream and a careful monitoring of the progress of the wound. The bleeding will probably stop in a short time.

Profuse bleeding is an emergency, usually indicating a wound that is sufficiently deep to need urgent veterinary attention. Steps to control the bleeding while on the way to the surgery are worthwhile, and may be life-saving. Tourniquets are no longer used, so do not attempt to make one. Instead, use a pressure bandage over the wound.

The rare need for a pressure bandage is one reason for the cotton wool and bandages in your first-aid

▲ *On warm days, even with a window open, a car will rapidly become an oven. Don't cook your dog.*

kit. When needed, take a large wad of cotton wool — as large as is available in your kit. Place it directly over the wound, and bandage firmly. If the wound is on a limb, bandage right down to the foot and include the entire leg below the wound in your bandage. Make sure the site over the wound is firmly bandaged, and then take the dog to the veterinary surgery.

BANDAGING AN EAR

1 Ears are often damaged in dog fights. Clean the wound, then place an absorbent pad behind the ear.

2 Carefully fold the ear back on to the pad. Place the pad over the folded-back ear.

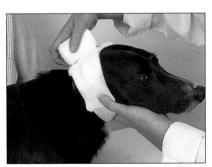

3 Start bandaging around the neck from behind the ear and work forwards, enclosing the ear, but not too tightly.

4 The unaffected ear should not be included in the bandaging.

HEAT EXHAUSTION

Some breeds of dog are more prone to heat exhaustion than others — Chow Chows and Bulldogs come to mind, but several other short-nosed breeds can also be affected.

The most common reason for heat exhaustion is human error. Dogs are too often left inside cars in summer without adequate ventilation. The owner is usually just thoughtless, or caught out by a change in the weather during a longer-than-expected shopping trip. The temperature inside a closed car in summer in even a temperate climate can kill a dog.

The signs of heat stress are obvious distress, heavy panting and an inability to breathe deeply enough, indicated by a half-strangled noise coming from the dog's throat. The dog's tongue looks swollen and blue.

Treat heat stroke as an immediate emergency, and do not attempt to take the dog to the vet until you have started its resuscitation. Plenty of cool (not cold) water and shade is the first-aid treatment. First, move the dog to a shaded area, with a breeze if possible, or use an electric fan. Apply plenty of cool water, especially to the head and neck. Continue with this treatment until breathing becomes easier, but avoid cooling the dog to an extent that it starts to shiver. Then take it to the veterinary surgeon.

The vet may put the dog on to an oxygen air flow, and will probably give it an injection to reduce the swelling in its throat, but unless the vet happens to be at hand, for example if the animal is at a dog show, this life-saving treatment needs to have been given before the dog gets to the surgery.

BANDAGING A TAIL

1 Successful tail bandaging is fraught with difficulty. First, enclose the tail lengthways in a bandage.

2 Lay strips of bandage along the length of the tail.

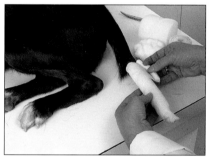

3 Bandage the tail around its length, whenever possible including some of the dog's tail hair within the turns of the bandage.

4 Cover the bandage with an adhesive dressing. Take the adhesive dressing well above the end of the bandage, and include strands of hair within each turn.

TREATING HEAT STROKE

1 The first signs of heat stroke in your dog are obvious distress and incessant heaving panting. This is a serious condition that needs quick treatment.

2 Cool the dog down immediately by sponging or spraying with cool (not cold) water, ensuring the head and neck are wet.

3 Allow the dog to drink a small amount of water. A wet towel, frequently changed, will help to cool the dog down, and may prevent heat stroke.

◄ *Sick dogs may be encouraged to eat but never force-fed. They should always have easy access to water.*

SNAKE BITES, AND STINGS FROM OTHER VENOMOUS CREATURES

These are often difficult to recognize unless the bite is witnessed. The degree of urgency depends on the type of venomous creature, where on its body the dog was bitten, and the age of the dog. Small puppies are obviously more at risk than older, larger animals.

The only venomous British snake is the adder. The risk is greater in areas with certain types of soil — sandy downs seem to harbour more adders than most other areas. In the USA, Australia and Africa, the most common snake bites in dogs are from the viperine snakes. Poisonous North American snakes include rattlesnakes and coral snakes. Snakes are often more likely to bite when they come out to sun themselves on a warm spring day and the dog goes to investigate. So, the dog is most likely to be bitten on the face, head or neck.

If the dog's face starts to swell up while you are out on a walk, the chance of a snake bite must be considered. Unless the swelling starts to cause obvious breathing distress,

TREATING EYES

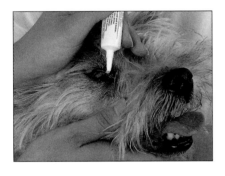

1 Take great care when administering eye drops or ointment. It is important to hold the dog's eyelids open so that the medication actually goes into the eyes.

2 After the drops have been put in, the eyelids must be gently massaged over the surface of the eye to encourage the spread of the medication.

BRUSHING TEETH

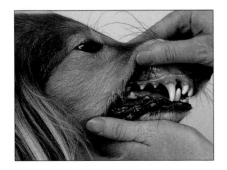

1 Regular brushing will slow up the formation of plaque and tartar.

2 Some dogs will resent the use of a brush, but toothpaste on the end of a finger can be almost as effective.

3 Specially made dog toothbrushes are often well tolerated.

▶ *Disturb an injured dog as little as possible, although be prepared to lift it carefully and take it to a vet.*

treatment is urgent, but this is not a life-threatening emergency. You can afford to walk back to the car – no need to run – but make sure the dog walks quietly. Exercise should be minimal. Carry a small dog. Take the dog straight to the veterinary surgery. Very few dogs in Britain die from the effects of adder venom, but many each year have distressing abscesses caused by a combination of the venom and infection. In the USA, Eastern diamondback and coral snakes are the cause of 20 per cent of dog fatalities from snake bites.

Bites from non-venomous snakes should be thoroughly cleaned, as the snake's teeth may be carrying bacteria, which could cause infection.

The only reason to include snake bites in the first-aid section is that there is a belief that the venom of a snake should be 'sucked out' of the wound. Do not attempt to do so.

Bee and wasp stings carry a similar risk of death to snake bites – generally, they are only likely to be lethal if the swelling from the bite blocks the dog's airway. The exception to this is the case of multiple stings, the shock of which can cause the death of the dog. However, such events are rare.

Venomous spiders are unknown in the United Kingdom and uncommon in the United States, although they do occur there. The Australian funnel-web spider, however, is an extremely venomous arachnid.

A single swelling from a bee or wasp sting does not usually require veterinary treatment, but home attention with a soothing cream will speed the dog's recovery, and possibly stop the 'sore scratch' cycle.

CHOKING

Some dogs are inveterate pickers-up of sticks and stones, or ball chasers. All carry the risk of getting an object stuck in the mouth or throat. A half-swallowed ball may be an emergency by reason of a blocked airway. First aid may be a two-handed job, as you could get bitten. If the dog seems to be choking, look in its mouth with care. A block of wood to prevent it closing its teeth over your fingers can help, with one person holding the dog's head while the other looks into its mouth. If there is a ball in the dog's throat, try to lever it out with a fine rod rather than with your hand.

A frequent occurrence is that a piece of wood becomes wedged across the teeth, or between the back teeth. Treat removal with similar caution, using some sort of lever to remove it. This type of incident not infrequently requires a trip to the vet and sedation to remove the object.

ROAD ACCIDENT

It is virtually certain that a dog involved in a road accident will not be under control. The first step, even before looking to see what may be wrong, is to leash the dog with whatever comes to hand. But you must do this without risk to yourself.

A noose needs to be made and slipped over the dog's head without actually touching the dog. The noose may be easily made from your own dog's lead or any other line, or even a piece of string.

▼ *Many road accidents and injuries to dogs may be avoided if the owner exercises the dog sensibly by restraining it with a lead.*

► *Large injured dogs may be carried with one arm at the front of their chest, under the neck, and the other looped through to allow the back legs to hang. A muzzle may be necessary.*

The next step, unless the dog is unconscious, is to muzzle the dog. Any dog that has been involved in a road accident is likely to be in shock, and even the most friendly can bite whoever is attending it, through pain or fear. You are unlikely to be carrying a proper muzzle with you. A cord, a dog lead or a bandage can be used. Only once the dog is secure, and you are unlikely to be bitten, should you try to examine the dog.

If the dog is not conscious, do not try to resuscitate it – get it to the vet as quickly as possible. If other people are there, ask someone to phone ahead to the surgery to warn them that you are coming.

A coat or blankets may be used as a makeshift stretcher, but only a dog that is so badly injured that it is unaware of its surroundings is likely to tolerate being carried in this way.

If the dog is bleeding heavily, use whatever is available to make a pressure pad; bind the wound and take the dog to the veterinary surgery immediately.

If the dog is carrying a leg, or is limping, there may be a fracture. Despite the first-aid warning about not moving an injured person, you are better to take the dog straightaway to the veterinary surgery than to wait while someone phones around to find a vet who can leave the surgery to attend the accident. There is no organized emergency ambulance service for animals.

Once the dog's mouth is bound and it cannot bite, it is almost always safe to carry the dog. If possible, let the affected leg hang free – you will avoid further damage and pain.

Dogs in road accidents will often run away, despite serious injury. If you see this happen, warn the police, who will at least be able to inform anyone who enquires about their missing dog. Sometimes the police will accept responsibility for the care of dogs involved in road accidents. If they are informed and are able to attend the scene, they will usually know the local veterinary surgeons and be able to advise on their phone numbers.

MUZZLING AN INJURED DOG

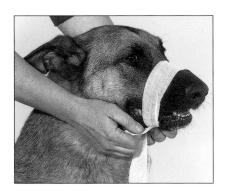

1 An improvised muzzle may be made with a bandage or almost any material. Make a loop, pass it over the dog's muzzle and under its chin.

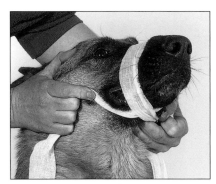

2 Take the ends of the material behind the dog's ears.

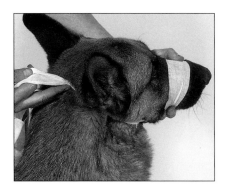

3 Tie the muzzle firmly behind the dog's head. An improvised muzzle must be tied tightly. It will not choke the dog.

POISONING AND COMMON POISONS

The poisons likely to be encountered by a dog are almost always those found around the house and garden. They include tablets and medicines intended for human consumption, or those not for internal use at all — household chemicals such as bleach or detergents, and garden chemicals.

Puppies will try anything. You must keep all potentially dangerous materials out of their reach, preferably in a locked cupboard.

If an accident does occur, and you think your dog has eaten something that could be poisonous, there are two things to do:

1 Make the dog sick. If this is to be of any help, it must be done before the poisonous substance has had a chance to be absorbed from the stomach, so do it before contacting

▲ *Cigarettes are toxic to dogs and might cause nicotine poisoning. Fortunately, however, few dogs will actually eat cigarettes.*

your veterinary surgeon. But if you know your vet is immediately available for advice, and you are certain what the dog has eaten, do not make the dog sick until you have spoken to the vet.

The most effective substance to use to make the dog sick is washing soda. Put two small crystals on to the back of the dog's tongue, and make the animal swallow them by

▲ *If poisoning is suspected, take the container and, if possible, some of its contents to the veterinary surgeon with the dog.*

holding its mouth shut and stroking its throat. Vomiting will take place within minutes, so be prepared with old newspapers to hand.

2 Contact your veterinary surgeon. Retain some of the poisonous substance, or at least its wrapping, to show them. There may be no ill effect, or immediate further treatment may be necessary.

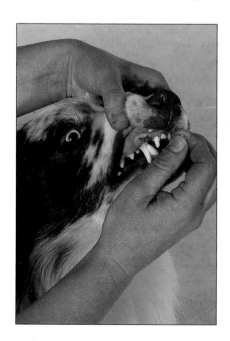

▲ *Do not make the dog vomit if the toxic substance is already being absorbed, which occurs within 30 or so minutes of ingestion.*

Some common poisons

• Rat poisons — all rat poisons are coloured to indicate the active substance. They are of low toxicity to dogs when used properly, but dogs may get hold of bulk quantities.
Blue: Anticoagulants
Brown: Calciferol
Green: Alphachloralose
Pink or grey: Gamma-HCH (Lindane)

If rat poisoning is suspected, the package or some of the suspect material must be retained for examination by the veterinary surgeon.

• Barbiturates — human sleeping pills
• Sodium chlorate — weed killer
• Detergents — usually safe, but if concentrated, they may cause external lesions, or vomiting if they are swallowed
• Antifreeze — Ethylene glycol
• Lead — old paint chewed by dogs
• Slug bait — Metaldehydrate, attractive to dogs; some brands now have an anti-dog component
• Cigar and cigarette ends — nicotine
• Organochlorine, Organo-phosphorus compounds — flea and lice killers
• Paraquat — herbicide
• Aspirin — if taken in large quantity
• Strychnine — vermin killer; dogs may get at carcasses
• Toad — from mouthing the toad; exotic toads are more venomous
• Tranquillizers

Inherited diseases

An inherited disease is one that may be passed from generation to generation through affected genes of the sire or the dam, or sometimes a combination of both. Genetics, the study of inheritance, is a highly complicated science, becoming increasingly so the more we learn of the subject.

There are two main problems in the control of inherited diseases in dogs. Some diseases are partly inherited, and partly occur as a result of some environmental influence, which is often difficult to determine precisely. The inherited element may depend on several inherited factors rather than a single gene.

Typical of this type of disease is hip dysplasia, probably the most widely known of all inherited diseases of the dog. It is a hind-leg lameness, caused by severe erosion and damage to the hip joint. It is generally considered that inheritance accounts for about 50 per cent of the clinical signs of hip dysplasia, and that the remainder is caused by some environmental circumstance – the dog's weight, exercise, diet perhaps – but precisely what is not known. In these circumstances, attempts at control are slow at best, depending on diagnosis of the disease and the avoidance of affected dogs in breeding. This may sound simple, but it is not.

▲ *The breeder carries a heavy burden of responsibility to produce a healthy, keen-to-please dog such as this German Shepherd Dog.*

The condition affects many breeds, mostly the larger ones, including the German Shepherd. Largely due to the efforts of German Shepherd breeders, control schemes have been operating in several countries for many years. Progress has been real but is slow, and sometimes heartbreaking for breeders, who may have used a dog and a bitch that both have excellent 'hip scores', only to find that the offspring are seriously affected.

The second problem is that the disease may not show itself until the affected animal is mature. The dog or bitch may well have been used in a breeding programme before any signs that it has the condition are seen. To some extent, this may be overcome by control schemes that do not give certificates of freedom from the disease until the dogs in the scheme are old enough for the particular

◀ *This Irish Setter is free from the distressing condition of Progressive Retinal Atrophy (PRA), which responsible breeders are doing a great deal to eliminate in the breed.*

before sale, not only for total deafness, but for partial deafness in one or both ears. There is evidence that partially deaf dogs can pass on partial or complete deafness to their offspring, and the numbers of dogs being tested are increasing rapidly in several countries. The test for dogs originated in the United States, which is probably leading the world in this area.

Almost certainly, studies of the 'genome' or genetic make-up of all species are resulting in a revolution in the study and control of genetic diseases. Once the precise positions of inherited diseases on the DNA molecule are known, specific action may be taken to eliminate the problem. This approach is no longer 'pie in the sky'. DNA testing has now become routine.

▲ *Until a specific gene test becomes practicable, it is important that not only this pregnant Dalmatian bitch but also the sire have been certified healthy.*

disease to have shown itself. Hip dysplasia is again an example: hip scoring is by an expert panel who examine X-rays of submitted dogs. These X-rays may not be taken until the dog is 12 months old.

There are several diseases that are known to be inherited in a straightforward way and are present at birth. These diseases can be controlled, depending for the success of the control scheme on the co-operation of the breeders, and their recognition that animals that show signs of the disease are actually afflicted, rather than the subject of mysterious accidents that merely mimic the condition.

The most outstanding example of breeder co-operation in the control of inherited disease must be the experience of Progressive Retinal Atrophy – night blindness – in Irish Setters. Thanks to the involvement of nearly all the breeders, and with recognition that the disease had a straightforward inheritance pattern, this condition has been virtually eliminated from the breed.

Another such scheme includes one to control deafness in Dalmatians. For many years, a proportion of Dalmatian puppies have been born deaf or partially deaf, but breeders were generally only able to recognize stone-deaf puppies, which were routinely put to sleep soon after birth.

Scientific testing, developed for use in people, has now enabled breeders to have their puppies examined

▼ *Dalmatians may be tested scientifically for deafness before they are six weeks old.*

Neutering, spaying and breeding

Being a responsible dog owner means that you will not increase the number of unwanted dogs being sent to rescue centres. Every year, thousands of dogs are put down because they are unwanted, but having your dogs neutered and spayed will stop unwanted pregnancies, and also provide health benefits. Such treatment can substantially lower the risk of prostate problems and testicular cancers in male dogs later in their life, and mammary cancers and pyometra (a life-threatening disease of the womb) in bitches. Neutering and spaying is the responsible, practical approach to dog ownership.

Health checks

There are health checks for certain breeds of dog: Labradors, Border Collies and Golden Retrievers are prone to hip problems, and the parents should be hip-scored. Hips can only be X-rayed when the dogs are 12 months old. The X-rays are examined by the vet and given a score on nine points of the hip joints. The lower the score, the better the hip joint (a perfect score is 0/0 and the worst is 53/53). Border Collies and Tibetan Rerriers need eye checks; Dalmatians are prone to deafness, and Cavaliers and Boxers are prone to heart issues and need checks before they are mated. In addition, the stud needs to be checked for potential problems, and both dog and bitch need a good temperament with no aggression.

NEUTERING AND SPAYING

It is often thought that castration will cure any problem with an adolescent dog, including jumping up and overexcitement, but in fact castration only helps with problem: directly related to testosterone (and definitely not those caused by attention-seeking). If testosterone levels are high, then roaming the neighbourhood looking for bitches (with the risk of getting run over and causing accidents), scent-marking, mounting inappropriate objects and people, and male-to-male aggression may be remedied, but extra training sessions will also be required. However, contrary to misconception, neutering and spaying does not alter the personality of the dog, nor does it make the dog fat (this is usually caused by a lack of exercise). Both operations will, however, make a dog a more content member of the family.

Spaying bitches will also halt phantom pregnancies, which can be upsetting for both the bitches and their owners. A bitch having a phantom pregnancy may carry a toy around in her mouth as a substitute for a puppy, become aggressive towards other dogs, be moody and withdrawn, and may stop eating.

People can have strong feelings for and against getting dogs and bitches neutered and spayed, but it's important not to confuse a human's response with what's best for your dog. As for the ideal age, the best advice is to wait until your dog has matured emotionally and physically, although if your male dog is beginning to show behavioural problems caused by high testosterone levels, you should castrate sooner rather than later.

▲ *Bitches can have as many as 12 puppies in a single litter.*

TO BREED OR NOT TO BREED

If you do decide to let a bitch have a litter, it's best to do your research. This is a responsible, time-consuming job. Your bitch will need a quiet room in the first weeks. If you think you can make a quick profit, this is not correct: breeding is an expensive business.

The first job is to check whether a Caesarean operation is likely, and to make sure you know what to do if there are any problems during whelping. The size of the litter can be 1–12 puppies, with larger dogs producing larger litters – and they all need to be cared for. You will have to start house-training them, oversee the first inoculation, let them socialize and keep them for eight weeks until they are ready to go to their new homes.

You'll also need to be sufficiently knowledgeable about dogs to impart all the relevant information to the new owners, from diet and worming to socialization and training – and field their emergency phone calls. If you do decide to breed from your bitch, check the suitability of prospective new owners by visiting them in their home. Finally, be prepared to take any of the puppies back into your care should anything go wrong along the way.

Alternative medicine

Modern conventional veterinary medicine is science-based. It depends on research that produces repeatable results in the hands of competent scientific investigators, and it is subject to a considerable measure of official control with respect to safety and efficacy. The science-based approach to illness is essentially that of treating the root cause of the disease itself. Critics of this approach worry that too little attention is given to possible side effects of often quite potent medicines.

Holistic medical practitioners, typified by homoeopathic doctors and veterinary surgeons, regard the symptoms as essentially the reaction of the animal's body to the disease. They aim to treat the whole animal, rather than the symptoms of the disease alone.

Some alternative therapies are difficult to assess scientifically. For

◀ Osteopathy may produce more satisfactory long-term results in musculo-skeletal problems in dogs than the continuous use of corticosteroids, with their risk of side effects.

Homeopathic remedies
- Arnica – bruising, shock and after injury
- Belladonna – aggressive behaviour, ear problems and acne
- Cantharis – cystitis and kidney problems
- Cocculus – travel sickness
- Gelsemium – nervousness and timidity
- Nux Vom – digestive upsets
- Pulsatilla – irregular seasons
- Rhus Tox – arthritis and rheumatism
- Scutellaria – nervousness, apprehension and excitability
- Sulphur – skin conditions

instance, the holistic approach may require an animal, with apparently the same set of symptoms as another, to be treated differently because it is perceived by the practitioner to have a different basic temperament.

HOMEOPATHY
Homoeopathy is based on an ancient medical practice of treating 'like with like'. There are three basic principles:
1 A medicine that in large doses produces the symptoms of a disease will in small doses cure that disease.
2 By extreme dilution, the medicine's curative properties are enhanced, and all the poisonous side effects are lost.

3 Homoeopathic medicines are prescribed following the study of the whole individual and according to basic temperament.

Conventional veterinary surgeons acknowledge that all side effects are removed in extreme dilutions, and to that extent, homoeopathic medicines are safe. Many argue that to be safe, if ineffective, by reason of the absence of any therapeutic substance is a spurious safety. Despite reservations about homoeopathy, it is almost certainly the most widely applied form of alternative therapy.

Homoeopathic remedies are invariably given by mouth, including the homoeopathic equivalent of vaccines, known as 'nosodes'. The medicines are either in tablet or powder form, with no unpleasant taste.

A few veterinary surgeons use homoeopathy exclusively, while a number use it regularly as part of their armoury of treatment. They tend to select cases that they consider likely to respond better to homoeopathy than to conventional medicine, often the more chronic conditions in which conventional treatments can only suppress the symptoms, sometimes with undesirable side effects.

Veterinary surgeons using homoeopathic medicine are usually known to their colleagues locally, who will happily refer patients to the appropriate practice on request.

ACUPUNCTURE

Acupuncture is another form of treatment with roots going back thousands of years. The practice originated in China.

Treatment involves the insertion of fine needles into the skin of the patient along what are known as 'meridians', which bear no relationship to recognized nerve tracks. Application of the needles reduces pain considerably, sometimes to the extent that surgery can be carried out without the patient experiencing discomfort.

Although for many years it was assumed by Western doctors that the effect was purely psychological, acupuncture appears to have definite analgesic properties in animals, rather giving the lie to the 'purely psychological' claim.

Many dogs seem remarkably tolerant of the application of acupuncture needles, and there is

a considerable body of empirical evidence that it can have a beneficial effect on musculo-skeletal problems in dogs, as well as a less-documented effect on other chronic diseases.

Acupuncture is a whole system of medicine in Chinese tradition, but in Western veterinary medicine, it's used as an auxiliary to other more conventional treatments.

There are few associations of veterinary acupuncturists, and practitioners of this skill in veterinary medicine are relatively uncommon. There are, however, sufficient vets with an interest in acupuncture to make it worthwhile asking your own veterinary surgeon for help if the occasion arises.

HERBALISM

Herbalism has probably the longest tradition of any system of medicine known to man. Plants have been used for their medicinal properties since time immemorial, and they have provided the basis of the modern pharmaceutical industry's research programmes since its foundation. Many modern drugs are derived from plant products.

It is inevitable that with a practice as steeped in antiquity as herbalism, different traditions have grown up in different parts of the world. For instance, there is a Chinese tradition, and Islamic influences in Western herbalism are clearly marked.

Herbalists differ from conventional therapists in their use of the whole plant, or unrefined extracts of parts of the plant, rather than specific chemical entities isolated from the plant. The best-known illustration of this difference in approach is the use of the foxglove plant. The foxglove

(*Digitalis purpurea*) was discovered to have a beneficial effect on some of the symptoms of heart disease many hundreds of years ago. An extract of the plant has been in use since the eighteenth century, but

▲ *Liquorice root has mild laxative properties to ease constipation.*

Common herbal remedies
- Buchu – diuretic and urinary antiseptic
- Cascara – laxative, bitter tonic
- Cayenne – circulatory stimulant
- Dandelion – liver problems
- Elderberry – rheumatism, anaemia
- Eucalyptus – bronchitis
- Garlic – infections, worm infestations
- Liquorice – anti-inflammatory, mild laxative
- Peppermint – colic, travel sickness
- Raspberry – reproductive problems
- Rhubarb – constipation and diarrhoea
- Skullcap – hysteria, anxiety
- Valerian – colic, travel sickness, behavioural problems

it has always been recognized as being dangerous in overdosage. Pharmaceutical chemists were able to isolate active elements in foxglove extracts, which enabled them more accurately to prescribe the drugs for control of heart disease. But *Digitalis*, the original extract of foxglove, still has its adherents in medical practice, who prefer it to the more refined alternatives, suspecting that the process of refinement removes some part of the efficacy of the original.

Compared with conventional medicine, herbalists have, once again, a more holistic approach, preferring to treat the whole animal rather than a specific disease.

Despite the holistic approach of the veterinary herbalists, some of their preparations have become so well established that they are regarded almost as conventional medicines. One remedy, available in Europe, with remarkable powers is rescue cream.

▲ *The leaves of the peppermint plant are mainly used for their effect on the digestive tract.*

▲ *Skullcap is a calming herbal remedy to reduce stress.*

This is a general salve that soothes and restores damaged skin. Its efficacy is at least comparable with many restricted, prescription-only skin preparations.

There are very few veterinary herbalists, but some countries have an official institute of medical herbalists, which could put you in touch with a practitioner.

AROMATHERAPY

Aromatherapy could be regarded as an offshoot of herbalism, in that the system uses extracts from plants, prepared as the essential oils of those plants, as a form of therapy. The oils are used either for massage or simply inhaled by a diffusion into the air, and are considered to be useful for a wide range of ailments.

Aromatherapy is rarely used by veterinary surgeons, although some owners are sufficiently knowledgeable to be able to use the therapy as an adjunct to conventional medicine.

OSTEOPATHY

Veterinary osteopathy is now well established as a supportive therapy in veterinary medicine.

Osteopathy, as originally understood, held that most or all diseases are caused by displacement of bones and are curable by manipulation. It is doubtful if any practising osteopaths now adhere totally to this doctrine, but it is certain that manipulation can effect considerable improvement in a number of chronic-disease conditions. Musculo-skeletal problems in the dog seem to be particularly responsive. As with the insertion of acupuncture needles, dogs seem to tolerate osteopathy remarkably well, although some naturally unruly dogs may need sedation before treatment.

PHYSIOTHERAPY

Physiotherapists have long had an association with conventional medicine. Their approach is more scientifically based than traditional osteopaths, and their training and work is medically supervised. Physiotherapy treats illness by physical measures. It includes massage and manipulation, in which respect it is like osteopathy, but also uses heat, electricity, and passive or active exercise. It aims to restore the functions of joints and muscles.

Many physiotherapists are involved in veterinary medicine, but there is no specific association. Vets usually know of a physiotherapist with an interest in veterinary work, and will happily refer a patient. Fractured legs on the mend often respond well to physiotherapy, which stimulates muscles and tendons that have tended to waste or lose their strength during the period of bone healing. Physiotherapy may be used in any circumstances where gentle, trained manipulation is likely to improve mobility.

Dogs and human health

There are some diseases that may affect both dogs and humans. The technical term for such a disease is 'zoonosis'. The most feared of these diseases is undoubtedly rabies, the reason for long-standing quarantine laws between the UK and all other countries, which have only recently been changed. The laws throughout the EU countries have now been dramatically relaxed for many domestic pets. It is now possible to acquire a 'pet passport', which allows owners to bring their pet into Britain. However, rules have changed since the UK left the EU, so make sure you check the government website.

The passport requirements are very stringent and include a full health check by a vet, which includes up-to-date immunizations against rabies and many other diseases. Animals must also have an identification chip inserted, a photo, current certificates and pet insurance.

When travelling in an area that is not rabies-free, consult a doctor immediately if you are bitten by a dog or any other animal.

Fleas, common on dogs (but most frequently actually the cat flea) will bite humans. It is unlikely that dog or cat fleas can survive on humans, so a few intensely itchy bites are the only likely problem. The presence of flea bites on you or your children is a timely reminder that flea control on your dog has, perhaps, not been as effective as you thought.

Rabbit mites frequently cause a skin rash in dogs. They are capable of biting humans, and may cause an itchy rash on the forearms from contact with the affected dog, however the rash is unlikely to spread.

Ringworm is not a common disease in dogs but, when it does occur, precautions should be taken to avoid its spread to human members of the family. It is a true zoonosis and can establish itself on the human skin. Affected areas are again likely to be those of contact – the hands and forearms in particular.

Toxocara, the most frequently encountered roundworm in puppies, and indeed almost universal in very young puppies, has been implicated in a rare specific type of eye disease in children. Roundworms that are ingested by a species other than their

◄ *The many benefits of association between children and dogs far outweigh the risk of cross-transmission of diseases. Sensible hygiene will almost always overcome the risks.*

◄ *Dogs should never be permitted to run freely where children may play, because of the risk that the animals may deposit faeces.*

▼ *Many local authorities provide dog litter bins, which should be used.*

normal host may encyst and settle in almost any part of the body, but are known to invade the eye. These cysts have been known to cause blindness. Such an occurence is extremely rare but, of course, a tragedy for the child and their parents if it happens.

Good hygiene and vigilance should prevent any child from coming into contact with dog faeces. Puppies must be wormed regularly, every three weeks until they are six months old. Their faeces must be collected, at home as well as on the street, and the puppy should be taught to defecate in a prescribed spot in the garden, not in a public place. If an accident does happen while you are out with your dog, scoop it up. Always go prepared. Legislation covers fouling by dogs in public places, and 'poop scoop' laws are in force in many areas.

Simple hygiene for children must be practised: they should always wash their hands after playing with the dog. But children should not be discouraged – there is so much to be gained from a happy association between child and dog that, provided risks are minimized by adopting sensible precautions, their close companionship should be encouraged. Remember, the dog is our oldest friend.

▲ *Owners must always collect faeces deposited by their dogs.*

► *Dogs should be discouraged from playing with the baby's toys.*

THE BREEDS

For thousands of years, dogs have been selectively bred to perform a function to assist mankind, and many can trace their lineage over several generations. This section looks at registered breeds — dogs with documentation to certify that they are a certain 'breed'. Breeds are generally grouped according to functional type, such as herding dogs, hunting dogs or guard dogs. From country to country there is great diversity within these groupings, with dogs not necessarily being in the same groups. For the purpose of this book, dogs have been placed in the group that is, overall, the most consistent grouping for that breed. These pages give a 'snapshot' of each breed, and the breed boxes provide statistics for the average dog. In some cases, there is a difference in size between dog and bitch, and where this occurs it has been indicated. It is strongly recommended that all potential purchasers contact responsible breeders to gain in-depth information prior to buying a dog.

◄ *Decades of careful selective breeding have gone into producing this stunning sled dog. Breeds that pull loads are in the Working Group.*

Dog breeds

The enormous number of breeds recognized today are derived from a creature that first associated with humans thousands of years ago. The precursor of the dog must have been keen to share the shelter, warmth from fires and left-over food that people provided. It was soon discovered that dogs could be put to good use as hunters, guards and companions. Humans realized that some dogs were better at one job than another, so they selected the best for each task and bred them together. This policy has been happening ever since.

Some breeds, such as the Ibizan Hound, are virtually unchanged from their predecessors thousands of years ago. Others breeds have developed very recently — the Eurasier has only been in existence since the 1960s.

A pedigree is the written record of a dog's genealogy for at least three generations. A purebred dog is a dog whose parents belonged to the same breed and who share unmixed descent since the recognition of the breed.

Dogs are divided into 'groups', and in some cases sub-groups, depending on type and the job they have been bred to do. There is a great variation within these groups worldwide. Some kennel clubs call the groups by different names, and dogs that are listed in one group may appear in a different group in another country.

For the purposes of this book, the dog breeds have been divided into seven broad categories: Hound; Gundog (Sporting); Terrier; Utility (Non-sporting); Working; Herding; and Toy. This is a generalization and should not be taken as a firm indication of the grouping of any particular breed. An eighth category looks at unrecognized breeds and hybrids.

HOUND

Dogs in this group are hunters. Sighthounds such as the Greyhound see their prey and chase. Scent hounds such as the Beagle sniff out a trail left by their target and follow it. The Tree Walking Coonhound is among a number of breeds that find and indicate the presence their quarry by barking. Generally, hounds are not known for their obedience, and are more intent on hunting than listening to their owner. Some have very loud voices indeed.

GUNDOG (SPORTING)

These dogs work in a number of ways, and help the hunter by seeking, indicating, flushing or retrieving game, as well as acting as decoys. The group contains kind and gentle creatures that adapt well to the role of family companion. They are not all suited to town living.

TERRIER

From the Latin *terra* meaning 'earth', terriers are the diggers of the dog world. They hunt anything that they consider fair game. If this means digging to get to their prey, so much the better. Feisty and trainable, they are sharp in character and appearance, if you have the patience.

▲ *Basenji — a sighthound.*

▲ *German Wirehaired Pointer — a gundog.*

▲ *Lakeland Terrier – a terrier.*

▲ *French Bulldog – a utility dog.*

▲ *Portuguese Water Dog – a working dog.*

UTILITY (NON-SPORTING)

This group is very varied among worldwide kennel clubs, and in some does not exist at all. It really is a grouping for breeds that do not fit comfortably in any other group. There is a great diversity of size, type and temperament among the utility breeds. Many of them are considered as companion dogs, and their suitability is discussed under the individual breeds.

WORKING

This is one of the biggest groups, and includes dogs that guard, pull loads, perform rescues from water, and even those such as the Portuguese Water Dog that assist fishermen. Sizes, temperament and trainability vary enormously within the group, as do exercise requirements. Many make excellent household pets and excel at canine sports.

HERDING

All the breeds in this group assist humans to move livestock. This is done in a variety of ways. Nipping at heels, imitating predators and/or barking are a few of the methods that are often employed. These are mainly high-energy, intelligent dogs, some of which are capable of performing their job independently from their owners. Breeds should be researched carefully before considering one as a family companion.

TOY

All the breeds in this group are small. They are usually kept as companions, but some make excellent watch dogs, too. Bright and trainable, they are happy in country retreats or town apartments. Activity levels differ, but even the least energetic will require daily walks and mental stimulation.

UNRECOGNIZED BREEDS AND HYBRIDS

Some dogs breed true to type but are not recognized by most kennel clubs. Others are hybrids and so-called 'designer dogs'. Incorrectly referred to as breeds by some, these are a first cross between two different breeds. A few popular ones are listed overleaf.

▲ *Border Collie – a herding dog.*

▲ *Belgian Griffon – a toy dog.*

▲ *Goldendoodle – a hybrid.*

Cavachon

The Cavachon is a hybrid, or first cross, between a Cavalier King Charles Spaniel and a Bichon Frise. Provided the sire and dam are as stated, the resulting Cavachon is a small dog with a soft and slightly wavy, silky coat. Coat colours vary, but include solid white, or white with black or apricot

Breed box
Size: 30–35.5cm (12–14in),
    4.5–9kg (10–20lb)
Grooming: Moderate
Feeding: Undemanding
Exercise: Medium
Temperament: Affectionate
    and playful

▶ *The Cavachon will not come with any registration papers, since it is not a pedigree dog breed.*

markings, as well as white, black and tan. Often incorrectly sold as non-shedding, the Cavachon will moult, but not as much as some other dogs. The coat will require trimming regularly, and the cost of professional grooming should be factored into your budget.

This type of dog is active and requires moderate daily exercise. It enjoys playing and learning tricks, but like many small dogs, it can be slow to house-train. It is generally good with children, dogs and other domestic pets, and can adapt to apartment living. The Cavachon makes an

affectionate family companion but requires early socialization and training, as with any dog. Potential owners should be aware that a Cavachon may possess the best traits of a Cavalier King Charles Spaniel and Bichon Frise, but it is equally likely that it will inherit the worst.

Cockapoo

The Cockapoo is a cross between a Poodle and either an American Cocker Spaniel or an English Cocker Spaniel. In many cases, but not all, the Toy Poodle or Miniature Poodle is used. There can be a great variation in the size of this type of dog, which depends on the size of the Poodle parent. In Australia, the Cockerpoo is known either as a Cockerdoodle or a Spoodle.

As with any first cross, this dog may take characteristics from either parent. Generally, Poodle crosses require regular trimming and will shed less than some dogs, but it is incorrect to say that they are non-shedding. The coat can be solid, patched, spotted, merle, brindle or ticked, and comes in a wide range of differerent colours. Weights and heights listed in the breed box are a rough guide only.

◀ *This is a hybrid that is trainable, very agile and often enjoys swimming.*

This is a moderately active and agile dog that requires regular exercise. It is loving and happy to join in with family activities, and it is good with children, other dogs and domestic pets, provided they have been brought up with them. The Cockapoo dislikes being left alone for long periods, and may suffer from separation anxiety.

Breed box
Size: 25–43cm (10–17in),
    5.5–15kg (12–34lb)
Grooming: Medium
Feeding: Moderate
Exercise: Medium
Temperament: Outgoing and
    friendly

Labradoodle

The best-known of the 'designer dogs', this hybrid is a first cross between a Labrador Retriever and a Poodle. The Labradoodle shot to fame after Australian breeder Wally Conron bred a litter for use by the Royal Guide Dog Association of Australia. He hoped to produce an assistance dog that was hypoallergenic. In fact, no dog is

Breed box
Size: Variable
Grooming: Variable
Feeding: Variable
Exercise: High
Temperament: Intelligent and
  playful

▶ *Ensure you know the size of the Poodle used in the cross, as this will affect the size of the adult hybrid.*

truly hypoallergenic, although some are low-shedding and produce less dander. Not all Labradoodles fall into this category.

Coats vary and might be straight, wavy or curly, and the hair can be soft or wiry. Colours include chocolate, cream, gold, black and parti. Height is dependent on the size of the Poodle used in the cross. Potential puppy purchasers should always request to see both parents and be aware that there is no consistency in type either in first-cross Labrador Retriever to Poodle or Labradoodle bred to Labradoodle.

This dog is generally energetic and playful, and good with children. It is intelligent and should be non-aggressive. The Labradoodle needs both physical and mental exercise and enjoys having a job to do, such as obedience, agility or flyball. Grooming requirements vary depending on coat type and texture.

Yorkie-chon

The Yorkie-chon is a first cross between a Yorkshire Terrier and a Bichon Frise, and is not a breed. It is listed under various other names, including Yorkie Bijon, Borkie and Yo-chon. It is often sold as a non-shedding dog, however this is untrue. All dogs shed, some more than others, and this cross may or may not be

low-shedding. As with all cross breeds, it is advisable to see both parents to ensure you know what you are getting.

Coats may be long and wavy, or long and woolly. Colours include solid white, solid black, white with coloured patches, gold or fawn with dark or black markings and tricolour. The coat will need regular grooming and trimming, as it will mat if left unattended. The services of a professional dog groomer may be required. Size and weight varies, even in the same litter.

◀ *Littermates – but what a difference! The puppy on the left closely favours the Bichon, while the right-hand puppy has a terrier head.*

Temperament depends on which parent the puppy takes after – the Yorkshire Terrier is feisty with a high prey drive, while the Bichon is a merry animal. The Yorkie-chon makes a good watch dog, but it may bark persistently for attention if it gets bored. It is good with children if brought up with them. Most are easy to obedience-train, but can be slow to master toilet training.

Breed box
Size: 23–28cm (9–11in),
  4.5–7kg (10–15½lb)
Grooming: High
Feeding: Undemanding
Exercise: Medium
Temperament: Variable

THE HOUND GROUP

The temperament of any breed should be as important to prospective owners as size or appearance, although it is one factor that cannot be exactly described or standardized. Official kennel club breed standards do contain clauses under the heading 'Temperament', but these describe the ideal. Included here are observed traits that may not always conform to the ideal. What is accepted by most dog-minded folk is that hounds are basically hunters that have been bred to work over all kinds of terrain searching out different quarries. To take on any hound as a companion or family animal and expect it not to behave as a hunter is misguided. Some hound breeds can more readily be taught new tricks than others, but it is never easy. Some breeds in the Hound Group, such as the Beagle and the Whippet, are extremely popular, while others are virtually unknown and unobtainable outside their country of origin.

◀ *The Greyhound is capable of travelling almost 20m (65ft) per second over short distances, making it one of the fastest dog breeds in the world.*

Afghan Hound

One of the most glamorous breeds, the Afghan has a superbly elegant, silky coat on an athletic frame, as befits a hunting creature originating in the mountains of Afghanistan.

Its expression is one of dignity and superiority, but it can have moments of hectic eccentricity, racing across gardens or fields. Not inclined to heed the wishes of an exasperated owner unless handled with firmness as it grows up, this is a dog that is not for the uncommitted. Treating one casually will not lead to a happy relationship in the household.

More than capable of acting as a watch dog, the Afghan may use its powerful teeth on intruders if its warnings are not heeded.

▲ The Afghan is an ancient breed that was discovered by the Western world in the 19th century.

In spite of standing over 70cm (27½in) at the withers, the Afghan is not a greedy feeder; in fact, it may be a little finicky if it is allowed to have its own way. It is an athlete and needs a lot of exercise to expend its copious, restless energy.

The Afghan's silky coat will not look its best without constant care. It needs regular and thorough grooming, and

Breed box
Size: Male 70–74cm (27½–29in), 27kg (59½lb); female 63–69cm (25–27in), 22.5kg (50lb)
Grooming: Frequent and thorough
Feeding: Medium
Exercise: Essential
Temperament: Wary of strangers

▲ One of the truly glamorous expressions of dogdom, the Afghan's eyes look straight through you; they seem to defy you to resist them.

any knots must be removed every day. The breeder from whom it is purchased will show the new owner how this is best done.

The Afghan is a dog for the true enthusiast who has the time and patience to get the best out of a canine glamour star.

◀ A shining silhouette characterizes one of the most dignified of all the breeds.

Basenji

The Basenji may have originally come from the Middle East, but it is regarded as being of Central African (Congo) derivation from some 300 years ago. Certainly, that is the area from which the breed was exported in the mid-1930s.

A neat dog of sharp outlines with stiffly upright ears, it has a square frame standing around 43cm (17in) high, ending with a tightly curled tail. It attracts a small but enthusiastic following with its gentle, friendly attitude. It has a questioning look on its wedge-shaped face and a wrinkled brow; its curiosity is a real feature of

◄ With sharp outlines on a neat dog, the Basenji is renowned for its cleanliness and for being odour-free.

Breed box
Size: Male 43cm (17in), 10kg (22lb); female 40cm (16in), 9.5kg (21lb)
Grooming: Minimal
Feeding: Undemanding
Exercise: Reasonable
Temperament: Intelligent and affectionate

its temperament. It is known for the unusual fact that it does not give voice by way of a bark, but has a yodel-type cry.

The Basenji's short, close-fitting coat is sleek and very easy to groom; it comes in variations of black and white, and red and white, with an occasional tricolour, and it has a

tendency to carry out its own grooming in the manner of a cat

The Basenji's movement is clipped in style and suggests that it is quite tireless, although it does not require an excessive amount of exercise. It will not cost much to feed. All in all, it is a dog that will suit most households, because it is thoroughly companionable.

◄ Poised to spring even from a lying position, the Basenji gives the impression of constant restlessness. It will hunt any form of vermin.

▲ The Basenji is always alert, with a permanent frowning, quizzical expression on its face.

Basset Hound

The Basset Hound is the best known of the Basset Group, originating in France. Its normal prey is the hare, which it follows in a persistent, lumbering fashion. It can break into a run, but its natural pace is steady over long distances.

In spite of the fact that it stands about 38cm (15in) at the withers, it weighs around 32kg (70lb), which makes it a big dog on short legs. If it has to be lifted into the car or on to the

◄ The Basset Hound is a cheerful character, even if its expression could be described as lugubrious.

Breed box
Size: Male 33–38cm (13–15in), 25–32kg (55–70lb); female 33cm (13in), 20–29kg (44–65lb)
Grooming: Relatively easy
Feeding: Has a hearty appetite
Exercise: Steady but necessary
Temperament: Placid but loud

veterinary consulting room table, it may present a problem to the slightly built owner.

The Basset Hound has a reasonably hearty appetite, which may lead it to put on an inordinate amount of weight, especially as it can be idle, given the opportunity. As befits a hunting hound with a big chest, its voice is akin to the sound of a ship's foghorn. This can come as a distinct surprise to those in the immediate vicinity, but it should never give the impression that it is of an unfriendly disposition.

At first sight, the Basset looks as if its skin was made for more dog than it contains, and there is a certain amount of wrinkles on its forehead. Its most exaggerated feature is the length of its ears; these have been allowed to increase to the extent that the dog can tread on its ears with ease. As a result, the flaps can be injured, and their weight can cause problems by interfering with the circulation of air into the ear canal. The droop of this breed's lower eyelids can also cause problems.

The Basset's forelegs tend to twist outwards below the wrist, and this may produce limb problems. Its short, smooth coat is easy to keep clean and wholesome, even if it does enjoy rolling in various offensive-smelling substances.

The Basset Hound is for the enthusiast who wants to take on a canine companion of great character as a member of the family.

► The Basset Hound usually comes in black, white and tan, or in lemon and white. Its coat is easily kept clean and tidy.

Grand Basset Griffon Vendéen

This breed is often referred to as a 'Grand', but despite the name it is really a medium-sized dog. There is also a 'Petite' or small, and 'Briquet' or medium-sized type of the hound. Used for hunting boars and deer, or to track hares and rabbit, this is a versatile hunter's dog.

With a sturdy body and short legs, this is a determined but athletic dog. Feet are large and well padded. The white coat is mixed with lemon, orange, tricolour or grizzle markings. A dense undercoat and wiry topcoat give it rather an untidy look, but this protects against thorny vegetation. The face is well covered with hair. Ears are long and should reach to the tip of the nose.

Increasingly popular, this exuberant hound can make a good companion. Since Grands are pack animals, they do not like being left alone for too long. They enjoy

◄ The GBGV has a merry disposition and takes to any sort of canine activity with great enthusiasm.

having the company of another dog, or even a cat. This is an intelligent dog that can become destructive if bored. Renowned for being a clever escapologist, a well-fenced garden is essential. Like all hounds, it will use its voice and easily become distracted by an interesting scent.

Breed box
Size: Maximum 45cm (18in), 18–20kg (39½–44lb)
Grooming: Relatively easy
Feeding: Undemanding
Exercise: Essential
Temperament: Friendly and humorous

Basset Fauve de Bretagne

This typical Basset-type breed, with its long back and short legs, comes from the Brittany area of France. The body shape makes it an ideal dog to flush game out from thick undergrowth and brambles. It is also known as the Tawny Brittany Basset. Until fairly recently, this breed was relatively unknown outside France, but is now becoming popular in other countries.

The thick and harsh coat provides excellent protection. The hair is varying shades of fawn, gold or red. With a wide chest and slightly barrelled ribs, the body gives the impression of great strength. The dog has a long muzzle with the ears set below eye level. The tail is set high and is thick at the base, tapering to a point.

It is a lively dog that can have its own agenda regarding obedience training. It enjoys physical activity but does not like being confined. It makes an excellent companion and would enjoy living with an active family, and is suitable for a small house.

Breed box
Size: 32–38cm (13–15in), 16–18kg (36–39½)
Grooming: Medium to easy
Feeding: Moderate
Exercise: Medium
Temperament: Lively and affectionate

► A harsh, tight coat on the Fauve de Bretagne makes this breed easy to groom wherever it hunts. A quick brush-over is all that is needed.

Petit Basset Griffon Vendéen

The Petit Basset Griffon Vendéen, or PBGV as it is known to its multitude of admirers, has rapidly increased in popularity since the 1970s, when it began to be exported from its native France. All French hounds are expected to be able to do their job, and this breed is no exception. It is a bustler of a dog, seemingly never able to sit still, so it is suitable for the active and tolerant owner only. Bred to hunt hares, this scent hound is easily distracted and won't always come when called.

▶ *Cheeky-faced PBGVs positively swarmed across the Channel between their native France and the UK in the mid-1970s, and it was not long before they migrated on to the United States.*

Breed box
Size: Male 34–38cm (13½–15in), 19kg (42lb); female 35.5cm (14in), 18kg (39½lb)
Grooming: Necessary
Feeding: Reasonable
Exercise: Essential
Temperament: Happy and extroverted

▲ *Fur on the face resembles a moustache and beard, and they usually have long eyelashes.*

The PBGV stands up to 38cm (15in) at the withers; its length is greater than its height, but not to an exaggerated degree — in other words, it does not suffer from problems with its intervertebral discs to any extent. On its sturdy, well-proportioned body it sports a rough, harsh topcoat with a thick undercoat, which together make it weatherproof. It is inclined to get muddy on its country rambles. It has lengthy eyebrows, so a curry comb is a good grooming tool. It needs good feeding to supply the energy that exudes from it at all times.

The PBGV is not a dog for a town-dwelling family that never visits the countryside. It is a breed that will use its voice and will howl if it gets bored or is left home alone.

▶ *The Petit Basset Griffon Vendéen is a rough-and-ready breed, built to face all weather and ground conditions.*

Beagle

As a breed, the Beagles produce their puppies easily in reasonable numbers and seem to accept a life in kennels in philosophical fashion. As a result, they have been bred extensively for use in medical/veterinary research laboratories, making them victims of their own friendly temperaments.

From the point of view of life as a member of a human household, they are similarly accommodating. They enjoy being part of a gang in much the same way as they make good team members of a pack hunting hares. They are tidy creatures, although they are not always easy to house-train. Their short waterproof coat makes them drip-dry in the foulest of weathers. Even after a day running across clay, a quick sponge-down soon makes them acceptable visitors to the kitchen.

The Beagle is not greedy, although life in hunt kennels tends to make it swallow its daily ration fast. It is not prone to veterinary problems, and lives to a reasonably ripe old age.

It is unusual to see a Beagle winning an obedience competition,

Breed box
Size: 33–41cm (13–16in);
male 10–11kg (22–25lb);
female 9–10kg (20–22lb)
Grooming: Easy
Feeding: Reasonable
Exercise: Considerable
Temperament: Genially stubborn

◀ *A natural hunter and explorer, the Beagle will need a well-fenced garden to keep it secure.*

as the breed has a tendency not to stay around for the recall once off the lead. This is a breed that pleases families who lead active lives.

▲ *Beagles are hunters with handsome muzzles designed to make a thorough job of sniffing out their quarry.*

▶ *Tough forelegs and tight feet make the Beagle able to last all day whatever the activity – in the field, the park or the garden – as long as there is human company around.*

Bloodhound

▼ *The Bloodhound's huge size requires solid bone. The 'Hound of the Baskervilles' of Sir Arthur Conan Doyle's book was based on this breed.*

The Bloodhound is a big dog with a mind of its own. As it stands some 66cm (26in) at the withers and can weigh up to 55kg (121lb), it is heavy. It is also clumsy, with a tendency to pursue its path regardless of obstacles such as ditches, walls and fences. Once on collar and lead, it may choose to take its handler on without great regard to physical or vocal opposition.

Most people will be familiar with the breed's appearance: the Bloodhound has a super-abundant quantity of skin overhanging its eyes, and this is often accompanied by sagging lower eyelids. Its ears hang low on its skull in pendulous folds, and these are said to sweep scents from the ground into its large nostrils and over its highly efficient olfactory mechanism.

The large body is supported by enormous bones, but the Bloodhound has suffered over the generations from hip joints that cannot always take the strain of conveying it along, head down on the scent. Over the past few decades, much has been done by dedicated breeders to improve this.

▼ *The deep chest gives this dog good lung capacity.*

Bloodhounds eat massively and greedily. As with other breeds that have deep chests and wide bellies, the Bloodhound suffers from more than its fair share of a condition called 'bloat', in which the gases in the stomach tend to be produced in great quantities. For various anatomical reasons these cannot be belched in the normal fashion and may lead to torsion of the stomach, which is rapidly fatal unless veterinary intervention is prompt.

The general advice is to feed small quantities several times a day, and not to take a Bloodhound out for exercise on a full stomach. It is wise to ask a breeder offering puppies for sale about the incidence of bloat in the ancestry of sire and dam. Bloodhounds, like most giant breeds, tend not to live to a ripe old age.

Most Bloodhounds are dignified and affectionate, but this is not a breed with which to take liberties, as they can take exception to undue familiarity. Properly handled by those who are prepared to understand them, they are a fascinating breed to live with and loyal, faithful companions.

▲ *Also known as the St Hubert Hound, this tracker dog's long ears are said to sweep scent from the trail up into its large nostrils.*

Breed box

Size: Male 63–69cm (25–27in), 41kg (90lb); female 58–63cm (23–25in), 36kg (79½lb)
Grooming: Easy but extensive
Feeding: Demanding
Exercise: Ponderous but considerable
Temperament: Requires understanding

Borzoi

The Borzoi, as befits a hound from Russia that was dedicated to hunting wolves, is tall, aristocratic in bearing, and possesses a pair of impressive jaws. Its height at the withers is a minimum of 68cm (27in), which makes it tall by anyone's standards. Added to its height is a lean head, shaped to give an impression of

▼ *Also known as Russian Wolfhounds, Borzois need their elegantly long and powerful jaws to snatch and hold wolves.*

Breed box

Size: Male 75–85cm (30–33in),
34–48kg (75–105lb);
female 68–78cm (27–31in),
25–41kg (55–90lb)
Grooming: Regular and thorough
Feeding: Not excessive
Exercise: Moderate
Temperament: Requires
understanding

supercilious aristocracy, carried on an arched, longish neck that runs into well laid-back shoulders, all of which produces a superlative representative of the sighthound group.

The silky coat varies in length over different areas of the body; it requires enthusiastic handling from an owner willing to learn from an expert.

These dogs are capable of running at tremendous speed but do not demand great amounts of exercise. A Borzoi does not have a large appetite and is not particularly choosy. It is

▲ *A gentle expression in the eyes belies the fact that the breed can have a slightly fierce temperament.*

usually faithful to its owner and reasonably biddable.

The Borzoi gives the impression of being fond of people, but it is wise not to take liberties with such a creature; it is capable, on occasion, of becoming dangerous if it is annoyed. Such behaviour is rare, but there is some suspicion that certain strains inherit a less than perfect temperament. It would be as well to look into this further before deciding whether to take on a Borzoi, especially as a family pet.

▶ *The immensely variable pattern of coat colours is one of the distinctive features of this noble Russian breed.*

Dachshund

The Dachshund breed comes in six varieties, each named according to its size and coat type: Standard Smooth-haired, Standard Long-haired, Standard Wire-haired, Miniature Smooth-haired, Miniature Long-haired and Miniature Wire-haired. The popular dogs vary in weight from 9–12kg (20–26½lb) in the case of the Standards, down to 4.5kg (10lb) in the case of the Miniatures.

All six varieties are similar in body shape, being low to the ground in order to be able to go to ground after their prey, which is generally considered to be the badger (though they will do an equally good job if required to go after a fox).

In the past, all the varieties suffered from severe problems with their backs, basically because there was a tendency to breed for longer backs without due consideration being given to the musculature needed to cope with that structural build. Today, there is a much better overall type, but it is wise to seek out breeders who can demonstrate a sound strain.

▲ *The head of all six varieties tapers uniformly to the tip of the nose.*

Grooming of Smooth-haired and Wire-haired varieties is straightforward, but the Long-haired has a soft, straight coat that does need regular attention.

Exercise is accepted readily by all six varieties, but they are not over-demanding on the matter. From the feeding viewpoint, they are all also undemanding, good eaters.

Temperamentally, they are sharp as far as acting as sentinels around the family premises and possessions is concerned, and they will not hesitate to use their teeth if pushed. They are loud barkers, and the smaller sizes have a tendency to yap, but they stop once the intruder has been pointed out. They make excellent companion animals and deservedly attract a large following of devotees.

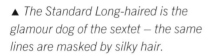

▲ *The Standard Long-haired is the glamour dog of the sextet – the same lines are masked by silky hair.*

Breed box
Size: Standard 20.3–22.8cm (8–9in), 9–12kg (20–26½lb); Miniature 12.7–15.3cm (5–6in), maximum 4.5kg (10lb)
Grooming: Varies with variety
Feeding: Undemanding
Exercise: Reasonable
Temperament: Independent

▼ *The Standard Smooth-haired – if any of the six varieties of Dachshund is to be considered the original, this is it. The body lines are neat and trim.*

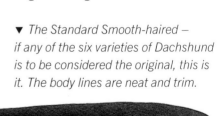

Elkhound

The Elkhound (Norwegian Elkhound) hails from Norway, where it hunts elk, known as moose in the USA. The hound has to be solidly built to take on such a large form of quarry. The attitude of the Norwegians to this native breed is that it should

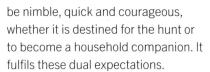

▶ *Elkhounds are solid, and their legs and feet must be powerful to carry them.*

be nimble, quick and courageous, whether it is destined for the hunt or to become a household companion. It fulfils these dual expectations.

Within the group, the spitz types have prick ears and tails that curl up over their backs. The Elkhound is a true spitz; it has another characteristic of the type – a loud voice, which it enjoys using. It is essentially friendly, but intruders could be forgiven for doubting this.

The Elkhound's coat, which is predominantly grey, makes it weatherproof. It is a delight to clean by sponging off the worst mud, letting it dry and then brushing it vigorously.

It stands around 52cm (20½in) at the withers, and its body is solidly chunky at 23kg (50lb). Elkhounds tend to live to a ripe old age and are a good choice for the active family.

Breed box
Size: Male 52cm (20½in), 23kg (50lb); female 49cm (19in), 20kg (44lb)
Grooming: Reasonably easy
Feeding: Has a reasonably hearty appetite
Exercise: Moderate
Temperament: Very companionable

Finnish Spitz

The Finnish Spitz is the national dog of Finland, and the Finns are fussy about

▼ *The Finnish Spitz's outline is as sharp as its hearing.*

its appearance, which is very striking. It is reddish in colour, with shades varying from bright red to chestnut or honey. When it grows up, the dog has stiffly pricked ears and a tail that curls up over its back. Its coat is easy to clean off and brush up.

It grows to a maximum of 50cm (20in), but weighs at best a mere 16kg (35lb). It is a pocket-sized athlete, the nearest thing to perpetual motion, and it loves to be part of a pack. It is used in Finland to search out the whereabouts of birds, most particularly the capercaillie (a large grouse), and is the only member of the Hound Group whose objective is a bird. Its reaction to a successful hunt is to tell the world in a strident voice, which it also uses at home.

The Finnish Spitz is not greedy; it lives a reasonably long life and it expects to be part of the household. In other words, it is a healthy extrovert and considers that its owners should be similarly healthy and extrovert. Whether the neighbours would agree is a point to be considered.

Breed box
Size: Male 43–50cm (17–20in); female 39–45cm (15–18in), 14–16kg (31–36lb)
Grooming: Easy
Feeding: Undemanding
Exercise: Moderate
Temperament: Noisy and needs understanding

Deerhound

▲ *The Deerhound has been used to hunt red deer for 1,000 years.*

The Deerhound, or Scottish Deerhound, is an ancient beed. It has a similar body type to a Greyhound, but is larger and heavier-boned. It is said that it has hunted deer for 1,000 years, and ancient depictions of it suggest that it has altered little over the centuries. It appears to capture the heart of all who fall under its spell, but in return it demands great loyalty.

It stands 76cm (30in) high and weighs around 45.5kg (100lb), so it is not a lightweight, but it has a surprising ability to curl up in a corner and not get in the way, even in a small house. It is not a big eater and gives the impression that ordinary oatmeal would be welcome, along with the venison.

Grooming should be regular, but this is not a chore as the harshness of the Deerhound's shaggy coat renders it relatively easy to keep tidy.

As far as its temperament is concerned, the Deerhound is a friendly, faithful creature with a dignified attitude to strangers. One of the most venerated among its current breeders travels with a team of Deerhounds from the outer regions of mid-west Scotland to shows all over Britain and does so by train, which must say something about the breed's charm and adaptability.

Breed box
Size: Male 76cm (30in), 45.5kg (100lb); female 71cm (28in), 36.5kg (80½lb)
Grooming: Moderate
Feeding: Medium
Exercise: Moderate
Temperament: Highly companionable

▲ *The shaggy coat comes in mainly pastel shades, from grey through brindle to fawn.*

▲ *The narrowish front of the Deerhound reveals the depth of chest that is displayed by all sighthounds.*

116

Irish Wolfhound

The Irish Wolfhound is the largest breed of dog known, if not necessarily the heaviest. A magnificent creature, it is well proportioned even for a dog that may reach 86cm (34in) in height and weigh a minimum of 54.5kg (120lb). Its expression of quiet

▲ ▶ This massive creature illustrates the range of chest and body sizes seen among the sighthounds.

◀ This is the largest dog breed in the world, but it has no air of menace, even if those jaws are believed to have cleared Ireland of its wolf population.

during the Wolfhound's youth. In adulthood, it will enjoy long rambles in the countryside, and it can achieve surprising speeds. The breed does not live to a ripe old age, but Irish Wolfhounds are such delightful dogs to live with that their devotees accept this with resignation.

Breed box
Size: Male minimum 79cm (31in), 54.5kg (120lb); female minimum 71cm (28in), 41kg (90lb)
Grooming: Regular
Feeding: Very considerable
Exercise: Regular
Temperament: Gently dignified

authority and its rough, harsh coat give it a look of invincibility, while its attitude towards people is kind.

It adapts to living under most circumstances, but those who own one must deal with the problems of transporting or lifting a dog of these dimensions, especially if it is immobilized by illness or injury. This breed is prone to suffer from bloat, and the feeding regime must be strictly observed to prevent it.

Rearing puppies of giant breeds is a skill in itself, and the advice of an intelligent, caring breeder should be followed closely. Growth is rapid, but over-feeding can cause as many problems as too low an intake, as can any tendency to over-exercise

Greyhound

The Greyhound is, of course, the template for what are collectively known as the sighthounds. There is a physical difference between those Greyhounds that course hares and those that are seen in the show ring, but they all have the same instincts.

Adult dogs that have been retired from chasing the electric hare make wonderful family pets, but they do retain their instinct to chase. This can mean that they may not be popular if let off the lead in public parks while

▶ The Greyhound is the fundamental sighthound – it is lithe, muscular, deep-chested and tight-footed.

◀ With its piercing searchlight eyes and an unwavering gaze, the Greyhound is also known as a 'gaze hound'.

surrounded by other dogs. Fortunately, however, they are easy to clean up after a long ramble down muddy lanes.

They stand as high as 76cm (30in), and can be surprisingly heavy for such a sleek dog. Their appetites are not excessive, but exercising them is fairly demanding if they have to be kept on a lead; owners need to be fit to walk fair distances each day.

A healthy Greyhound is beautifully proportioned and a fine sight, although as in all breeds of similar style, the pups go through a gawky, loose-limbed stage.

Breed box
Size: 71–76cm (28–30in),
    36.5kg (80½lb)
Grooming: Minimal
Feeding: Medium
Exercise: Essential
Temperament: Affectionate and
    even-tempered

◀ The Greyhound is an ancient breed that may have originated in the Middle East.

▶ All colours – red, white and blue – are in favour. Anything goes, as long as it is fast.

Hamiltonstövare

The Hamiltonstövare is alternatively known as the Swedish Foxhound, and there is considerable similarity in type between this breed and the English Foxhound. In its native country, the Hamiltonstövare is a very popular hound indeed. It has a style of its own, with a mixture of black on its back and neck, and its mainly rich

▶ *The Hamiltonstövare presents a wonderful contrast of colours in a classic pattern.*

▲ *A white blaze down the centre of the skull and around the muzzle is the typical head-marking.*

Breed box
Size: Male 50–60cm (19½–23½in); female 46–57cm (18–22½in), 23–27kg (50–59½lb)
Grooming: Easy
Feeding: Medium
Exercise: Necessary
Temperament: Even-tempered

It has an appetite to go with its lifestyle, and it does not cause too much difficulty being cleaned up after a country ramble in mid-winter. This dog can be stubborn to train and requires patience and consistency, but it makes a thoroughly good canine companion for an energetic family.

brown head and legs. The white blaze on its head, down its neck, coupled with white paws and tail tip make it instantly recognizable.

It stands around 57cm (22½in) at the withers, but does not have quite as much body substance as the English version. It is a hunter with the same urgency in the chase as many other hounds. As such, it is truly a dog for the countryside, but it is very civilized if circumstances force it to become a temporary town-dweller.

◀ *Although the Hamiltonstövare is just a touch lighter-framed than the English Foxhound, note the same classic white paws and tail tip.*

Ibizan Hound

The Ibizan Hound is classified as a primitive type and has an ancient lineage. The life-sized gold statue of Anubis in the tomb of Tutankhamun is identical to the dog we see today. Hannibal took these hounds with him when he journeyed across the Alps.

Breed box
Size: 56–74cm (22–29in), 19–25kg (42–55lb)
Grooming: Easy
Feeding: Medium
Exercise: Essential
Temperament: Reserved and independent

This very fast dog will hunt and kill rabbits. The female is considered a better hunter then the male. In the USA, they compete at lure coursing and straight or oval racing.

The dog is elegant and exotic, with red and white, white and tan, or red or white colouring. There are three coat types: smooth, wire, and very rarely long-haired varieties. Amber eyes are set in long, lean heads topped with large, erect ears. The nose, eye rims, inside the ears and pads are tan in colour. Moving with a springy trot and able to clear 1.5m (5ft) from stationary, they need a well-fenced garden.

Unsuitable for outdoor living, this kind dog is good with children and

▲ *The Ibizan Hound has a restless energy and can clear high fences from a standing start.*

makes an ideal home companion, but does have a high prey drive – it will chase rabbits, cats and rodents, and not return for hours. It is sensitive and responds to calm but firm (as opposed to harsh) commands.

Pharaoh Hound

One of the oldest domesticated dog breeds, archaeological evidence suggests that this hound has lived alongside humans since 3000BC. Writings and artefacts show that dogs of striking similarity were kept by the kings of Egypt. It is thought that the Phoenicians

◀ *The general appearance of the Pharaoh Hound is one of power, grace and speed.*

colonized the Isle of Malta around 1000BC, taking their hounds with them. The Pharaoh Hound is the national dog of Malta, where it is called Kelb Tal-Fenek, which translates as 'dog of the rabbit'. This breed is both a sight and scent hound.

With a clean outline and straight front legs, this tall, elegant dog is a true athlete. The red or tan coat is smooth and glossy. White markings are permitted, and show judges prefer a white tip to the whip-like tail. The ears are erect and broad at the base, tapering up to a point. Both the Pharaoh and Ibizan Hound 'blush' when they are excited, with the skin on their nose and ears turning a pink.

This dog is suited to indoor living, as it is liable to feel the cold outside. While some males can be dominant,

it is generally good with other dogs. Liable to chase small animals, it should not be let off the lead unless it is in a safe, enclosed space. Willing to please, this is not only an excellent hunter but it can also be seen in the competition obedience ring. Although hardy, the Pharaoh Hound can be sensitive to insecticides and some types of medication.

Breed box
Size: 20–25kg (44–55lb); male 56cm (22in); female 53cm (21in)
Grooming: Easy
Feeding: Reasonable
Exercise: Medium
Temperament: Alert and intelligent

Norwegian Lundehund

Once a common sight in Norway, this little spitz dog was selectively bred over generations to hunt and retrieve puffins for its owner. However, when puffins became a protected species in

▼ *This breed has a gentle expression and fun-loving personality.*

the early 1900s, Lundehund numbers declined dramatically. After World War II, five dogs were found on a Scandinavian island. These formed a breeding nucleus that saved this hound from total extinction.

Listed as one of Norway's national treasures, this dog is totally unique within the canine world. It has the ability to bend its neck backwards so that the top of the head touches the backbone. It can fold its erect ears closed, either forwards or backwards, at will. Each foot has at least six toes, and the front legs rotate slightly when moving. These characteristics are thought to be a process of adaptation that enables the dog to climb steep, rocky cliffs in pursuit of puffins.

Although recognized by many kennel clubs, it is quite a rare sight. It loves the company of people and is good with children. This dog will alarm-bark and requires early socialization. It is agile and needs at least one long walk every day. House-training can be a challenge.

Breed box
Size: 31–39cm (12–15½in), 6–9kg (13–20lb)
Grooming: Moderate
Feeding: Undemanding
Exercise: Medium to high
Temperament: Friendly and demanding

Segugio Italiano

Once used to flush out boar, wild sheep and deer, the Segugio now mainly hunts rabbit or hare. It gets its name from the Italian word *seguire* meaning 'to follow', and works in a very distinctive manner by herding prey back to the hunter. This is the most popular hound in Italy for hunting, as it is versatile and capable of working all day.

There are two coat varieties: smooth or wiry. In Italy, the smooth-coated dog, the Sleuth, is classified as a separate breed, but the only difference between the two hounds is the coat type. Colours range from fawn and red to black and tan. White markings on the head, chest, feet and tail tip are permitted but not desirable. The head is narrow and elongated,

▶ *The length of ears is exaggerated to sweep scent up in front of the nostrils.*

with triangular ears that hang close to the cheek. This hound has a square outline and a muscular body. With a very fast galloping gait and a high-pitched bark, it is a very distinctive dog.

Early socializing is required, as the Segugio is cautious in nature. It is a gentle and affectionate hound that is generally good with children and other dogs. Trainable but with a keen nose, this dog requires a lot of exercise. This is best undertaken on the lead to avoid the dog following an interesting scent at high speed. The Segugio is an ideal jogging companion. It is an intelligent and active breed that will become destructive and bark if bored.

Breed box
Size: 18–28kg (39½–62lb); male 52–59cm (20½–23in); female 48–52cm (19–22in)
Grooming: Easy
Feeding: Moderate to demanding
Exercise: High
Temperament: Cautious and affectionate

Otterhound

The Otterhound is a large dog with a rough, shaggy, oily coat. It is native to the UK and listed as a Vulnerable Native Breed by the KC. It is believed that there are fewer than 1,000 dogs in existence worldwide. The decline in numbers is largely due to the dramatic decline in otters, which are classified as a protected species within the UK, making the breed redundant.

Otterhounds seem to amble somewhat casually, and they give the impression of being extremely laid-back in their behaviour. Owners should have a love of exercise and a relaxed view about dogs bringing twigs, mud and the like into the kitchen after a family outing.

The Otterhound is a typical pack hound in some ways, but unusual in being shaggy, massive and well attuned to the role of a house-dweller.

Breed box
Size: Male 67cm (26in), 40–52kg (88–115lb); female 60cm (24in), 45.5kg (100lb)
Grooming: Fairly demanding
Feeding: Considerable
Exercise: Essential
Temperament: Even-tempered

▲ *Otterhounds are able to track a scent in both mud and water, even when the odour is several days old.*

▶ *The Otterhound's imposing head has intelligent, gentle eyes, and its jaws are capable of a powerful grip on its prey. It loves water but tends to be a messy drinker, so it might not be ideal for the house-proud owner.*

▶ *Otterhounds have webbed feet. At their smartest, these dogs are still not stylish, but their genial character and adaptability make them a good choice for an energetic family with space to spare.*

Rhodesian Ridgeback

The Rhodesian Ridgeback is a solidly built, upstanding dog of considerable presence. It is characterized by a dagger-shaped ridge of hair along its back from its withers to just above its tail root, which gives it its name.

In its native country, it is a guard dog, and its height — at close to 67cm (26in) — coupled with a very solid frame make it extremely powerful. Its quarry as a hound includes lions, and its dignified bearing suggests that it would not flinch from this task.

Without a difficult coat to keep clean, it will appeal to those who want an impressive canine member of the household. Nobody in their right mind would contemplate breaking into a house in the knowledge that there was a Rhodesian lurking within. This breed enjoys its exercise and its food; and it makes a handsome companion.

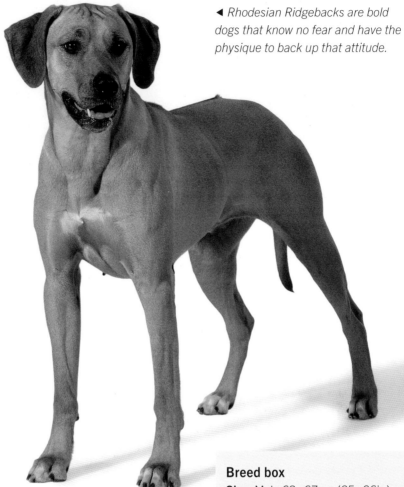

◄ *Rhodesian Ridgebacks are bold dogs that know no fear and have the physique to back up that attitude.*

▲ *The Rhodesian's expression sometimes gives the impression of being able to hypnotize.*

▼ *While these puppies are charming, they will grow into large, powerful dogs. With their ancestry as hunters and guards, it may not be wise to choose one as a first dog or as a companion for small children.*

Breed box
Size: Male 63–67cm (25–26in), 36.5kg (80½lb); female 61–66cm (24–26in), 32kg (70lb)
Grooming: Simple
Feeding: Fairly demanding
Exercise: Necessary
Temperament: Aloof and dignified

Saluki

The Saluki, or Gazelle Hound, is a dog of Middle Eastern origin. It is an elegant creature coming in a variety of colours, from white through cream and golden-red to black and tan and tricolour. It sports a smoothly silky coat that carries longer feathering on the backs of its legs and also from the upper half of its ears. It stands as tall as 71cm (28in) at its withers, but it is

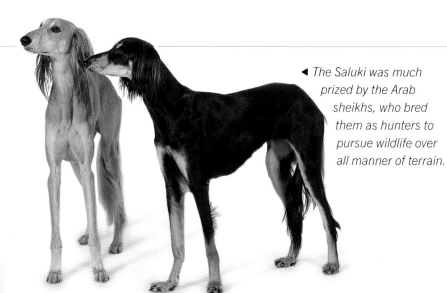

◄ *The Saluki was much prized by the Arab sheikhs, who bred them as hunters to pursue wildlife over all manner of terrain.*

Breed box
Size: Male 58.4–71cm (23–28in), 24kg (53lb); female 57cm (22½in), 19.5kg (43lb)
Grooming: Essential
Feeding: Demanding
Exercise: Demanding
Temperament: Very sensitive

lightly built, carrying very little fat – the dividing line between accepted and under-nourished is sometimes hard to assess. In spite of this, it has great stamina in the chase.

Its expression suggests that it is looking into the distance, and it

certainly has a very acute sense of sight. It is not a dog for a rough-and-tumble family, as it is sensitive to loud voices and vigorous handling. It is admittedly highly strung, but its devotees rate it as extremely faithful to those whom it trusts.

Sloughi

The Sloughi is an Arabian hound from North Africa and is also known as the Berber Greyhound. It is thought to have originally come from the Far East or Ethiopia, and travelled with early traders. This sighthound is fast and sure-footed. It was originally bred to

► *The Sloughi was once known as the Arabian Greyhound. Although similar in type, it is not related to the Saluki.*

hunt jackal, gazelle, wild pig and hares. It is a popular breed in the European show ring and is seen in increasing numbers in the USA, but it is still relatively uncommon in the UK.

With its melancholy expression, this tall hound is elegant yet robust. Body and legs should show a defined bone structure. Muscles are long and flat, and not as rounded as seen in most other sighthounds. Feet are lean, with the middle two toes distinctly longer than the others. The coat is smooth, fine and tough. Permitted colours are sable, fawn, brindle, or black with tan points.

The Sloughi is a gentle dog that is quiet and calm in the house. It will chase small furry animals and is best exercised on the lead. Responsive to training, it will make a good companion if treated kindly.

Breed box
Size: 12.5–13.5kg (27½–30lb); male 70cm (27½in); female 65cm (25½in)
Grooming: Easy
Feeding: Undemanding
Exercise: Necessary
Temperament: Indifferent to strangers

Whippet

▼ *This dog is a devoted, affectionate companion that is good with children.*

Affectionately referred to as the 'poor man's racehorse', the Whippet is the most popular of the sighthounds. This medium-sized dog is the fastest domestic dog of similar weight. It is capable of achieving speeds of up to 56km/h (35mph), with some animals able to run 180m (200yd) in 12 seconds. The breed is a mixture of Greyhound, terriers and the Italian Greyhound. It was popularized by English coal miners in the 19th century, who used them to race, kill vermin and catch rabbits. It is also known as the Snap Dog, because of its ability to 'snap up' rabbits.

This breed has long legs, a lean physique and powerful hind quarters, giving a balanced and graceful outline. A very deep chest provides plenty of heart room. The head is long and lean,

Breed box
Size: 12.5–13.5kg (27½–30lb);
    male 47–51cm (18½–20in);
    female 44–47cm (17–18½in)
Grooming: Easy
Feeding: Undemanding
Exercise: Average
Temperament: Gentle and
    affectionate

▼ *One of the most companionable of all the hounds, the Whippet comes in a great range of colours.*

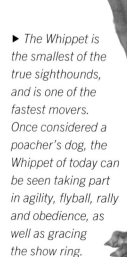

▶ *The Whippet is the smallest of the true sighthounds, and is one of the fastest movers. Once considered a poacher's dog, the Whippet of today can be seen taking part in agility, flyball, rally and obedience, as well as gracing the show ring.*

and set on an arched neck. It has a short coat that is soft and silky, and can be solid-coloured, parti-coloured or brindle, in almost any shade or combination. This dog rarely barks.

Still used for hunting, coursing and racing, this breed is also a popular competitor in the show ring. As a companion, the Whippet is undemanding – provided it gets a good walk, it is happy to come home and sleep for hours. A warm and soft bed should be provided, otherwise it is liable to sleep on its owner. This dog is not suitable for outdoor living, as it feels the cold. It is an affectionate hound that is gentle with children and makes a devoted companion.

THE GUNDOG (SPORTING) GROUP

Dogs from this group are the most recognizable of all the breeds. The purpose of every breed in the group is to assist in hunting and retrieving game, be it furred or feathered. Common points include their very easy-going temperaments (although there are slight variations), and the fact that they do not make much noise. They range in size from the Irish Setter at 65cm (25½in) down to the Sussex Spaniel at 38cm (15in). One characteristic seen in several breeds is that the strains that are most successful in the shooting field are not necessarily similar to those that find favour in the show ring. It would be wise to ask the breeder about this if you are buying for a particular purpose. However, a high percentage of gundogs of every strain retain the intelligence and willingness to please for which they were originally selected.

◀ *The Golden Retriever is extremely popular worldwide, both as a working dog and a family pet. It is tolerant and intelligent, making it very responsive to training.*

Bracco Italiano

The breed has been in existence at least since medieval times, and there is some evidence that it may date back to the 5th century BC. Also known as the Italian Pointer, this is the gundog that looks most like a hound. The Bracco is a very versatile worker that will hunt, point and retrieve.

It is a large, athletic dog that is almost square in shape. A drooping lower lip and long ears give the Bracco a very serious expression not unlike that of a Bloodhound. Coats are dense, short and glossy. White or white with orange, chestnut or amber markings are acceptable colours. Any black in the coat is considered a fault.

◄ *This is a multi-purpose dog that will fetch and carry for as long as it is asked to do so, with evident enjoyment.*

Breed box
Size: 25–40kg (55–88lb);
   male 58–67cm (23–26in);
   female 55–62cm (22–24in)
Grooming: Easy
Feeding: Medium
Exercise: High
Temperament: Loving and active

Grooming is easy, as a weekly rub over with a hound glove is all that is required. Ears must be kept clean to reduce the risk of infection.

This dog loves the company of humans, especially children, and will form a very strong bond with its family, making it an ideal companion.

Brittany

The Brittany or Brittany Spaniel comes from north-west France, and has been used as a hunting dog since the 17th century. As with many dog breeds, the Brittany suffered a serious decline during World War II. Numbers have greatly increased since then, as this

is a very popular working gundog and competitor in most canine sports.

There are two types, although both are the same breed: the 'French Brittany' works close to the gun, while the larger 'American Brittany' is faster. Coats are liver and white, black and white, orange and white, liver tricolour or black tricolour. The Canadian and USA Kennel Clubs do not recognize black colouring.

◄ *The Brittany is a superb setting and flushing dog, as well as a retriever.*

This is an active breed, sometimes termed as hyperactive. If not given enough exercise, it can become destructive and neurotic. It excels at agility, flyball and hiking, and is affectionate. It is not suited to families with young children as it may knock them over. It requires time and commitment to care for this dog.

Breed box
Size: 43–53cm (17–21in),
   14–18kg (31–40lb)
Grooming: Medium
Feeding: Moderate
Exercise: High
Temperament: Energetic and busy

English Setter

The English Setter is a tall, handsome creature of comparatively slight build. It gives the impression that it knows it is attractive and intends to be noticed by all and sundry. As it stands 68cm (27in) tall, it is easily seen; it has a gloriously long, silky coat that can be a mixture of black, orange, lemon or liver with white. Like all such coats, it requires dedication to keep it clean after a day's work. The breed has a long, lean aristocratic head set on a long, muscular neck.

The English Setter can be trained to work in the field with speed and intensity, quartering large tracts in search of pheasant, partridge or grouse; once its relatively long nose recognizes an exciting scent, the dog comes to a rapid stop and sets on to the object.

The sight of well-trained setters at full gallop suddenly screeching to a halt is, to say the least, memorable. There is no huge difference in shape and style between the show and working strains, but hunters have selected more for brains than beauty.

As a family dog, the English Setter is a natural because of its friendly nature, however it has a wildish streak in its make-up, even if it is not as

▼ The flecked colours in the coat are referred to as 'belton', so you may have a lemon belton or an orange belton dog.

▲ Over the years, the English Setter has been bred in large numbers by top breeders, who have produced their own very characteristic styles, but the soft eyes are obvious in all strains.

marked as in its Irish counterpart. It needs a firm, calm hand to turn it into a house dog, and it is not ideally suited to life in the suburbs. That said, it has a host of urban-dwelling admirers who will disagree with this personal verdict.

Breed box
Size: Male 65–68cm (25½–27in), 28.5kg (63lb); female 61–65cm (24–25½in), 27kg (59½lb)
Grooming: Demanding
Feeding: Reasonable
Exercise: Demanding
Temperament: Friendly

▲ This familiar pose is adopted by many dogs that are waiting for their owner to suggest a bit of action.

German Shorthaired Pointer

Of the three German pointers, the Shorthaired Pointer (GSP) is the best known. The mix of dogs that produced this breed is unknown, but is thought to include the English Pointer, Foxhound, Bloodhound and the German Bird Dog. The result is a superb all-round sporting dog that can

Breed box
Size: Male 59–64cm (23–25in), 25–32kg (55–70lb); female 53–58cm (21–23in), 20–27kg (44–59½lb)
Grooming: Easy
Feeding: Moderate to high
Exercise: High
Temperament: Boisterous and trainable

▶ *These dogs are strong swimmers. They have webbed feet, and delight in retrieving objects from water.*

retrieve, point and track. The GSP will retrieve from thick cover, open ground or water. Although predominantly a bird dog, it will hunt rabbits and racoons as well as trail deer.

Elegant and slightly streamlined, the GSP is striking. The short coat is solid liver, solid black, liver and white, or black and white. The American Kennel Club does not recognize any black colouring, and would consider this a cause for disqualification. The hair forms a water-resistant layer. This enables the dog to stay warm when working in water or cold weather. The GSP has a broad muzzle, so it is able to retrieve large game.

This is a very energetic breed. It is best suited to active owners who can take it for long, daily walks. It is generally good with children, but may not be the best choice for a young family. Care should be taken when introducing it to cats or other pets, as it has a strong hunting instinct.

Gordon Setter

Originating in Scotland, the Gordon Setter is the heavyweight of the setter section. It stands 66cm (26in) tall, but it is more solidly built than any of the others. As a result, it tends to move more steadily but still with considerable drive. It is a tireless

▶ *Setters vary in style, but nobody can fail to recognize the Gordon's solid build.*

Breed box
Size: Male 66cm (26in), 29.5kg (65lb); female 63cm (25in), 25.5kg (56lb)
Grooming: Reasonable
Feeding: Fairly demanding
Exercise: Reasonable
Temperament: Dignified and bold

worker that likes and needs its exercise; it does enjoy its food and can be heavy when fully grown.

It has a long, silky-textured coat of shining black with a pattern of chestnut-red tan on its muzzle and limbs. It grows slowly, as do all the setters, through a leggy, gawky stage,

during which it can be the despair of its owner, but eventually it matures into a sound, dignified dog.

Grooming has to be thorough, but is not over-demanding. This dog can make a good-natured companion as well as a reliable worker both in the field and on the moors.

German Wirehaired Pointer

The breed was developed in the early part of the 1900s by crossing the German Shorthaired Pointer with a number of other breeds, including the Griffon. The aim was to produce a dog that was a robust and versatile hunter that could work in any terrain. Like all German Pointers, this dog has webbed feet. The coat is an important factor in the breed. It is made up of two layers — the outer is weather-resistant, and the undercoat is dense in the winter to provide insulation. This almost disappears in the warmer months. Dead hair needs to be removed to keep it looking tidy.

◀ *Although recognized as a breed in Germany in 1870, this dog is still relatively uncommon today.*

Breed box
Size: 27–32kg (59½–70lb); male 60–67cm (24–26in); female 56–62cm (22–24in)
Grooming: Easy
Feeding: Medium to high
Exercise: High
Temperament: Playful and energetic

This is an affectionate and energetic dog that is loyal to its owner. It loves human companionship and, if properly trained, is tolerant towards children. It is prone to roaming and can become difficult to manage if not given enough exercise.

German Longhaired Pointer

This breed is rare and seldom seen in many parts of the world. It was devised in the 19th century by crossing German Shorthaired Pointers with English Pointers and Setters to produce a dog that could indicate by pointing the presence of flying prey. It is closer to a setter then a GSP in appearance, with a medium-length, shiny coat. The fur can be solid liver or any combination of liver and white. It is an athletic dog that moves with a graceful gait. It is a very trainable and extremely affectionate dog that is prone to separation anxiety. Provided it is not left alone for long periods and has long daily walks, the GLP make a good family companion. This is a playful breed that gets on well with children.

◀ *The hair on the ears, tail, belly, chest and backs of the legs is longer than that on the body.*

▲ *Clean ears regularly to prevent a build-up of dirt and wax.*

Breed box
Size: 30kg (66lb); male 60–70cm (24–28in); female 58–66cm (23–26in)
Grooming: Moderate
Feeding: Medium to high
Exercise: High
Temperament: Athletic and friendly

Hungarian Vizsla

The Hungarian Vizsla (often just called Vizsla) is a spectacularly coloured hunting, pointing and retrieving (HPR) breed from Central Europe. The short, dense coat of rich red russet only needs polishing with a cloth to keep it at its glorious best.

The breed stands up to 64cm (25in) at the withers, weighs some 28kg (62lb), and is strongly built with well-

Breed box
Size: 20–30kg (44–66lb);
    male 57–64cm (22½–25in);
    female 53–60cm (21–23½in)
Grooming: Easy
Feeding: Medium
Exercise: Medium
Temperament: Lively and fearless

▶ *With one of the handsomest heads, the Vizsla is keen-eyed and has an intelligent expression.*

muscled limbs and a noble head that is not over-fleshed.

The Vizsla is a worker with a great reputation in its native Hungary as both a pointer of game and a reliable retriever; it takes special delight in going into water in its quest for a shot bird. As a companion, it is a good,

▲ *The sight of a Vizsla in bright sunshine is a flash of the richest red.*

affectionate member of the household, but it can be fairly protective so it needs a firm hand. Easily trained by those who set their mind to it, it is a truly all-purpose dog.

Hungarian Wire-haired Vizsla

The Hungarian Wire-haired Vizsla is another HPR breed, very much like the Hungarian Vizsla, with the exception that the coat is harsh. It sports definite eyebrows, which give it a sterner expression. Its height is the same as the Vizsla's, as is its weight, and it demonstrates much the

same characteristics of temperament. The coat on its legs is short and harsh, and possibly makes its limbs appear larger.

▼ *The harsh coat is the same russet red as that of the Hungarian Vizsla.*

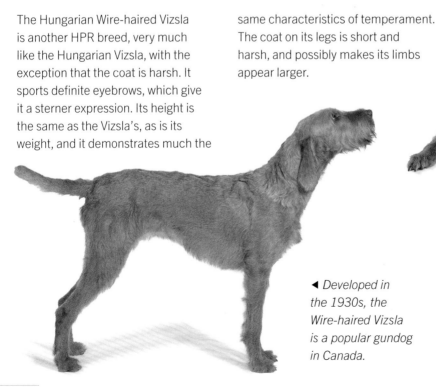

◀ *Developed in the 1930s, the Wire-haired Vizsla is a popular gundog in Canada.*

Breed box
Size: 20–30kg (44–66lb);
    male 57–64cm (22½–25in);
    female 53–60cm (21–23½in)
Grooming: Relatively easy
Feeding: Medium
Exercise: Medium
Temperament: Lively and fearless

Irish Setter

The Irish Setter is known to its friends as the Mad Irishman, with a devil-may-care way about it. It is certainly beautiful, but to keep that long, silky coat of deep chestnut gleaming requires thorough and regular grooming, and the occasional bath.

▶ *The Irish Setter first appeared in recognizable form in the early 18th century.*

Breed box
Size: Male 65cm (25½in), 30.5kg (67lb); female 26kg (57½lb)
Grooming: Demanding
Feeding: Reasonable
Exercise: Demanding
Temperament: Affectionate and racy

It stands around 65cm (25½in), but the official breed standard does not contain a height clause because, according to those who have bred it all their lives, a good Irish Setter can never be a bad height. It is allowed to have a small amount of white on the front of its brisket, but nowhere else.

The Irish Setter does not carry a great deal of flesh, but its musculature has to be powerful because it is expected to work at top speed in the shooting field. It is not expensive to feed, although it can burn up a lot of calories, and it expects to be well exercised. It can be trained to curb its wildness, and its attitude to one and all is of sheer friendship and *joie de vivre*. The recall exercise is not easily mastered by this dog.

Irish Red and White Setter

The Irish Red and White Setter comes as a surprise to those who have always recognized the traditional Irish Setter, often incorrectly called the Red Setter. In fact, the Red and White is reputed to have been the original, but it was largely unknown outside Ireland for much of the early 20th century.

Its success since the start of the 1980s has been gradual as breeders have become more selective and people have begun to notice this large red and white dog. It is similar in appearance to the Irish Setter but has a broader head and is more heavily built.

It stands up to 65cm (25½in) at the withers and has a base colour of white with solid red patches on the head and body, and mottling on its limbs.

This breed enjoys human company and it makes a friendly family dog but its coat needs careful attention. It can be quite a handful to control, and its training requires firmness.

▶ *The Irish Red and White Setter is a strong, athletic dog. It is good-natured and affectionate and is growing in popularity, but this breed requires patience to train it.*

Breed box
Size: Male 65cm (25½in), 29.5kg (65lb); female 61cm (24in), 25kg (55lb)
Grooming: Demanding
Feeding: Reasonable
Exercise: Demanding
Temperament: Cheerful and biddable

Italian Spinone

The Spinone is an ancient breed from the Piedmont region of Italy. This hunter is capable of working on almost any terrain, and will point and retrieve. The breed name may have come from the word 'spino', which is a type of thorn bush that coarse-coated hunting dogs could push through without harm. The Spinone is often confused with the German Wirehaired Pointer, but it is very different in working style and character.

With a solid, well-muscled body and strong bone, it is easy to see how this dog can work in challenging undergrowth. The coarse white, orange and white, brown and white, orange roan or brown roan coat

▶ The Italian Spinone has recently arrived in North America, where the breed already has its devotees.

protects the skin from brambles and thorns. The Spinone has pronounced eyebrows, and the hair on its muzzle forms a beard that provides additional protection to the face. Paws are large with webbed toes.

Not as fast or as energetic as many of the gundog breeds, the Spinone is well suited to life as a family dog.

Breed box
Size: 55–71cm (22–28in),
27–38.5kg (59½–85lb)
Grooming: Easy
Feeding: Demanding
Exercise: Medium
Temperament: Loyal and placid

Kooikerhondje

This dog has many different names, including Small Dutch Waterfowl Dog, Kooiker Hound, Kooiker Dog and the Dutch Decoy Dog. Popular in the 17th and 18th centuries, it was used to lure ducks into traps, by dancing around and waving its tail in front of them. The ducks would follow the dog and, once in the trap, could be caught by the hunters. This method of hunting

is not used now, but the Kooikerhondje is still used for luring ducks into traps for conservation and environmental purposes.

This beautiful medium-sized dog is red-orange and white in colour, with a well-plumed white tail. Some have a black ring encircling the tail, where the red-orange meets the white. The ears should have long black hair at the tips, which are called 'earrings'. Other black markings are not permitted, but puppies are often born with black hairs on their bodies that fall out as the puppy coat is shed. The unique adult coat can take two years to develop.

This dog is active outdoors but settled within the home. It is affectionate and curious, investigating every new object that it finds. It is wary of strangers and will need

▲ The Kooikerhondje's active frame is ideal for agility training.

socialization to overcome this. It does not like excessive handling, but with sympathetic training it will make a loving, loyal companion. It is not recommended with small or noisy children. With training, it excels at activities such as dance and tracking.

Breed box
Size: 36–41cm (14–16in),
9–18kg (20–40lb)
Grooming: Moderate
Feeding: Medium
Exercise: Medium
Temperament: Sensitive and affectionate

Lagotto Romagnolo

The name of this dog is descriptive: *lagotto* is the Venetian for 'duck dog', and Romagna is a region in Italy that the breed comes from. The breed type has been in existence in Italy since the 7th century BC. As marshlands were drained, the need for duck-hunting dogs diminished. But the Lagotto, with its exceptional scenting ability, was found to be able to 'sniff out' truffles. It is now the only breed of dog in the world that is recognized as truffle hunter.

It is an avid swimmer that has webbed toes and thick hair on the underside of the ear to prevent water from entering the inner ear. Eyes are large and round, and vary in colour

◄ *This breed has been employed for centuries in Europe and Scandinavian countries to hunt for truffles.*

◄ *Bright and happy, this dog responds well to training for a variety of activities.*

from dark brown to dark yellow. The Lagotto has a curly, non-shedding, waterproof coat that provides protection against thorns. This will require clipping several times a year. Left untrimmed, the hair on the head will grow across the eyes. Coat colours range from solid white, brown or rust to white with rust or brown patches.

Provided that it is given sufficient exercise, this dog is an affectionate and loyal family companion. It is an intelligent breed that enjoys taking part in canine sports such as agility and flyball. It gets on well with other dogs and is tolerant towards children. It is a great digger, and will dig up the lawn in a matter of minutes given the chance. The territorial Lagotto will bark to sound an alarm, making it an excellent watch dog. Puppy socialization and training classes are strongly recommended.

▲ *The Lagotto Romagnolo is often misidentified as a Poodle because of its similar coat.*

Breed box
Size: Male 43–49cm (17–19in), 13–16kg (28–35lb); female 36–41cm (16–18in), 11–14kg (24–31lb)
Grooming: Extensive
Feeding: Medium
Exercise: Medium
Temperament: Robust and intelligent

Large Munsterlander

The Large Munsterlander is a hunting, pointing and retrieving (HPR) dog that comes from the Munster region of Germany. It is a fearless hunter that has a total disregard of even the worst of weather conditions. Its boundless stamina and energy means that it is happy to work all day on the hunting field. Predominantly a bird dog, it will also hunt rabbits, hares and deer.

This breed has a black head and a white body that is flecked, ticked or patched with black. A solid black coat is considered a fault. Ears, tail and legs are feathered. There is a clear difference between males and

▶ *Excelling at obedience competitions, this breed is also used successfully as a therapy dog.*

females – the former are larger, with bigger heads, more feathering on the legs and longer hair on the chest. The Large Musterlander has a noble expression and moves in a fluid and effortless manner.

It is a very active breed that has a high exercise requirement. It is not suitable for an inactive owner, but ideal for someone who likes to spend a lot of time outdoors. A bored or under-exercised Musterlander can become destructive and may bark when left

alone in the home. This dog is very active both inside and outdoors. It is good with children, but unless properly trained to be calm in their presence, it may knock toddlers over. It is a keen hunting dog that must be taught not to chase livestock and other domestic pets. The breed is highly trainable, provided that the owner is consistent, and responds well to reward-based training.

▼ *The Large Munsterlander is a keen, all-purpose gundog with a good nose and excellent stamina. Brown and white coats occur, but are uncommon.*

Breed box
Size: 58–65cm (23–25½in), 23–32kg (50–70lb)
Grooming: Medium
Feeding: Moderate to high
Exercise: High
Temperament: Active and trainable

▲ *This breed always has a black head, but the expression is alleviated by the gleam in those golden-brown eyes.*

Nova Scotia Duck Tolling Retriever

The word 'toll' means 'to lure', and that is what the Nova Scotia Duck Tolling Retriever does. It rushes about in a playful manner at the water's edge while a hunter waits in a hide. Ducks are attracted to the spectacle, and swim towards the shore. When in range, the hunter stands up, causing the birds to take flight, and then shoots the ducks. The Toller retrieves the fallen birds from the water.

Breed box
Size: 43–55cm (17–21½in),
   17–23kg (37½–50lb)
Grooming: Medium
Feeding: Medium
Exercise: Medium to high
Temperament: Jaunty and trainable

It is a medium-sized breed with a fox-like head. The coat is double, soft and water-repellent, and comes in rich shades of red. White markings are permissible on the feet, chest, tail tip and as a blaze on the head. The tail is well plumed and held high when active. The dog should be well muscled with medium to heavy bone. Tollers make a distinctive noise when excited; it is a cross between a bark and a howl, and is called the 'Toller Scream'. The breed is often mistaken for a small Golden Retriever.

The Toller is well suited as a family companion. It is a breed that enjoys the company of children, especially if they throw things for the animal to retrieve – this dog will retrieve for hours. It is a hardworking, intelligent

◄ *The main purpose of this spritely breed is to tempt waterfowl to within range of a hunter.*

and trainable dog that is devoted to its family. Excelling in canine sports, it can be seen enjoying obedience, dock diving and agility.

Pointer

The Pointer is an instantly recognizable breed. The clean-cut lines of its lean frame covered by a short, shining coat make a beautiful silhouette on grouse moor and in city parks alike, although it better suited for the countryside.

Breed box
Size: Male 63–69cm (25–27in),
   29.5kg (65lb); female 61–66cm
   (24–26in), 26kg (57½lb)
Grooming: Minimal
Feeding: Demanding
Exercise: Medium
Temperament: Kind and
   reasonably biddable

At 69cm (27in) in height, the Pointer is quite a tall dog. It does not carry much surplus flesh, so gives the impression of being bony. Its movements are fluent and athletic. This breed is not a big eater, it is a very easy dog to clean after a day's work, and it is relatively easy to teach it reasonable manners, though it is unlikely to win a top-standard obedience competition.

While most paintings depict the Pointer as white with a number of liver or black patches, it also comes in lemon and orange patterns. A kindly, gentle dog, it should appeal to the active owner.

► *The Pointer is built for speed and endurance.*

Chesapeake Bay Retriever

The Chesapeake Bay Retriever is a strong, muscular dog. It stands up to 66cm (26in) high, which does not make it a giant among dogs by any means, but its purpose in life is retrieving ducks from its native Chesapeake Bay, which is usually cold. For this it needs much subcutaneous fat and a thick, oily-feeling coat, all of which add up to a look of substance.

It comes in a colour that is somewhat unromantically described as 'dead grass' (straw to bracken). It can also be red-gold or brown.

Its ability to work is prodigious. It loves people and is always ready to please, but it is not meant for the idle; rather it will suit a family that enjoys the countryside and does not mind having a fair amount of it brought into the

▶ *The Chessie is a burly dog that delights in leaping into water, whether asked to or not.*

house along with the dog. A very stiff brush and a chamois leather will repair the worst damage to its coat, but possibly not to the best carpet or the antique chairs!

▶ *The head shape is not very different from that of its Labrador cousin.*

▶ *There's no getting away from the fact that, of all the basic retrieving dogs, the Chesapeake Bay Retriever is the heavyweight. Its thick, oily coat protects it in the water and dries quickly, preventing it from getting a chill.*

Breed box

Size: Male 58–66cm (23–26in),
    31kg (68lb); female 53–61cm
    (21–24in), 28kg (62lb)
Grooming: Fairly demanding
Feeding: Considerable
Exercise: Demanding but simple
Temperament: Alert and cheerful

Curly Coated Retriever

The Curly Coated Retriever is obviously unusual in style, as its body is covered with tight, crisp curls, even down the length of its tail. The only part of the dog with smooth hair is its face and muzzle. It is most often seen in black, but liver is not uncommon either.

Its height is up to 69cm (27in), and it is well proportioned, so its powerful shoulders and loins do not make it appear clumsy or coarse. Those who employ it as a worker swear by its intelligence and ability in water, nosing out shot birds and bringing them to hand rapidly; it is noted for its prodigious shake.

It is energetic but not a greedy feeder. It makes a good guard for a retriever, it is not hard to control, and makes a good family dog.

Breed box
Size: 34kg (75lb); male 69cm (27in); female 63.5cm (25in)
Grooming: Fairly demanding
Feeding: Reasonable
Exercise: Demanding but simple
Temperament: Friendly and confident

▲ The coat is the mark of this calm, powerful water dog, with a mass of curls that lie tight to the skin.

▲ The aristocratically chiselled muzzle is smooth-haired. The head is wedge-shaped with ears set below eye level.

▶ It is thought that the Curly Coated Retriever originated in Britain as the result of crossing the now-extinct English Water Spaniel with a Retrieving Setter and the later Lesser Newfoundland, which arrived in Britain in 1835 with the cod fishermen.

Flat-coated Retriever

The Flat-coated Retriever is one of the lightest built of all the retriever family, and is a very agile dog. It is sociable and good-humoured, and always eager to please. The breed is most commonly black, but there are also a fair number of liver-coloured dogs. The odd yellow-coloured variation is frowned on by enthusiasts.

Breed box
Size: Male 58–61cm (23–24in),
  25–35kg (55–77lb); female
  56–59cm (22–23in), 25–34kg
  (55–75lb)
Grooming: Medium
Exercise: Medium
Feeding: Medium
Temperament: Kindly

▶ *The Flat-coated Retriever has a lighter body than other retriever breeds. It is a dog for the country rather than the town.*

Standing at almost 61cm (24in) at the withers, it is not heavily built in the loins and hindquarters, hence its lighter appearance. Its coat is dense and flat, and positively shines with health after a good grooming. It is not a demanding dog to feed.

The Flat-coated Retriever is an excellent household dog who loves human company; its tail wags incessantly, and its intelligence is plain to see whether it is asked to work in the shooting field or play in the park.

▲ *This type of retriever has a less square foreface than other retrievers. Its deep bark gives a good warning of visitors or strangers.*

▶ *Flat-coats originated in Britain as the result of crossing several other breeds, including the Lesser Newfoundland. They originally had wavy coats.*

Golden Retriever

The Golden Retriever is a canine all-rounder. It can turn its talents to anything, from its natural retrieving to acting as a guide dog for the blind, a detector of drugs or explosives, a reasonably laid-back obedience worker, or just being a most attractive member of a household.

Breed box
Size: 29.5kg (65lb); male 56–61cm (22–24in), 34kg (75lb); female 51–56cm (20–22in)
Grooming: Fairly demanding
Feeding: Demanding
Exercise: Demanding
Temperament: Intelligent and biddable

It stands 61cm (24in) at its tallest, but gives the impression of being a solid, comfortable dog. It is inclined to get its snout into the trough as often as possible, and owners need to watch its waistline. There is often quite a difference in appearance between those retrievers used in the shooting field and the type that are bred for showing and the home.

The Golden Retriever has a dense undercoat with a flat, wavy topcoat; the colour varies from cream to a rich golden, which is sometimes very deep.

It is easy to train, but needs to be kept interested because it is easily bored. Its ability as a guide dog for the blind demonstrates its temperament, as the work involves a great deal of steady, thoughtful walking.

It is one of the most popular household dogs because of its generous, loving nature.

Such popularity is often a

▲ *The Golden Retriever, one of the most popular of all dogs in the world, is a wonderful all-purpose breed, although guarding is not its forte.*

curse, however, because dogs are bred by people who are not always conscientious in their dedication to producing truly healthy stock. As is true of any breed of pedigree dog, the best source of supply is direct from a reputable breeder who has the welfare of the dogs they produce at heart.

▶ *This breed was developed in Britain in the late 19th century. Becoming popular rapidly, it was imported to the USA, Canada, South America, Kenya, India and parts of Europe by the 1930s.*

▲ *These dogs have generous, soft muzzles that are able to carry shot birds, hares or even the newspaper without leaving a mark.*

Labrador Retriever

The Labrador Retriever is instantly recognizable. Thought to have originated in Greenland, it is a stockily built dog; its coat is short and hard to the touch, and it is entirely weather-proof and drip-dry. At one time, the black coat was the best known, but yellow (not golden) became more widely seen from the 1940s onwards. Today, there is quite a trend for chocolate, which is also called 'liver'.

▶ *Labradors were brought into the UK in the 19th century by the Earl of Malmesbury, to work the water meadows of his estate.*

Breed box
Size: Male 56–57cm (22–22½in), 30.5kg (67lb); female 54–56cm (21–22in), 28.5kg (63lb)
Grooming: Easy
Feeding: Reasonable
Exercise: Demanding
Temperament: Friendly and intelligent

▲ *Wisdom in a canine expression is difficult to define, but the true Labrador seems to get as near as any.*

The Labrador stands as high as 57cm (22½in), which is not very tall, but its body is extremely solid. Another characteristic is its relatively short, thick-coated tail, which is known as an 'otter' tail. Like the Golden Retriever, it is a multi-talented dog, being much favoured as a guide dog for the blind. (In fact. these two breeds are regularly crossbred to utilize their combined skills.) It is also useful in drug-searching, and has been used by the army as a canine mine-detector. Undoubtedly its greatest skill is as a retriever from water.

The Labrador Retriever seems capable of taking all the knocks of a rough-and-tumble family, which is why it rates so highly as a household member. Its temperament is such that it does not seem to take offence at any insult.

It can consume any quantity of food, so needs rationing if it is not to put on too much weight. It must have exercise and, although it can live in town surroundings, it should not be deprived of regular, long walks. Without these, it can rapidly become an obese couch potato, with all the health implications this implies.

▶ *With a frame like this, it is easy to see why the breed is famous for its stamina.*

Clumber Spaniel

The Clumber Spaniel may only stand around 42cm (16½in), but it is a lot of dog. Admittedly, it was never expected to rush around the fields in the manner of the Cocker or the Springer, but it has increased in weight over the years up to 36kg (79½lb) or even more, and thus moves at a somewhat ponderous pace.

Its temperament is kindly even if a trifle aloof at times; it can be an attractive member of the household, but it should live in the country. Its mainly white coat, with some lemon or orange marking, is close and silky in texture, but abundant in quantity. This breed is not difficult to groom. Despite its size, it is not a particularly greedy dog, but it does need exercise.

Breed box
Size: 42–45.4cm (16½–18in); male 36kg (79½lb); female 29.5kg (65lb)
Grooming: Reasonable
Feeding: Medium
Exercise: Medium
Temperament: Kind and reliable

▲ *These dogs will trundle through a day's shooting at a steady pace and never lose their cool.*

◄ *This breed has loose skin on its forehead, and it suffers from drooping lower eyelids. Both of these traits can cause veterinary problems.*

► *The Clumber was bred at Clumber Park, Nottinghamshire, England, in the 19th century. It is thought to have originated in France, and includes the Basset Hound in its ancestry, hence its long back.*

American Cocker Spaniel

The American Cocker Spaniel is a derivation of the English Cocker Spaniel. In both countries, their own nationality is dropped in the official name of the breed.

The process of selection from the original stock has gone quite a long way. The American version has a very different head shape from the English – the muzzle is shorter and the skull is domed to the point of roundness, while the eyes are fuller and set to look straight ahead. The other huge difference is in the coat,

Breed box
Size: 11–13kg (24–28½lb); male 36.5–39cm (14½–15½in); female 33.5–36.5cm (13–14½in)
Grooming: Extensive
Feeding: Small
Exercise: Medium
Temperament: Cheerful and intelligent

which is exaggeratedly long and profuse on the legs and abdomen of the American Cocker Spaniel. If left untrimmed, this coat is impractical for the working dog. As a member of a household, its coat is likely to present a problem if it is not kept well groomed. The dog comes in a range of very handsome colours, including black, black and tan, buff, parti-colour and tricolour.

▲ *Nobody could fail to remember a dog with a coat like this, but you should keep the grooming requirements in mind before succumbing to the enormous charm of those eyes.*

▶ *Note the characteristic peak to the hair over the eyebrows. This is one of the most popular breeds in the USA.*

◀ *These dogs were developed in the USA in the 19th century to flush out and retrieve quail and woodcock.*

This breed is a thoroughly cheerful dog that does not eat ravenously. It enjoys its exercise, but is easily trained to behave in a suitable manner for suburbia. As it stands a mere 39cm (15½in) at its tallest, it does not need a mansion, but will be happy to live in one if given the opportunity.

English Cocker Spaniel

The English Cocker Spaniel is the original of the American breed. It stands around the same height as the American Cocker Spaniel at 41cm (16in), but its coat is shorter and therefore nowhere near such hard work to keep well groomed, provided adequate attention is paid to its fairly hairy feet and its longish ears. It can be found in whole colours such as red (gold) and black, and also in black and white, and in multi-colours.

A thoroughly busy dog, it is always searching and bustling around in the grass and bushes. Its name comes

◀ The orange-roan colour is one of a huge range that this neat dog comes in. The breed is the basis of several of the land spaniels.

from its ability to flush out game, particularly the woodcock. It also delights in carrying objects about, whether on command or purely voluntarily. It is often portrayed as the original slipper-fetching dog sitting by its owner's fireside, its tail wagging furiously. There is a clear difference between the heavier show English Cocker and the leggier working type.

▼ Low-slung ears with long hair make regular grooming a must for this dog.

Breed box
Size: 12.5–14.5kg (27½–32lb);
 male 39–41cm (15–16in);
 female 38–39cm (15–15½in)
Grooming: Regular
Feeding: Small
Exercise: Medium
Temperament: Merry and exuberant

▼ The Cocker's job is to flush ground game for its handler. The tight body is essential for its bustling way of moving.

▲ This example shows a differently shaped eye, but still the gentle, relaxed expression.

145

English Springer Spaniel

The English Springer Spaniel was bred to flush or 'spring' game, hence their name. Flushing dogs, similar in looks to today's Springer, were in existence many years before the gun was invented. They would 'spring' on small game or birds to flush them out of cover so that they could be caught by hawks, hounds or in nets.

Nowadays, there is a clear difference in both appearance and working ability between English Springers bred for the field and those produced for the show ring. Potential owners should satisfy themselves that they are buying from the correct bloodlines for the type they require.

▶ The breed name 'Cocker' comes from this dog's use as a hunter of woodcock in England.

▶ Do not be deceived – this is a high-energy dog and requires long walks.

This is a compact, medium-sized dog that has a very gentle expression and is well proportioned and balanced. Show-bred dogs are heavier and have longer coats and ears than the field-bred type. Working types may be smaller and lighter than the guides given in the 'Breed box' on this page. In both types, the coat is black and white, liver and white or tricolour. The white may be flecked or ticked. There is feathering on the ears, chest, belly, legs and tail.

This is an extremely popular breed worldwide. Affectionate and friendly, this dog makes a good companion in both the home and hunting field. It has great stamina and needs a lot

▲ The Springer has a charm that it is quite capable of using to its own ends. The coat requires daily grooming.

of exercise. It is generally tolerant with children, other dogs and small pets. Eager to learn, the breed excels in obedience, flyball and agility. The English Springer loves to work, and is used for drug and bomb detection, and also search and rescue.

Breed box
Size: Male 46–51cm (18–20in), 23–25kg (50–55lb); female 43–48cm (17–19in), 16–20kg (36–44lb)
Grooming: Moderate
Feeding: Medium
Exercise: High
Temperament: Affectionate and tolerant

▶ The thoroughly balanced shape of the Springer means it is able to move rapidly and easily.

Field Spaniel

This dog was once considered to be the same breed as the English Cocker Spaniel. It is said by some that due to the considerable diversity in size of the Cocker, it was decided in the early 20th century to split the breed. Dogs weighing above 11kg (25lb) were considered as Field Spaniels, while those weighing less remained as Cocker Spaniels. Although the breed

▼ *The Field Spaniel is a dog for the country-dwelling family. It is steady and trainable.*

has changed since then, there are still some similarities to the working-type Cocker. This dog will retrieve from land or water, flush, hunt and track, as well as being a good watch dog. It is quite rare and is listed by the KC as a Vulnerable Native Breed.

The coat is silky and coloured roan, solid black or solid liver. White markings are permitted on the throat and chest. Some dogs have tan points. The coat is darker with less white than other spaniels. The ears, chest, belly and the back of the legs are feathered.

Breed box
Size: 43–46cm (16–18in), 18–25kg (39½–55lb)
Grooming: Moderate
Feeding: Medium
Exercise: High
Temperament: Docile and intelligent

Irish Water Spaniel

The Irish Water Spaniel is one for the connoisseur. It is tall by spaniel standards, as it reaches 58cm (23in). The fact is that it is much more of a retriever than a spaniel. It is covered with tight liver-coloured ringlets,

Breed box
Size: Male 53–58cm (21–23in), 27kg (59½lb); female 51–56cm (20–22in), 24kg (53lb)
Grooming: Medium
Feeding: Medium
Exercise: Medium
Temperament: Affectionate if aloof

except for its muzzle, the front of its neck and the last two-thirds of the tail. When it gets wet, its shake is a spectacular sight.

Aficionados regard it with great affection and enthusiasm, and consider that it has a good sense of humour. It is certainly energetic and revels in any amount of exercise, whether it is asked to be a household companion or fulfil its traditional role.

Grooming this spaniel requires skill and knowledge of the correct technique, as well as determination. Feeding is not a problem, as this dog is not greedy. It is a breed that could achieve greater acclaim.

▲ *Grooming is no easy task, and the art must be acquired from the start.*

Sussex Spaniel

▼ *The Sussex Spaniel has a heavier build and shorter legs than most other spaniels.*

This dog is designated as a Vulnerable British Breed by the KC. After World War II, there were thought to be only about seven Sussex Spaniels remaining. Numbers increased when breeding programmes were put in place, but this is still a fairly rare dog. It is a steady and careful hunter that is mainly used for flushing and retrieving upland game, and is a good watch and tracking dog. Unusually, it is the only gundog that bays when hunting.

It is a powerful, low and compact dog with a long body similar to that of the Clumber Spaniel. While being generally slow-paced, it can have bursts of extreme activity. Its rich red-gold coat is double, with a silky top layer and a dense water-resistant undercoat. The neck, chest, belly, legs and tail are feathered. Ears hang down, and are covered with silky hair.

This breed can be noisy, especially when bored or short of exercise. Training will teach the dog when this is appropriate and when it is not. It is generally accepting of children, other dogs and cats, and is calm in the home – not as active as other spaniels. It is a good companion breed, but can be stubborn to train if not properly socialized. The breed is not recommended for an inexperienced owner with small children, as this dog needs a person who is strong-minded with plenty of time to spare. The Sussex is prone to gaining weight if not getting sufficient exercise, so food rations need to be carefully monitored.

Breed box
Size: 38–40cm (15–16in),
   18–20kg (39½–44lb)
Grooming: Moderate
Feeding: Medium
Exercise: Medium
Temperament: Calm and steady

Welsh Springer Spaniel

This breed is similar to the English Springer Spaniel, but is smaller and has a finer head. The 'Welshie' is used to find and 'spring' or startle game to take flight. Fallen game is then retrieved by the dogs. The Welsh Springer has great stamina and can do this job all day long.

With its red and white coat and fringed ears, the Welshie is a striking dog. The coat is soft and lies flat to the body. Legs, chest, belly and tail are feathered. Eyes are almond-shaped and brown. Nose leather should be black or brown.

Friendly and loving towards family members, the Welshie can be wary of strangers. It is a fine companion, provided that owners are prepared to give it long daily walks. It is good with children, other dogs and pets. It does not like being left alone and can exhibit signs of separation anxiety. It needs early training to ensure it comes when called. The Welsh Springer Spaniel does well in the show and obedience ring, agility, flyball and tracking, and as a therapy dog.

◀ *This is a gentle breed that is used for therapy work.*

Breed box
Size: 16–20kg (36–44lb);
   male 46–48cm (18–19in);
   female 43–46cm (17–18in)
Grooming: Moderate
Feeding: Medium
Exercise: Medium to high
Temperament: Loyal and willing

Weimaraner

The Weimaraner is an outstanding dog. It stands tall in the Gundog Group at 69cm (27in). A highly unusual colour, the Weimaraner is nicknamed the 'Grey Ghost', although the grey can be slightly mousy rather than the silver-grey that experts crave. Possibly its most outstanding feature are its eyes, which can be either amber or blue in colour.

This is a hunting, pointing and retrieving (HPR) breed that originated on the European mainland. Its coat is short, smooth and sleek, although there is a rare version which sports a longer coat. In the more usual coat, it is no problem to groom – it is more a matter of polishing! Even when a Weimaraner spends a long day in the shooting field or on a country stroll through winter mud, it does not bring the outside world into its home.

This dog is not a big feeder, although it appreciates and needs a generously filled bowl on a cold winter's day. It does need exercise, because it has a temperament that requires plenty to occupy its very active mind. It can be trained fairly easily, but does not suffer fools gladly. It has a friendly attitude towards people but will act as an

▲ The long-coated Weimaraner is less common than the ordinary short-coated dog, but is a very attractive variant of this breed.

impressive guard if its home or family are threatened. It is not a fawning, easy-going type of dog, even if it comes from a group that appears generally placid.

▲ This dog's piercing eyes are a distinctive feature. Normally shades of amber or blue-grey, they may appear black when dilated with excitement.

Breed box
Size: Male 61–69cm (24–27in), 27kg (59½lb); female 56–64cm (22–25in), 22.5kg (50lb)
Grooming: Easy
Feeding: Medium
Exercise: Demanding
Temperament: Fearless and friendly

▶ The truly stylish 'Grey Ghost' is built on racy lines, but with a stamina and turn of speed that emulate the thoroughbred stayer of the horse world.

THE TERRIER GROUP

The breeds that comprise this group are the pest-controllers of the canine world, having originally been used to find and kill rodents of all shapes and sizes. They possess fairly similar temperaments – they have to be tenacious as well as sharp in movement and reaction. They are inclined to act first and think afterwards, they tend to argue with the dog next door, and they are not often the delivery man's best friend. But a terrier that is properly introduced is a delight as far as humans are concerned. A family who is seeking an alert, playful and affectionate friend will be well satisfied with a member of this group. The Terrier Group may be thought to include one of the most popular of all dogs, the Jack Russell Terrier, although this is, in fact, a cross-breed and therefore not registered by either the British or American Kennel Clubs. Nevertheless, we've included it in this chapter since it is such a common breed.

◄ *Although the Terrier Group is very diverse in type, size and weight, all have quick reactions and often act before they think. These are American Staffordshire Terriers.*

Airedale Terrier

Originating from northern England, the Airedale is the largest of the terriers, by some degree. It is a splendid animal with a genuine style about it that entitles it to its nickname, 'King of the Terriers'. It stands as tall as 61cm (24in) and has a head with an expression suggesting total command of any situation.

◄ *These three youngsters will eventually grow into king-sized Airedale Terriers. They will reach maturity at about two years old.*

that can be very convincing to any intruder. It is not a greedy feeder, but at the same time it is a well-built dog and naturally needs an adequate supply of nutrition.

◄ *The Airedale greets friends with a laughing expression on an impressively bearded face.*

Breed box
Size: 21.5kg (47½lb); male 58–61cm (23–24in); female 56–59cm (22–23in)
Grooming: Medium
Feeding: Medium
Exercise: Reasonable
Temperament: Friendly and courageous

The Airedale is somewhat less aggressive towards other dogs than some breeds in the group, but it will not back down if challenged. Few would dare to challenge it! It is reputed to be intelligent, but can be stubborn unless handled in a firm manner.

It has a black saddle, and the rest of it is mostly tan; the tan can be a gloriously rich colour. Its coat is harsh and dense and grows impressively, but can be kept tidy with regular brushing. It sheds its coat twice a year, and at such times it is good for it to be trimmed or stripped by a professional. The experts will frown on the use of clippers, but these can be an alternative if the dog is destined to be a household companion, not a show dog.

It makes a very good guard dog as it considers that its owner's property is its to look after. It has a loud voice

◄ *This splendidly elegant, mature dog is ready to stand up to rat or human intruder alike. Although unable to go to ground, the Airedale displays all other terrier characteristics in abundance.*

Australian Terrier

Initially called the Rough Haired Terrier, the Australian Terrier is thought to have originated from a cross of British northern terriers that travelled to Australia with the early settlers. This dog was bred to hunt and kill rats and mice. The breed is recognized by the kennel clubs of all English-speaking countries.

▶ *In Australia, these feisty little terriers are prized for their ability to kill snakes.*

Breed box
Size: 25cm (10in), 6.5kg (14lb)
Grooming: Reasonable
Feeding: Small
Exercise: Undemanding
Temperament: Extroverted and
   friendly

This is an alert, small dog of great character. It stands a mere 25cm (10in) high to the shoulder. The body shape is round rather than deep, with plenty of space for good lungs, which it needs in order to be as active as it always seems to be. The coat is relatively short and is harsh in texture, making it easy to groom. The dog has an intelligent expression and carries its ears pricked. The coat can have either steel blue on its saddle with tan on the rest of it, or an all-over red. The blue and tan-coated dogs are often born with a blue-black coat that changes colour at around nine months of age.

Either way, the Australian Terrier is a smart little dog that is tractable and anxious to please, although it can be bossy. It can be useful as a watch dog and is able to use its vocal chords in the home. Like all terriers, the male dogs can be aggressive in the absence of early socialization and training.

Bedlington Terrier

This dog comes from the northern counties of the UK, possibly Northumberland, and was bred to chase and catch rabbits and other small rodents. Often owned by poachers, it has also been known as the 'Gypsy Dog'. In the 19th century, this fast breed was used by factory workers to race, sometimes even against Whippets. Nowadays it is seen mainly as a family pet.

The Bedlington Terrier is a very distinctive dog with a somewhat tucked-up loin and an unusual non-shedding coat. The fur, sometimes described as 'linty', stands away from the dog's body and has a tendency to twist. Because this dog does not moult in the normal manner, it is considered less likely to cause allergic symptoms in susceptible people. The coat requires regular grooming and clipping, and when properly presented, this terrier looks like a shorn lamb. All Bedlingtons are dark in colour when born but lighten as they grow, and they become very pale shades of blue or sand that may appear white.

As this dog has a very strong prey instinct and is liable to chase other small furry animals, including cats, it requires a well-fenced garden.

▶ *Correctly presented, the Bedlington Terrier has a very distinctive, attractive trim.*

Breed box
Size: 41cm (16in), 8–10.5kg
   (18–23lb)
Grooming: Reasonably
   undemanding
Feeding: Small
Exercise: Undemanding
Temperament: Mild

Border Terrier

The Border Terrier is originally from the borders of England and Scotland, and is popular as both a worker and a family dog. The fact that many veterinary surgeons choose to own this breed speaks volumes about the temperament and lack of hereditary health problems found in the Border Terrier. It is a friendly breed that appeals to many different people.

The maximum weight is just over 7kg (15½lb). This is a dog who is expected to work, however much it is adapted to living as a family companion. It fits that bill excellently. It has a cheeky otter-like head, a sound body clothed in a harsh, dense

▶ *The Border Terrier is described as 'racy', which means it gives the impression of speed but without loss of substance.*

coat, and its legs will carry it across country or urban park for as long as its owner requires. The official standard states that the dog should be capable of following a horse,

hence its sufficient length of leg. It is not quarrelsome, but it is game for anything. It likes being with people.

The Border Terrier comes in a variety of colours, including red, wheaten, grizzle and tan or blue and tan. It is light enough to be picked up easily, and it does not require a great deal of food. It has a lot going for it.

◀ *One of the most cheerful and companionable of all dog breeds, the Border Terrier makes an excellent family dog.*

Breed box
Size: Male 30.5cm (12in), 6–7kg (13–15½lb); female 28cm (11in), 5–6.5kg (11–14lb)
Grooming: Undemanding
Feeding: Small
Exercise: Medium
Temperament: Game and friendly

▶ *This breed has changed little since it first appeared in the late 18th century. It has found much favour in the show ring, but has still remained true to type. The breed standard describes it as having a head like an otter.*

Bull Terrier

The Bull Terrier is an odd one out in the Terrier Group. It is not a pure terrier, even though its name is a combination of 'bull' and 'terrier'. In fact, it was originally more of a dog fighter than a small pest-controller.

The breed's shape contrasts with other terriers'. The Bull Terrier is much more burly, and it has an egg-shaped

▲ White is the most common colour for the Bull Terrier, often with coloured markings on the head.

▲ The egg-shaped head of the modern Bull Terrier is hard as a bullet if the dog runs into you at speed.

▼ There is no wasted space on this power-packed bitch – just solid quality in the muscled flesh.

head and a Roman nose. It gives the impression of being ready for anything and is nicknamed the 'Gladiator of the Terriers', a description that fits it perfectly.

Bull Terriers are the only dogs to have triangular eyes, which are dark in colour and deep-set. Ears are erect and set to the side of the skull. The tail should be horizontal when on the move, but carried lower when at rest.

The Bull Terrier is usually thought of as white, but even the white ones often have patches of red, black or brindle on the head. The dog can also appear as black, red, fawn or brindle,

Breed box
Size: 45cm (18in), 33kg (72lb)
Grooming: Easy
Feeding: Medium
Exercise: Medium
Temperament: Even but obstinate

with a certain amount of white mainly on its head, neck or limbs.

Its coat is short and flat, with a feel of harshness about it. It is simple to groom, by sponging the dirt off and then rubbing it down with a cloth.

The Bull Terrier is a very active dog. It likes its exercise and food, and is a grand dog to have about the home because it loves people – but woe betide any burglar!

The Pit Bull Terrier, originating in the United States, was also bred for fighting. As the result of deliberate training for illegal dog fighting, this breed has been deemed dangerous and has been banned in many countries throughout the world.

Cairn Terrier

The Cairn Terrier is an engaging creature. Coming from the Highlands of Scotland, it is one of a group of breeds that is small in stature but large in heart. It stands a mere 31cm (12½in). Its coat, which is harsh and weatherproof, ranges from cream through red or grey to almost black. The essential feature is that the dog

Breed box
Size: 28–31cm (11–12½in),
   6–7.5kg (13–16½lb)
Grooming: Medium
Feeding: Small
Exercise: Reasonable
Temperament: Fearless

▶ Most Cairns carry more coat; this example is in between coats, but shows the neatness of line and length of leg.

should end up looking shaggy even after it has been groomed.

Its prick ears on top of a small, sharp-featured head give it a look of alert gameness, which is absolutely justified. It bustles everywhere at great pace, tending to catch unawares any small rodents that it chases. It is a tireless animal with an impressively sharp voice, and delights in accompanying its human family, whether going on a country walk or a shopping foray. It lives a long life, eats whatever it is offered, and has a disposition that combines a devil-may-care attitude with a great love of people.

Czesky Terrier

The Czesky (pronounced 'cheski') originated in the Czech Republic. It is a kind dog with a coat colour varying from black through dark grey to a silvery look. Sociable and relatively obedient, it tends to be less aggressive than many of the other terrier breeds.

It stands up to 35cm (14in) high and is slightly longer in the back than it is tall. Its coat is not shed and needs trimming regularly with attention from brush and comb. It is not greedy, but eats well. It enjoys exercise as a family companion.

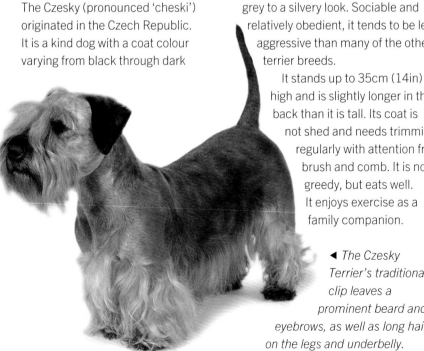

◀ The Czesky Terrier's traditional clip leaves a prominent beard and eyebrows, as well as long hair on the legs and underbelly.

▲ The Czeskys were bred for underground burrowing work.

Breed box
Size: 35cm (14in), 5.5–8kg
   (12–18lb)
Grooming: Medium
Feeding: Small to medium
Exercise: Reasonable
Temperament: Cheerful but
   reserved

Dandie Dinmont

The Dandie Dinmont is a terrier whose appearance comes as something of a surprise. It has an expression that can only be described as soulful, with large, round eyes peering out of an equally large head that is covered with what seems to be a huge soft cap or top-knot of hair. The breed comes in two distinct colours: a reddish brown

▶ *The Dandie Dinmont is more docile than other terriers, but has a surprisingly deep and loud bark.*

▲ *This breed was named after one of Sir Walter Scott's characters in his novel* Guy Mannering, *written in 1814 – Dandie Dinmont was a farmer who kept these dogs.*

Breed box
Size: Male 28cm (11in), 10kg (22lb); female 20.5cm (8in), 8kg (18lb)
Grooming: Medium
Feeding: Small
Exercise: Reasonable
Temperament: Independent and affectionate

through to fawn, which is dubbed mustard; and a bluish-grey, which is known as pepper.

The dog is longer in its body than it is high at the withers. It may weigh up to 10kg (22lb), so is not a heavy dog. It is also not a big eater. It thrives on human companionship and certainly makes an attractive household member. It never looks as if it would do anything in a hurry, but it can be roused to action by the sight of any rat or squirrel unwise enough to invade its territory.

▶ *A faithful houshold member, the Dandie Dinmont has gentle eyes, a soulful expression and is good with children and a watchful guard dog.*

Smooth Fox Terrier

The Smooth Fox Terrier is a smart, alert dog. It stands about 39.5cm (15½in) at the withers and always gives the impression of being right up on the tips of its toes. A lethargic dog of this breed would be most unusual. It is typical of all the square-built terriers, ready to stand its ground

Breed box
Size: 39.5cm (15½in); male 7.5–8kg (16½–18lb); female 6.5–7.5kg (14–16½lb)
Grooming: Undemanding
Feeding: Medium
Exercise: Medium
Temperament: Friendly and fearless

▶ *Most breeds of terrier came from somewhere in the British Isles; this one is the original hunt terrier used alongside packs of Foxhounds.*

and argue with any dog who may challenge it, but not the one to start proceedings. Its small to medium size and sharp warning bark makes it excellent as a house dog.

The Smooth Fox Terrier will take all the exercise offered, but will not spend any time nagging its owner to fetch its lead. It carries enough flesh to have a well-covered frame, but does not run to fat unless over-fed and under-exercised. It is not a dog to leave loose near livestock unless it has been very well schooled. It is easy to maintain in an urban area, and will keep the rodent population down.

Grooming its basically white coat, with tan or black markings, is simple – use a stiff brush followed by a comb and finish

off with a cloth. This regular routine will keep the dog looking very trim throughout its long life.

▼ *The sharp outline and the way in which colour appears in distinct patches on an otherwise all-white dog is typical of this breed. This is a tough, no-nonsense dog.*

▼ *Once known as the English Terrier, this is an intelligent dog that is quick to learn and delights in any form of work.*

Wire Fox Terrier

The Wire Fox Terrier is the rough-haired version of the Smooth Fox Terrier, with the same aptitude for rat-catching. It measures up to 39cm (15½in) and is square-built. Its harsh, wiry coat is white, usually with a black saddle and black or tan markings, or a combination of the two. The coat grows thick and it should be trimmed fairly regularly. This is probably best done by a professional, but it is perfectly possible for an owner to learn the art, given a good teacher. Well trimmed, this is a very smart dog indeed.

The Wire Fox Terrier is not a greedy dog and does not run to fat unless it is given insufficient exercise. A very good house dog, it will guard its domain noisily. It imagines that its family is there purely to provide it with company and fun, irrespective of whether it lives in the town or the country.

▶ *The Wire Fox Terrier is the wire-haired version of the Smooth Fox Terrier, with the same balanced body, short back and sharp features.*

▼ *The breed may be derived from the old Black and Tan Rough-haired Terrier of Wales and northern England, or some people consider it to have Foxhound and Beagle in the mix. It is one of the oldest terrier-type breeds.*

▲ *The small, dark eyes of this breed are full of fire and intelligence.*

Breed box
Size: 39cm (15½in), 8kg (18lb)
Grooming: Medium
Feeding: Medium
Exercise: Medium
Temperament: Friendly and fearless

▶ *This is a bold breed that can be noisy and wilful, and it also loves digging. Affectionate and loyal to its owner, it is quick and intelligent, and it enjoys learning tricks, as well as taking part in a range of dog sports. It can become destructive if it is bored or stressed.*

Irish Terrier

The Irish Terrier stands up to 48cm (19in) at the withers. It sports a harsh, wiry coat of a sandy red colour, which may on occasion tend to be a paler wheaten tone. It is not hard to keep it looking neat, although it needs an occasional smartening trim.

Breed box
Size: Male 48cm (19in), 12kg (26½lb); female 46cm (18in), 11.5kg (25lb)
Grooming: Medium
Feeding: Medium
Exercise: Medium
Temperament: Good with people, but fiery with dogs

▶ *This dog bristles through and through with a love of action. It is still used as a working terrier in Ireland, and is popular for field trials and lure coursing in the USA.*

As a result of not being thick-set, it does not need a lot of food to sustain its frame. It enjoys exercise, but this should be under strict control if there are likely to be other dogs about. It makes a fine house pet.

Glen of Imaal Terrier

The Glen of Imaal Terrier is the shortest and rarest of the Irish terrier breeds, and comes from County Wicklow. Used to control vermin, including foxes and badgers, this terrier is brave and fearless.

Although it is still found working on Irish farms and smallholdings, it is little known outside its country of origin.

▶ *Short legs enable this fearless dog to pursue its quarry underground.*

Numbers remain low, but there has been a small increase in recent years. This dog is recognized by the KC and AKC and a few other kennel clubs around the world.

Standing roughly 36cm (14in) at the withers, its back is long in proportion to its height. Small ears hang naturally on a powerful head that has a pronounced stop and tapered muzzle. Feet are slightly turned out with black nails, and the front legs should be slightly bowed to assist the dog while digging. The coat is wiry and not over-long, with a soft undercoat. It comes in shades of blue, brindle or wheaten. This sturdy dog has a 'shaggy dog' appearance that requires little grooming other than a daily brushing.

The Glen of Imaal Terrier is not a striking dog, but it has a happy and charming personality that makes it an attractive family pet. An affectionate and playful nature also makes this dog an ideal companion, but like most terriers the Glen, it will not back down in a fight. At home, this calm dog is very loyal and loving towards its owner, and is not as yappy as most other small terriers.

Breed box
Size: 35–36cm (14in), 16kg (35lb)
Grooming: Medium
Feeding: Medium
Exercise: Medium
Temperament: Game but docile

Kerry Blue Terrier

This blue-coloured Irish terrier originated from County Kerry, hence its name. It was once considered to be a mascot for the Irish patriots, and is now the national dog of Ireland. Initially bred to hunt badgers, foxes and otters, it is thought to have bloodlines back to Irish, Bedlington and Bull Terriers. This dog is an excellent all-rounder capable of guarding, hunting, retrieving and herding, as well as being a good swimmer.

Breed box
Size: Male 46–48cm (18–19in), 15–17kg (33–37½lb); female 46cm (18in), 16kg (35lb)
Grooming: Medium
Feeding: Medium
Exercise: Medium
Temperament: Game

All puppies are born black and should change to a shade of blue within the first 18 months of their life. A small patch of white on the chest is allowed. The profuse, fast-growing coat is soft and silky with no undercoat, and does not shed. This dog has a strong neck, lean head and powerful jaws, and the overall body is square in shape.

This dog requires extensive grooming and regular clipping or trimming. The beard will need constant attention to keep it neat and clean. The time and expense of trips to the groomer or the purchase of grooming equipment should be factored in when considering this breed.

The Kerry Blue is generally good with children and is very playful, but retains strong guarding qualities.

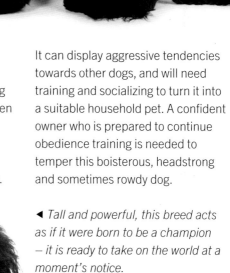

◄ The Kerry Blue was first introduced to the breed ring in the USA in the early 1920s.

It can display aggressive tendencies towards other dogs, and will need training and socializing to turn it into a suitable household pet. A confident owner who is prepared to continue obedience training is needed to temper this boisterous, headstrong and sometimes rowdy dog.

◄ Tall and powerful, this breed acts as if it were born to be a champion – it is ready to take on the world at a moment's notice.

▼ This terrier is capable of catching and killing an otter in deep water.

Manchester Terrier

The Manchester Terrier is a fair height, 41cm (16in), and looks as if it has a bit of Whippet in its make-up. It is jet black and tan in colour, and its coat is smooth, shining glossily after a good, hard polish with a cloth.

This dog does not eat a great deal, and might give the uninitiated the impression that it is a dilettante in its approach to life, but it was bred as

◄ This breed is well loved by many devotees. With its Whippet connection, it is an unusual type for a terrier.

▲ *In Victorian England, this dog was called the 'Gentleman's Terrier', as it was more well-mannered than most of the other terrier breeds.*

a ratter and, given the chance in modern society, will prove it still retains its old skills.

It is a sporting sort that delights in family activities, whether in town or the country. It is not aggressive either to human or dog, and it makes a good companion for anyone who likes a dog to be a bit out of the ordinary.

▼ *Being good with children and responding well to training make this breed an ideal choice for a novice dog owner.*

Breed box
Size: Male 41cm (16in), 8kg (18lb); female 38cm (15in), 7.5kg (16½lb)
Grooming: Easy
Feeding: Undemanding
Exercise: Reasonably undemanding
Temperament: Companionable and relatively quiet

► *There is an obvious likeness in this stylish pair of Manchester Terriers.*

Norfolk and Norwich Terriers

The Norfolk Terrier and its older cousin, the Norwich Terrier, each bear the name of their place of origin in England. They are breeds of extremely similar type and style. They are eager, bustling, little dogs, low to the ground and thick-set in body. The essential difference is that the Norfolk Terrier's ears drop forward at the tip, whereas the Norwich Terrier's ears are pricked.

Their aim in life is to hustle foxes, badgers, rats and anything that moves in the countryside, except farm animals and people. In fact, they are both capable of keeping their family companions on the move, but from in front rather than behind.

They stand 25cm (10in) at the withers, with hard, wiry coats that tend to be rougher around the neck and shoulders. The coat is red, wheaten, black and tan or grizzle, and it gives the impression that it is warm and thorn-proof. It does not present a problem when it comes to grooming, and after a country walk or a busy session down a handy hole, the coat is easily returned to its rough neatness.

The two breeds are exhibited at shows separately in spite of the fact that there is little or no difference between them, except the ear carriage.

In either guise, aficionados have adopted the attitude that docking of the tail is optional, and more are being seen with this appendage left as nature decreed it. Both terriers are good rough-and-tumble dogs with kindly personalities, and they will not go around looking for a fight.

▼ *Both the Norfolk (here) and Norwich are small, solid terriers and great diggers.*

▲ *There's a gleam in this Norfolk's eyes that speaks of fun and frolic.*

Breed box
Size: 25cm (10in), 6.5kg (14lb)
Grooming: Simple
Feeding: Undemanding
Exercise: Medium
Temperament: Alert, friendly and fearless

▼ *Wearing the look of a fun-loving breed, this is the Norwich Terrier looking its sharpest.*

▲ *An alert expression with prick ears is the hallmark of the Norwich.*

Jack Russell Terrier

Often confused with the Parson Russell Terrier, the Jack Russell Terrier originates from dogs bred by Reverend John Russell in the early 19th century. This small terrier is thought to trace its origins to the now-extinct English White Terrier. Bred to bolt foxes from holes, it is a feisty

and diligent hunter. It is not generally recognized as a breed by most kennel clubs, as breeders and breed clubs consider their working ability more important than a standardized size and conformation.

This dog is generally white with patches of black, tan or black and tan. Brindle and black and tan colouring does occur, however this is rare. The coat can be rough or smooth. Almond-shaped eyes are dark, and the nose leather should be black. Ears are small and fold forwards close to the head. Height and weight can vary.

This is an energetic, compact and muscular dog with a very high prey drive. It will chase rodents, cats and other small domestic or wild animals. This loving and intelligent

◄ This group of Jack Russells display a range of ear carriages, coat types and colours.

dog is strong-willed and needs an experienced owner. It can be aggressive with other dogs, so early socialization is vital. Some are very good with children but others will snap if they feel that their space is invaded. A well-fenced garden is essential, as this little dog is capable of jumping over 1.5m (5ft) high and is an industrious digger. It can be a persistent barker if bored. With the right owner and sufficient exercise, it is highly trainable and excels in canine sports such as flyball and agility.

Breed box
Size: 25–38cm (10–15in), 5.5–9kg (12–20lb)
Grooming: Easy
Feeding: Undemanding
Exercise: High
Temperament: Feisty and fearless

Parson Russell Terrier

▼ This breed has sparkling eyes and an intelligent-looking head.

The Parson Russell Terrier is descended from the type of Fox Terrier favoured by a famous sporting parson from the West Country of England in the second half of the 19th century. Parson Jack developed what he considered to be the ideal hunt terrier, one that stood about 36cm (14in) high and weighed 6.5kg (14lb), easy enough to carry on his saddle and able to earth to bolt a hunted fox.

First given breed status in 1990, this dog has rapidly gained in popularity. It is now recognized by most kennel clubs worldwide.

It has longer legs and is squarer in shape than the Jack Russell Terrier. Ears are V-shaped and drop down, with the tips pointing towards the eyes. Nose leather should be black in colour. The coat is either smooth or broken (i.e. smooth with some longer hair on the face, legs or body). Curly or rough coats are incorrect, according to the breed standards.

This is a feisty breed that requires both physical and mental exercise to prevent it from becoming bored and destructive. It is very energetic and excels in most canine sports, especially

agility and flyball. Provided it is well trained and socialized, the Parson Russell can make a good family pet, but it should not be trusted with small pets such as rabbits or hamsters.

Scottish Terrier

The Scottish Terrier has been popular for many years, but is not seen quite as frequently as it used to be. It stands some 28cm (11in) at the withers and gives the impression of being a neat, powerful dog for its size. It has a harsh, wiry and weatherproof coat that benefits from being kept tidy, whether professionally or otherwise.

The 'Scottie' has fairly large prick ears and carries a good deal of coat on its longish muzzle in the form of a beard. Most people would know it as black or very dark brindle, but on occasion it does come in wheaten

◀ Tall, erect ears of a neatly sculptured head are the essence of the Scottie, once known as the Aberdeen Terrier. This breed is popular in North America.

◀ The wealth of beard is one of the factors that sets this breed apart from the Cairn and West Highland White Terriers. Eyebrows are kept long.

▼ Solid and thick-set, the Scottie is surprisingly agile and active for such a short-legged dog. It is a proud dog that is very dignified in nature.

as well. Its well-boned legs look almost thick-set, and its deep frame makes it appear to be close to the ground. The Scottie moves with a smooth, level gait as if it is very important and, although normally gentle, this is not a dog with which to pick a fight.

Breed box
Size: 8.5–10.5kg (19–23lb);
  male 28cm (11in); female
  25.5cm (10in)
Grooming: Medium
Feeding: Reasonable
Exercise: Undemanding
Temperament: Bold and friendly

Sealyham Terrier

The Sealyham Terrier is a small, sturdy terrier from rural Wales. It should not grow taller than 31cm (12in) at the withers, and the length of its body should be slightly greater.

It has a longer coat than some terriers, but it is also wiry. Since it is basically white with small patches of lemon or badger usually on its head and ears, it is not simple to keep clean in the breed's natural country home, especially if the weather is wet. For this reason, it does benefit from occasional professional attention.

The Sealyham can be a trifle cautious with strangers, but it is a superb companion or house dog and a very effective alarm-raiser. It is known as a self-sufficient dog that makes its own entertainment.

▶ *The Sealyham is named after the Welsh village from which it originated. It has a marked independence of nature.*

◀ *The curtain of hair on this breed's face conceals a pair of very bright eyes that will not miss anything.*

Breed box
Size: 31cm (12in); male 9kg (20lb); female 8kg (18lb)
Grooming: Medium
Feeding: Reasonable
Exercise: Undemanding
Temperament: Alert and fearless

◀ *A sturdy body on short legs tends to make it difficult to keep this breed's coat clean, but the Sealyham does like living country-style.*

Skye Terrier

The Skye Terrier was developed from the same root-stock as the Scottish Terrier. It is a very long dog, being only 26cm (10in) at the withers but twice that from stem to stern.

The coat is hard and straight as well as long, and covers its eyes. It needs constant attention, which can be demanding, so it is something of a specialist's dog. The Skye Terrier

▼ *Most Skye Terriers have prick ears that are gracefully fringed with hair.*

Breed box
Size: Male 25–26cm (10in),
    11.5kg (25lb); female 25cm
    (10in), 11kg (24lb)
Grooming: Demanding
Feeding: Medium
Exercise: Medium
Temperament: Distrustful of
    strangers

is cautious of people it does not know, while being very loyal to its own family. It is very striking to look at and is certainly a good watch dog. It is designated by the KC as being a Vulnerable Native Breed.

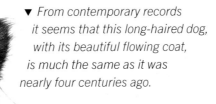

▼ *From contemporary records it seems that this long-haired dog, with its beautiful flowing coat, is much the same as it was nearly four centuries ago.*

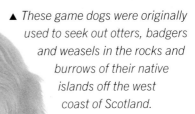

▲ *These game dogs were originally used to seek out otters, badgers and weasels in the rocks and burrows of their native islands off the west coast of Scotland.*

Soft-coated Wheaten Terrier

The Soft-coated Wheaten Terrier, as its name implies, sports a soft and silky coat that is always wheaten in colour. It stands up to 49cm (19in) at the withers. It originally came from Ireland, where it was a hunter, guard dog, herder and a companion to farmers. In 1943, it was registered with the Kennel Club in Great Britain, and in 1973 with the American Kennel Club. Today, it is recognized as an attractive pure-bred dog.

This breed has a good-natured temperament: it loves people and seems to get on well with other dogs, too. It enjoys plenty of exercise – the rougher the better. In spite of the length of its coat, it is not hard to keep in order. It needs as little trimming as possible, and it only eats enough to keep its prodigious energy levels up to par. This is an easy-going breed, but due to its mud-trapping coat, it is possibly not one for the house-proud.

Breed box
Size: Male 46–49cm (18–19in),
  16–20.5kg (36–45lb); female
  45.5cm (18in), 16kg (35lb)
Grooming: Medium
Feeding: Medium
Exercise: Medium
Temperament: Good-natured
  and spirited

▲ The breed retains its happy-go-lucky charm, even in full show trim.

▲ It is hardly surprising that the Soft-coated Wheaten Terrier is sometimes referred to affectionately as a 'mop-head'.

▶ This square-built power-pack of a dog is full of confidence and humour. It makes a delightful companion.

Staffordshire Bull Terrier

The Staffordshire Bull Terrier is not just a breed; it is a cult. The devotees of this smooth, shiny-coated dog from central England often appear to be blind to the existence of any other sort. The breed is renowned for its courage, and certainly if any dog would be willing to defend owner and house to the death, this is the one. All it asks in return is adequate rations and a lot of love.

Officially, the 'Staffie' measures up to 41cm (16in) tall, but many bigger dogs are seen. Its head is fairly big, without being exaggerated. It views

▶ *This solid-boned and well-muscled dog was originally bred for fighting and ratting.*

life as if everything is entirely for its own benefit. Its body is built on the lines of a muscled midget, and it walks with a swagger — for prodigious distances if invited.

It can be groomed in a minute because it is short-coated, and it is brimming with vitality into the bargain.

It comes in red, fawn, black or brindle, with varying amounts of white. The colours can be predominantly in patches, sometimes over the eyes.

▼ *The Staffie needs early socialization. A lack of training accounts for the high numbers seen in rescue centres.*

▲ *The power of the Staffie should never be underestimated. In the company of other dogs or animals, the Staffordshire Bull Terrier may need to be carefully controlled.*

Breed box
Size: Male 35.5–41cm (14–16in),
    12.5–17kg (27½–37½lb);
    female 35.5cm (14in),
    11–15.5kg (24–34lb)
Grooming: Easy
Feeding: Medium
Exercise: Medium
Temperament: Fearless and
    dependable

Welsh Terrier

The Welsh Terrier is a square-built breed from Wales, referred to by diehards as being built like a miniature Airedale, standing up to 39cm (15½in) tall. It has a coat of the same abundantly wiry type, and it requires the same professional care. It also comes with a similar black saddle and tan head and legs.

Perhaps slightly thicker-set than the Lakeland Terrier, it has that breed's style of standing right up on its toes. It enjoys exercise; it delights in its family and all their occupations, including any form of game. Above all, it is as biddable as any in the Terrier Group, and it is not fussy over food.

◄ This is an old breed that was originally known as the Old English Wire-haired Black and Tan Terrier. It is possible that the Welsh and the Lakeland Terriers have common ancestry from pre-Roman Britain.

Breed box
Size: 39cm (15½in), 9–9.5kg (20–21lb)
Grooming: Medium
Feeding: Easy
Exercise: Medium
Temperament: Happy and fearless

▲ The set of the ears betokens intelligence and alertness. The hair around the muzzle is trimmed to form a beard.

◄ Standing four-square on tight paws, this is a neat, cheerful, workman-like dog, and also a good rat-catcher.

West Highland White Terrier

The West Highland White Terrier, or 'Westie', has pushed its way steadily up the popularity charts, and this is no wonder – it is a handy size to pick up and carry when necessity requires, it has an outgoing manner, it loves people, and, although it will not buckle under when challenged, it does not go out of its way to pick a quarrel with other dogs.

It stands a mere 28cm (11in) at the withers, but packs a great deal of spirit into its small frame. It is not as stocky as the Scottish Terrier. As the name implies, the Westie's coat is white and can get dirty very easily, so this breed needs regular bathing.

Breed box
Size: 28cm (11in); male 8.5kg
  (19lb); female 7.5kg (16½lb)
Grooming: Medium
Feeding: Easy
Exercise: Undemanding
Temperament: Active and friendly

It is also prone to brown tear stain marks if the area around the eyes isn't frequently cleaned. The coat is harsh and recovers its quality surprisingly quickly after a shampoo, but Westies do need a trim every now and then to keep them looking neat.

The Westie uses its sharp voice to warn off strangers, so it makes a good guard dog. It also makes a great family friend or a companion *par excellence* for someone living on their own.

◄ *The various predecessors of today's Westies were known as Poltalloch, Roseneath, White Scottish and Little Skye. These variations were all merged under one name, the West Highland White Terrier, in 1904.*

▲ *The West Highland White Terrier shares common ancestry with the Cairn. These were selectively bred to be white by the Malcolm family of Poltalloch in Argyllshire, Scotland.*

▼ *The Westie has a merry expression and loves company and attention. A devoted family member, its small size will not prevent it from fiercely protecting its hearth and home.*

THE UTILITY (NON-SPORTING) GROUP

This group includes dogs of all shapes, sizes and functions, from the Dalmatian at the large end of the scale to the Lhasa Apso at the small. There are two common explanations for the composition of the group. The first is that the breeds cannot be fitted into any of the other five groups, which is quite an unflattering explanation. The second is that they are all companion dogs, which may sound politer but also suggests that the members of the other groups are not companions. To complicate matters, not all countries include the same breeds in this group. For example, the Japanese Akita Inu is classed as a utility breed in the UK but a working breed in the USA. Looking through this section will undoubtedly give you some sympathy for those who had to solve the problem of how to classify such a varied assortment.

◄ *In the past, the Chow Chow been used as a hunter, guard dog and as a food source, but now is firmly a member of the Utility Group.*

Boston Terrier

The Boston Terrier is a strikingly handsome dog. It is often described as the national dog of America, although its short muzzle confirms that it has Bulldog in its ancestry.

It stands around 38cm (15in) tall; it can vary considerably in weight – around the 9kg (20lb) mark – but it is easily handled and picked up. Its coat is short and shiny, and can be kept that way with the minimum of fuss. As its colour scheme requires brindle or black with white markings, it is instantly recognizable.

The Boston Terrier is compactly built with a square-shaped head, wide-set, intelligent eyes and prick ears. It is both dapper and boisterous, without being too short-bodied; it is strong-willed but nevertheless a thoroughly good-natured house pet.

▶ *Today's Boston Terriers are the result of a cross between the Bulldog and the English White Terrier (now extinct).*

▼ *Intelligence and watchfulness are the Boston's hallmarks.*

Breed box
Size: 23–38cm (9–12in); lightweight under 6.8kg (15lb); middleweight 6.8–9kg (15–20lb); heavyweight 9–11.3kg (20–25lb)
Grooming: Simple
Feeding: Undemanding
Exercise: Undemanding
Temperament: Determined

▶ *Boston Terriers were originally bigger and heavier, but careful selective breeding has produced the clean-cut dog of today.*

▲ *The Boston Terrier has a characteristically short muzzle and a square head.*

Bulldog

The Bulldog, often referred to as the British Bulldog to distinguish it from any other, is instantly recognized by eveyone who sees it.

It has a friendly if stubborn nature. Its devotees will not hear a word against it, but those who fancy taking one on must understand its special needs. Its physical characteristics, for example, mean that a walk should not be conducted at a great pace, especially in the heat of the day. The shape of its head and its breathing apparatus mean that it can easily become short of breath; it can, on occasion, put in a surprising burst of

▲ ▶ The Bulldog today is radically different from the bull-fighting dog of the past. The ferocity and viciousness of the breed have been bred out.

speed, but over-exertion on a hot day can, and does, have serious side effects. In addition, it tends to breathe quite noisily.

The Bulldog was bred to get to grips with bulls by grabbing their noses using their front teeth. The design of the jaw for which it was bred, in the days when bull-baiting was legal, has been considerably exaggerated in recent times, even though it is no longer necessary to fulfil that role.

◀ Affectionately nicknamed 'Old Sourmug', the Bulldog's face is definitely its fortune because of its uncompromisingly upturned chin. It has an undershot bite.

Its coat is short and easily kept clean; it can be all manner of colours, from red through fawn to white or pied. It is a massively built dog, giving the impression that its muscles have been built up like those of a human weight-lifter. It weighs 25kg (55lb), sometimes more, and eats as befits its size. It is a superb guard dog and it adores children. It is reasonably good with other dogs as it simply appears to ignore them, but it can give a show of aggression towards strangers, human or canine, if provoked.

Breed box
Size: Male 55–70cm (22–28in), 25kg (55lb); female 52–65cm (20–25½in), 22.5kg (50lb)
Grooming: Simple
Feeding: Medium
Exercise: Undemanding
Temperament: Affectionate and determined

Chow Chow

One of the first primitive dog breeds to have descended from the wolf, the Chow Chow is believed to have come from Mongolia or northern China. In China it is called 'Songshi Quan', which translates as 'puffy lion dog'. It has been used for hunting, pulling sleds, as a war dog, temple guard and as a source of food. In more recent times, it is primarily a companion dog.

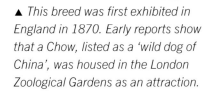

▲ *This breed was first exhibited in England in 1870. Early reports show that a Chow, listed as a 'wild dog of China', was housed in the London Zoological Gardens as an attraction.*

▲ *The Chow Chow, Shar Pei and polar bears all have black tongues. Puppies are born with pink tongues.*

Legend has it that the first teddy bear was modelled on a Chow Chow puppy belonging to Queen Victoria.

It is a sturdy, square dog with a broad skull and small, triangular pricked ears that are rounded at the tip. It is the only breed of dog to have a blue-black tongue, lips and oral cavity. The Chow has very straight hind legs that give it a stilted action. The profuse coat comes in two types: rough and smooth. Both types are very dense and stand away from the body. Thick fur around the neck forms into a ruff or mane.

This a dominant breed that needs early and continual socialization and training. Ground rules must be clear and adhered to. Although not overly active, the dog will require a daily walk. This breed can be stubborn, and this trait appears to increase with age. It is very protective and may be hesitant with strangers. The hunting instinct is still strong, so exercise on the lead is recommended. Some Chow Chows may show aggression towards other dogs.

◄ *The Chow Chow is a distinctive Chinese breed with a scowling expression and upright gait.*

Breed box
Size: 43–51cm (17–20in);
male 25–32kg (55–70lb);
female 20–27kg (44–59½lb)
Grooming: Intensive
Feeding: Moderate
Exercise: Low to medium
Temperament: Protective and quiet

Dalmatian

The Dalmatian is as distinctive a breed as any. With its white base colour and plethora of black or liver spots all over its head, body and limbs, it is the original 'spotted dog'. It has been known in the UK for well over a century, and was originally used as a carriage dog; it has a penchant for running between the wheels of a horse's carriage quite undaunted by the close proximity of the flashing hooves. In the USA, it was used to control the horses that pulled fire appliances, and it is still a well-known firehouse mascot.

◄ The essence of the Dalmatian is that no part of the dog is ever still, especially its long and tapering tail.

◄ The Dalmatian is always ready for its next walk.

The Dalmatian is a handsome dog that is up to 61cm (24in) in the UK, or 58.5cm (23in) in the USA. It could not be more friendly to people. It lives to a ripe old age and never seems to slow down. It loves running and needs plenty of exercise, so owners need to be fit. Its coat, being short, is no problem to groom, and in spite of its size, it does not over-eat.

▼ This bitch is a youngster; a full-grown dog can be a handful to control.

▲ This is a dog of ancient ancestry and uncertain origins. The first undisputed record of it is in Dalmatia on the Adriatic coast, hence its name.

Breed box
Size: Male 58.5–61cm (23–24in), 27kg (59½lb); female 56–58cm (22–23in), 25kg (55lb)
Grooming: Easy
Feeding: Medium
Exercise: Demanding
Temperament: Outgoing and friendly

French Bulldog

The French Bulldog is the French version of the British Bulldog. It has a similar square face, but without the exaggeration of the shortened muzzle. It carries its large ears erect, well up on its skull. Its dark eyes are full of expression – usually kindly, but capable of a glint that suggests it does not suffer fools gladly.

It can weigh up to 12.5kg (27½lb) and enjoys its food, so its diet must be controlled. It comes in dark brindle,

◀ *French Bulldogs can move very much faster than their solid frame might suggest.*

fawn or pied, and its coat is short, close and shiny, and is therefore easily groomed. It is compactly built with a slight concave curve over its loins and, like its British cousin, it has a short tail which can be corkscrew-shaped.

It rushes about when taking exercise, but finds hot days hard

going, tending to breathe noisily when under severe stress. It makes a charming house pet and gives the impression that it would guard hearth and home with its life. This breed has become increasingly popular recently.

▲ *The large, upright ears tend to swivel to pick up every sound.*

▶ *These dogs both have pied coloration; the most desired pattern comes with a neat central band down the forehead.*

◀ *French Bulldogs are one of the few breeds that have their loins higher than their withers; this helps them to launch themselves vertically, as if on springs.*

Breed box
Size: 30.5–31.5cm (12–12½in); male 12.5kg (27½lb); female 11kg (24lb)
Grooming: Easy
Feeding: Undemanding
Exercise: Undemanding
Temperament: Cheerful and intelligent

German Spitz

The term 'German Spitz' refers to both a type of dog and a breed of dog. The German Spitz type includes a number of breeds as diverse as the Wolfspitz and the Pomeranian. All have similarities in body shape and coat.

The registered breed now termed 'German Spitz' is subdivided into two sizes, the Mittel and the Klein. In conformation there is no difference between these, other than body weight and height, with the Mittel being the larger of the two. Both are alert, curious dogs that have a long lifespan and are game for anything.

▲ *A pair of perky Kleins with intelligent eyes and good bone structure.*

▶ *This is a typical German Spitz head, which is fox-like in appearance.*

▼ *A coat like this Klein's will cope with the bitterest of winter weather.*

German Spitzes are prick-eared, sharp-featured dogs with compact bodies and tightly curled tails. They have thick, harsh-textured coats that keep them warm in the coldest of winters. They come in many colours, from chocolate to white, as well as in all sorts of combinations. Their coats look marvellous after grooming, but they are not for the lazy owner. These sturdy, cheerful dogs are friendly but will alarm-bark at strangers. They make good companions for all ages.

▲ *No matter which size you have, a German Spitz carries a great deal of coat, which needs a lot of grooming. This example is a Mittel.*

Breed box
Size: Mittel 30–38cm (12–15in), 10.5–11.5kg (23–25lb); Klein 23–29cm (9–11½in), 8–10kg (18–22lb)
Grooming: Demanding
Feeding: Undemanding
Exercise: Medium
Temperament: Happy and lively

Akita

The Akita, or American Akita, is subject to debate. The American and Canadian Kennel Clubs consider the Akita and Japanese Akita to be two varieties of the same breed, but all the other clubs, including the Japanese Kennel Club, state that they are two separate breeds.

The Akita is a large, strong dog that is capable of hunting and holding an Asian black bear at bay. This brave hunter was also bred as a fighting dog. The Akita found favour with US servicemen stationed in Japan during World War II, many of whom brought dogs home with them.

This powerful dog is solidly built with a heavy bone structure. The head is large and bear-like, and set on a thick, muscular neck. Ears are upright and hooded. The coat comes in two types: standard or long. Long coats are considered a fault and are

Breed box
Size: Male 66–71cm (26–28in), 45–59kg (100–130lb); female 61–66cm (24–26in), 35–45kg (70–100lb)
Grooming: Medium
Feeding: Demanding
Exercise: High
Temperament: Dominant and fearless

not accepted in the breed show ring. Both coats are very dense and can be any colour, including pinto. Some dogs have black masks.

Classified in some countries as a 'dangerous dog', this breed needs an experienced owner who will become the pack leader. The Akita is territorial

▲ *The name 'Akita' comes from the northern mountainous Japanese province where these dogs originated.*

and reserved with strangers. It is very dominant and can show aggression to other dogs, especially those of the same sex. A clean and fastidious breed, it can make a good companion with the right owner. As with all dogs, the Akita should be closely supervised around children and other animals.

▼ *The head of this dog is massive, but it must be in proportion to the body.*

◄ *The Akita became very rare during the 1930s, and the breed nearly died out.*

Japanese Akita Inu

The Japanese Akita Inu, or Akita Inu, differs from the Akita or American Akita in two main respects: size and coat colour. The Akita Inu is smaller, lighter and has a more fox-like face. The Japanese Akita Inu is at least 10kg (22lb) lighter and not as heavy-boned as the Akita.

The coat is very thick, and comes in red, fawn, sesame or brindle. All colours have *urajio* markings, a whitish colouring on cheeks, muzzle, jaw, neck, chest, body, tail and inside of legs. Black masks are not permissible.

Very dominant and challenging, this dog is not suitable for a first-time owner. The Japanese Akita Inu rarely exhibits body language, so it can be difficult to predict. Some are food protective and aggressive towards other dogs. This dog is classified as a 'dangerous dog' in some countries.

Breed box
Size: Male 64–70cm (25–27in),
   32–39kg (70–85lb); female
   58–64cm (22–25in), 23–29kg
   (50–65lb)
Grooming: Medium
Feeding: Moderate
Exercise: High
Temperament: Protective and
   dominant

▲ *The Japanese Akita Inu comes in a series of striking colours and patterns. White on the body is undesirable.*

Japanese Shiba Inu

The Japanese Shiba Inu, or Shiba Inu, stands up to 39.5cm (15½in) tall. It is much the same shape as the Akita, including the hooded ears that tip sightly forward, continuing the topline of its neck. It has the same plush feel to the coat, but comes in less striking colours, including red, black, black and tan, and brindle, which do not have the same brilliance.

Its temperament is not as dominating, although its intelligence is just as obvious; a Shiba will think its way through to getting what it wants. It is not noisy but will spot the invader of its owner's property without making a scene about it.

It loves its family and joining in all activities, but this breed is not a restlessly demanding dog. It is trainable and enjoys learning.

▲ *This is the smallest of the Japanese dog breeds, and is of ancient origin.*

◄ *The Shiba Inu's plush coat comes in a variety of colours. Note the hooded ears.*

Breed box
Size: 8–10kg (18–22lb); male
   39.5cm (15½in); female
   36.5cm (14in)
Grooming: Reasonable
Feeding: Reasonable
Exercise: Reasonable
Temperament: Bright and
   intelligent

Japanese Spitz

The Japanese Spitz breed was developed as a companion in the 1920s, and is now well established. Standing about 36cm (14in) tall, it is a neat, sharply outlined dog with a stand-off coat that is never anything but brilliant white. Considering the thickness of its coat, it is not too difficult to groom or even to keep clean, although it will obviously need regular attention.

It is not overly noisy indoors or outside, but makes a good sentry. It is capable of being an extremely

▶ *This breed is recognized by major kennel clubs, with the exception of the American Kennel Club who consider it to be too similar to the white Pomeranian, American Eskimo Dog and Samoyed.*

Breed box
Size: 30–36cm (12–14in),
  5–6kg (11–13lb)
Grooming: Medium
Feeding: Undemanding
Exercise: Medium
Temperament: Affectionate
  and alert

companionable and nimble character, whether it lives with a large family or a single householder. It is not greedy, and is not a picky feeder for what, at first sight, looks like a dainty dog.

The Japanese Spitz is a very proud, noble character who takes readily to training for a variety of canine sports. The breed standard regarding height varies from country to country, but it is always classified as taller than its close relation the Pomeranian. This energetic dog is good with children and other dogs. It would suit an active family, being happy to join in with all games and activities.

▲ *The pointed muzzle should be neither too thick nor too long.*

◀ *Three delightful Japanese Spitzes, with their coats gleaming like freshly fallen snow. It is possible that these small, nimble dogs have the same ancestry as Samoyeds.*

Keeshond

The Keeshond is a spitz-type dog that comes from Holland, where it guards farms and barges, and is also known as the Dutch Barge Dog. It has smallish prick ears, a compact body and the most tightly curled tail of all the spitzes. It stands around 46cm (18in) and is solidly built; it can be a greedy feeder and needs rationing if it is not to put on excess weight.

Its harsh coat is thick, and it comes in what is officially called silver-grey – but in fact it sports long guard hairs that have black tips. It withstands freezing temperatures and snow, regarding them with contempt, and considers central heating in its owner's house to be a sign of weakness! Grooming it is hard work, but it has the sort of coat that rewards those who are conscientious and dedicated.

It loves human company and the exercise that goes with a busy family, but it is not demanding. It has sharp hearing and responds noisily to the arrival of visitors or the intrusion of strangers. Socialization is required.

◀ *The Keeshond is a very solidly built, hardy dog that can live happily in the toughest of weather conditions. It was used as a guard dog and vermin catcher in its native Holland.*

▼ *Thoroughly trusting and cheerful, the Keeshond loves being with people.*

◀ *The coat does not look as good as this one unless someone has made a great deal of effort grooming it.*

Breed box
Size: Male 44–48cm (17–19in), 19.5kg (43lb); female 40–46cm (16–18in), 18kg (39½lb)
Grooming: Demanding
Feeding: Medium
Exercise: Medium
Temperament: Friendly and vociferous

Lhasa Apso

The Lhasa Apso is a native of Tibet, where these dogs were originally kept as indoor guards. With their intelligence and sharp hearing, they were ideally suited to the task. Their long, hard coats protected them from the severities of the climate. Nowadays, a Lhasa Apso can be glamour personified, the colour of the coat ranging from gold to grey, but that show-ring gleam is not

▼ *The long hair falling over the Lhasa Apso's eyes protected them from the wind and glare in their native Tibet.*

achieved without regular shampoos and lots of hard work.

The Lhasa Apso stands around the 25cm (10in) mark at its withers, but it sports a back that is a little bit longer than its height, although not as exaggeratedly as to make it prone to a weakened spine. Its appetite is appropriate to its small size. Its head, under all the hair that often covers its

▲ *With the hair swept back from the eyes, the Lhasa Apso has a soulful expression and dark brown eyes.*

Breed box
Size: 25–28cm (10–11in),
  6–7kg (13–15½lb)
Grooming: Demanding
Feeding: Undemanding
Exercise: Undemanding
Temperament: Companionable
  but haughty

face, is much more like that of one of the smaller terriers than one would expect.

It is tough in cold weather, and it will cheerfully walk for long distances. It has an independent nature and is wary of strangers, although very affectionate with its owners. It makes a delightful family companion.

◄ *The Lhasa Apso must be seen on the move to realize just how active the dog under that mass of coat really is. The long, dense, straight coat should never be woolly or silky, but fairly harsh to the touch. The tail is carried over the back.*

Schnauzer – Standard

The Standard is the middle size of three Schnauzers (Giant, Standard and Miniature). This German breed has been known since the 15th century, and the name comes from the German word for 'snout', referring to the beard on the muzzle. It was initially used as a farm dog for driving livestock, guarding, catching rats and pulling carts. All three Schnauzers are interesting in that they are not all in the same Kennel Club group, and the grouping varies greatly from country to country. (In this book, the Giant Schnauzer is included in the chapter on the Working Group.)

Salt and pepper or black in colour, the coat is double with a soft undercoat and a wiry topcoat. White markings are not permitted. The Schnauzer has a stubby moustache and whiskers on the chin, which form the beard. Long hair over the eyes gives the impression of fringed eyebrows. Neat and triangular ears drop forward towards the muzzle. The chest is broad and deep.

This terrier-type dog does not have a terrier temperament. Energetic, friendly and loving, it makes a good companion. Most enjoy the company of children and are gentle and patient. They will alert owners of potential danger, making them excellent watch dogs or guard dogs. This can lead to

▲ *The Standard Schnauzer is a lively and trustworthy companion.*

persistent barking if they have had inadequate training or socialization. The Schnauzer is an intelligent breed that needs daily exercise but is happy to join in with games and learn tricks. It excels at agility and tracking, and is used as a search and rescue dog.

Breed box
Size: Male 48.5cm (19in), 18kg (39½lb); female 45.5cm (18in), 16kg (35lb)
Grooming: Straightforward
Feeding: Medium
Exercise: Medium
Temperament: Alert and reliable

Schnauzer – Miniature

The Miniature Schnauzer, one of the three Schnauzer breeds, gives the impression that it should be grouped together with the square-built members of the Terrier Group, which indeed it is in the USA. It stands around 36cm (14in) in a coat that is harsh and wiry.

To achieve the look that you see in the show ring takes a professional touch; for the companion at home, all that is required is a good instructor and a wire glove. The breed comes in black, black and silver or, most commonly, what is officially termed 'pepper and salt', but to most people this is actually a dark grey.

What makes the Schnauzer family so distinctive is their ears, which are set up high on the head and tip forward towards the temple; and their luxurious eyebrows and beards.

The Miniature Schnauzer enjoys exercise but does not grumble if it is not out and about all the time. It is not noisy. It makes a handy-sized companion for people of all ages, from the busy family to the solo owner.

◄ *Combing the whiskers and leg hair daily will keep the dog's coat looking neat.*

Breed box
Size: Male 36cm (14in), 9kg (20lb); female 33cm (13in), 7.5kg (16½lb)
Grooming: Straightforward
Feeding: Undemanding
Exercise: Medium
Temperament: Alert and intelligent

Poodle — Standard

Although the Poodle is the national dog of France, it actually originated in Germany. It was first known as a Pudelhund, which roughly translates as 'splash-about dog'. It was bred as a water dog to retrieve game from lakes and rivers. Documentary evidence proves the existence of this breed as far back as the 15th century, and its use as a water dog declined through the ages until it was just thought of as a companion.

The Poodle comes in several sizes, with the Standard being the largest. This size is now making a comeback as a water dog in Northern America, where it can be seen on the hunting field and taking part in hunting tests.

All sizes of Poodle have the same body shape and conformation. They are very elegant dogs with a square-shaped outline. The Standard is

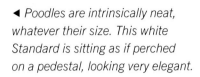

38cm (15in) or more in height (except under FCI rules, where the minimum height is 45cm/18in), but in reality it is usually considerably taller. The Poodle is clever, and is regarded as second only to the Border Collie in intelligence and aptitude. The Standard is considered to be a better family dog

▼ *This is the best-known show cut, and is meant to protect the dog's chest, kidney and leg joints.*

◄ *Poodles are intrinsically neat, whatever their size. This white Standard is sitting as if perched on a pedestal, looking very elegant.*

than the smaller sizes because it is thought to be more tolerant. It is good with children and loves playing games, and this breed does not like to be left alone. The Standard Poodle is an active companion that is happy to take part in various canine sports, including agility, flyball, dock jumping, tracking and even Schutzhund, as well as competing in the breed show ring.

▲ *An old breed from Germany, the Standard Poodle was originally a water-retrieving dog.*

Breed box
Size: 38cm (15in) or over; (FCI 45cm/18in and over); weight dependent on height
Grooming: Intense
Feeding: Moderate
Exercise: Medium to high
Temperament: Intelligent and quick-witted

Poodle — Miniature and Toy

Most kennel clubs classify Poodles in three sizes: Standard, Miniature and Toy, with Standard being the largest and Toy the smallest. The FCI is the exception, including a medium-size that is halfway between Standard and Miniature. It is thought that the original Poodle was a large dog and the smaller sizes were bred down, but this is disputed by some parties. The Miniature was widely used for scenting out and digging truffles, an edible fungus, in the 1700 and 1800s. Both the smaller sizes were favoured by upper-class Georgian and Victorian

Breed box

Size: Miniature 28–38cm
  (11–15in); Toy under 28cm
  (11in); these heights given as
  guidelines only as they vary
  within different kennel clubs;
  weight dependent on height
Grooming: Extensive
Feeding: Undemanding
Exercise: Medium
Temperament: Alert and active

▼ *Underneath the huge coat of this Miniature Poodle is a dog that measures less than 38cm (15in) high.*

ladies as a lap dog. These dogs had their fur dyed and sculptured into unusual shapes to match their clothing, and as a fashion statement.

The Poodle is often described as a non-shedding breed, but this is untrue. It does shed its coat, but at a slower rate than many other breeds. Because the coat is curly, dead hair and dander does not fall away, but is matted into the living hair. For this reason, the Poodle is less likely to cause allergies then most other breeds. The coat is solid-coloured or parti-coloured and comes in a wide variety of colours. Some colours or combinations are not accepted in the breed show ring.

Both the Miniature and Toy tend to live longer than the Standard. Bright and active, they are highly trainable and make lovable companions. The smaller sizes are less tolerant than the Standard, and may sometimes snap when afraid.

◄ *All Poodles dislike being left alone, and can become anxious if not properly socialized. Toys have the same herding, guarding and water-retrieving background as Standards.*

Schipperke

There is much discussion as to the original use of the Schipperke. Some believe that this breed is a small shepherd, while others think that it was bred as a barge dog. It does make an excellent boat dog, but will also guard and protect its family. It was used by the Belgium Resistance during World War II to carry messages from one group to another without detection by the Nazis.

This small fox-like dog has a double coat with a distinctive ruff of longer hair around the neck. This makes it look heavier at the front. The longer hair on the hind legs is referred to as 'culottes'. The coat can

▶ *Sometimes known as the Belgian Barge Dog, the Schipperke is both neat and sharp.*

be black, cream or gold solid in colour. The ears are pricked and carried high on the head. Some Schipperkes are born without a tail, while those born with one carry it loosely curled over the back. Sometimes the tail is docked, but this is now illegal in many countries.

Alert and active, this dog can be mischievous and stubborn. It is a naturally curious breed, and early socialization and training are

essential. It is loyal to its owner and generally good with children, with whom it usually forms a strong bond. It can be overly protective of places and property.

Schipperkes are fast and will chase small animals, so they require a well-fenced garden. If bored or allowed to dominate, they can be demanding barkers. They are better suited to an owner with some experience.

▼ *If asked to be on guard, this breed can stand like a sentry. They will bark to warn of an approaching stranger.*

▲ *This breed is sometimes referred to as the 'Little Skipper'.*

Breed box
Size: 21–33cm (10–13in),
    5.5–8kg (12–18lb)
Grooming: Medium
Feeding: Undemanding
Exercise: Moderate
Temperament: Active and
    mischievous

Shar Pei

The Shar Pei, also known as the Chinese Shar-Pei, is a breed of great distinction. It has become well known because of its unusual appearance, with its characteristically wrinkly skin and frowning expression.

Its head shape is rectangular, with little taper from the back of the head to the nostrils, and its lips and muzzle are well padded. It has inherited a tendency to be born with in-rolling eyelids (entropion), and this can cause problems. It is also born with very wrinkled skin, and unfortunately these remain into its adult life; skin problems can occur as a result. The earliest exports were not blessed with the most perfect of temperaments.

Those people who like the breed obviously appreciate the Shar Pei's unusual appearance, while those who find it ugly will steer clear. The dog stands up to 51cm (20in) tall and is powerfully built, mounted on reasonably firm legs.

In any country where there is a very small pool of breeding stock, faults will multiply. Although the breed has improved in recent decades, it is wise to decide on this dog only after careful consideration and research. It is essential that the Shar Pei is given

▲ *The loose skin and wrinkles are abundant in Shar Pei puppies, but may be limited to the head, neck and withers of an older dog.*

early socialization and training if it is to be a family pet. Loving and loyal towards its owner, this breed is wary and very suspicious of strangers and any unusual situations.

▲ *This breed has a large head and a well-padded muzzle.*

Breed box
Size: 46–51cm (18½–20in),
   16–20kg (36–44lb)
Grooming: Medium
Feeding: Medium
Exercise: Medium
Temperament: Independent
   but friendly

◄ *The Shar Pei almost became extinct in its native China following the prohibition of dogs. Breeders in Hong Kong kept the line going.*

Shih Tzu

The Shih Tzu is thought to have originated in Tibet and then been developed in China. It has a host of admirers who greatly appreciate its wide-eyed expression and distinctly cavalier attitude. It views the world from a fairly small frame, which is only some 26.5cm (10½in) high, but it gives the impression of mental superiority in no uncertain terms.

▶ *Shih Tzus are sturdy, bouncy extroverts that make delightful family companions.*

▲ *The golden head typifies a breed that is convinced of its own distinction.*

The breed has a long, dense coat, which rewards hard work and gets distinctly ragged if neglected. It comes in a glorious variety of colours, often with a white blaze to its forehead, and it carries its high-set tail like a banner over its back. It definitely enjoys being part of the family, but this does not necessarily mean it is keen to partake in long, muddy tramps across the fields. It takes a fair deal of cleaning up if it does feel an urge towards outdoor forays in the middle of winter.

Breed box
Size: 4.5–7.5kg (10–16½lb); male 26.5cm (10½in); female 23cm (9in)
Grooming: Demanding
Feeding: Reasonable
Exercise: Reasonable
Temperament: Friendly and independent

▼ *This beautiful coat gives a good idea of the work involved in grooming a Shih Tzu to show standard.*

▲ *The hair grows upwards on the bridge of the nose, giving this breed its characteristic 'chrysanthemum' look.*

Tibetan Spaniel

The Tibetan Spaniel is a neat, tidy dog standing only 25.5cm (10in) high. Its coat is longish and silky, but does not take as much grooming to keep it looking good as you might expect.

This breed turns up in all sorts of colours, but a golden-red is the most common. It also comes in a mixture of

◄ This is an unfussy breed that does not demand endless grooming. A brush-through is all that is required.

▼ This dog's original purpose was to act as a companion and watch dog in the monasteries of Tibet.

fawn and white. It has slightly bowed front legs, but this trait should not be an excuse for it to be unsound.

It is accommodating in the household, being happy-go-lucky. It takes to climbing over garden rockeries with abandon, or rushing around the garden with its family. It does not spend its time looking for food, and makes a delightful household companion.

Breed box
Size: 25.5cm (10in), 4–7kg
  (9–15½lb)
Grooming: Medium
Feeding: Reasonable
Exercise: Undemanding
Temperament: Loyal and
  independent

Tibetan Terrier

The Tibetan Terrier is a profusely coated, square-built dog, standing as high as 40cm (16in). Its coat is fine, although with hard brushing it can be made to gleam like silk. It comes in a range of colours, from white to

► A terrier does not usually have such a shiny coat as this, but the Tibetan Terrier is, in fact, more of a guard dog. It will bark as a warning.

black, including golden. It loves people, enjoys plenty of exercise and is extremely nimble and energetic. It eats well, but not greedily. It will act as quite an impressive guard to house and family.

◄ The coat needs regular grooming, which, together with its boundless energy and enthusiasm, means that this good-natured dog may be rather overwhelming for some.

Breed box
Size: 35.5–40cm (14–16in),
  8–14kg (18–31lb)
Grooming: Fairly demanding
Feeding: Medium
Exercise: Demanding
Temperament: Outgoing and
  intelligent

THE WORKING AND HERDING GROUPS

This Working Group of dogs was selectively bred to undertake a job of work to assist their owners. Most dogs in this group are large, and so may not be suitable for all homes. Many are protective, strong and very intelligent. Without correct training and early socialization, some can become difficult and even dangerous. The majority are highly or moderately active, requiring safe places to run. Service and security dogs generally come from this group.

The Herding Group is a collection of breeds that help move animals and is variable according to different kennel clubs. Some split them into sub-groups, while others use a different collective name, such as the Pastoral Group. All are high-energy and require a lot of exercise. Most are responsive to training, but a herding instinct may mean that they try to round up people instead of animals.

◄ *The Working Group contains many giant breeds, such as the St Bernard, which was originally developed to guard the grounds of the Swiss hospice St Bernard.*

Alaskan Malamute

The Alaskan Malamute is a big dog. At 71cm (28in), it does not stand as tall as some other giant breeds, but it is massively built as befits a dog that is designed to pull heavy weights over snow-covered terrain for vast distances in sub-zero temperatures. It can weigh in excess of 56kg (123½lb). Temperamentally, it is normally friendly to people, but it can take umbrage with other dogs. A Malamute in full cry after a canine foe is an awesome sight, and requires strength and experience in those who have to apply the brakes.

This is a superbly built, handsome breed. Its relatively short, harsh, dense coat can be any shade of grey through to black, or from gold through red to liver, with areas of white on its underbelly, mask, legs and feet.

The breed was developed over many generations in Alaska and the Arctic fringes of Canada as a 'workhorse', and it uses its ability to

◄ The heaviest of the sled dogs, the Alaskan Malamute has a distinctly watchful air.

pull to great effect when it is on the end of a lead. It needs training from early puppyhood to be controllable in a household situation, so training classes are essential.

This dog enjoys its food and needs a great deal of exercise from those owners capable of handling such a giant; it is a delightful dog for anyone who is ready for a challenge.

Breed box
Size: 38–56kg (84–123½lb);
  male 64–71cm (25–28in);
  female 58–66cm (23–26in)
Grooming: Medium
Feeding: Demanding
Exercise: Demanding
Temperament: Reasonably
  amenable

▶ The Alaskan Malamute is a powerful, dignified dog. Named after an Inuit tribe called the Mahlemuts, it was used as a draught animal long before Alaska became an American state.

▲ This dog displays a thoroughly handsome and trusting expression, but it is not an animal to be treated in a casual fashion.

Anatolian Shepherd Dog

The Anatolian Shepherd Dog comes from Turkey. It is known to its familiars as the Karabash ('Blackhead'), the Turkish term for its best-known feature. The dog is cream to fawn in colour, and sports a black mask and ears.

Many European and Asian countries use two distinct types of dog with their flocks of sheep, one for herding and another for guarding. The Anatolian Shepherd performs the latter duty, protecting flocks against marauding wolves and also marauding humans in the form of rustlers.

The Anatolian's height at 81cm (32in) puts it into the range of the awesome; it weighs accordingly, and therefore takes a good deal of feeding.

Its coat is short and dense, and not difficult to keep tidy. It likes its exercise, but because its ancestors were expected to amble about with the shepherd as the flocks moved from pasture to pasture, it is not often in a hurry.

This breed needs understanding; it makes a good family dog, but the family needs to accept that their pet's sole purpose in life is to guard. A few generations of living a softer life has not obliterated the results of careful selective breeding since this mastiff type evolved.

▲ *This is a breed of ancient origin that is regarded as a national emblem in its Turkish homeland.*

▼ *This family group exhibits the prized black mask that gives the breed its popular name of Karabash.*

Breed box
Size: Male 74–81cm (29–32in), 50–64kg (110–141lb); female 71–79cm (28–31in), 41–59kg (90–130lb)
Grooming: Easy
Feeding: Demanding
Exercise: Demanding
Temperament: Bold and independent

Australian Cattle Dog

This dog has many names, including Australian Heeler, Blue Heeler and Red Heeler. Bred to move stock over long distances, it possesses great stamina and endurance. It is believed to have the Dingo, Kelpie, Bull Terrier and Dalmatian in its ancestry.

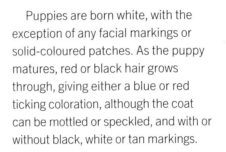

▶ *This workaholic is used as a therapy dog and by the police for drug detection.*

Breed box
Size: 43–51cm (17–20in), 15–22kg (33–48½lb)
Grooming: Easy
Feeding: Moderate
Exercise: High
Temperament: Protective and trainable

Puppies are born white, with the exception of any facial markings or solid-coloured patches. As the puppy matures, red or black hair grows through, giving either a blue or red ticking coloration, although the coat can be mottled or speckled, and with or without black, white or tan markings.

Needing lots of exercise and a job to do, this dog is not suitable for an inactive or inexperienced owner. Since it herds by nipping at the ankles, it is only suitable for families with older children. A Heeler forms a very strong bond with its owner and can become overly protective.

Australian Shepherd Dog

Despite the name, this dog does not come from Australia. It is thought to have originated from the French/Spanish Pyrenees. Basque shepherds exported flocks of Merino sheep to America and took dogs with them; these Spanish dogs would have crossed with native dogs and collie types, producing a versatile stock dog. This herding dog has been known as a Spanish Shepherd, Pastor dog

▶ *To keep coats in prime condition, time must be put aside for regular grooming.*

and Bobtail. It is uncertain why the breed is called an Australian Shepherd.

There is a pronounced difference between the size and build of male and female dogs. The medium-length double coat is weather-resistant, and can be red or blue merle, red, black or tricolour. Eye colour varies, and is generally related to coat colour. Dogs may have two different-coloured eyes; this does not affect the dog's sight. The tail is long and plumed, but some puppies are born with a natural bobtail.

This is a very high-activity dog that is even-tempered and loving. It is suitable as a companion, provided that socialization and training are ongoing. It can try to round up people and may be destructive if bored, so it needs long daily walks and company. It develops a strong bond with those it includes in its family pack.

Breed box
Size: 14–29kg (31–65lb); male 46–58cm (18–23in); female 46–53cm (18–21in)
Grooming: Medium to high
Feeding: Moderate
Exercise: High
Temperament: Energetic and easy-going

Bearded Collie

The handsome Bearded Collie possesses bewitching eyes. It can make the toughest heart melt just by standing still and looking soft, hence its enormous popularity. Standing up to 56cm (22in) tall at its withers, it moves with athletic grace on legs

▶ *The Bearded Collie has pure Scottish ancestry and retains the basic instincts of a worker.*

◀ *Keen, observant eyes are one of the breed's most attractive features.*

and feet which, like its whole body, are covered with a harsh, shaggy coat underlaid by a soft, close undercoat.

The coat takes plenty of effort to groom, as it is capable of picking up a good deal of the countryside in which it prefers to spend its days. Colours range from all shades of grey, through black, blue and sandy, all with white

on the head, brisket and lower limbs; it is rounded off with the typical beard after which it takes its name.

The Bearded Collie looks what it is – a cheerful, fun-loving rogue – and has converted well from its original role as a farm worker to make a superb companion and family friend.

Breed box
Size: 18–27kg (39½–59½lb);
 male 53–56cm (21–22in);
 female 51–53cm (20–21in)
Grooming: Demanding
Feeding: Medium
Exercise: Demanding
Temperament: Lively and cheerful

▶ *Quiet while lying waiting, these dogs will move like a flash when the order is given.*

Belgian Shepherd

There are four varieties or breeds of Belgian Shepherd: Tervuren, Malinois, Groenendael and Laekenois. In some counties, including Belgium, they are regarded as being four variants of the same breed, while others consider some, or all, as separate breeds in their own right. All are large to medium in size, rather square in shape, and have erect ears. The only difference between types is the length and texture of the coat.

The Tervuren gets its name from a village in the province of Flemish Brabant. It has a medium-length double coat that is generally mahogany, but can also be sable, sand or grey. This breed or variant should have an overlay of black and a black mask. A small amount of white on the chest and tips of the toes is permissible. The coat on the chest and around the neck forms a mane. Potential puppy purchasers who wish to show their dog in the breed ring should consult the breed standard for their kennel club, as there is a worldwide variation in permitted colours.

▲ *In Belgium, the four types of Belgian Shepherds are classified as separate breeds. In the USA, the Groenendael is the Belgian Sheepdog, and the Laekenois is not recognized.*

▶ *For many devotees, the most glamorous of all the Belgian Shepherds is the Tervuren.*

The Malinois has a short fawn, red or brown coat. The tips of the hair are black, forming a darker overlay. All colours have a black mask. Often confused with the German Shepherd Dog, the Malinois is smaller and squarer in shape, and has a lighter bone structure and finer chiselled head. This dog gets its name from a club that was set up in the city of Malines in 1898. The aim of the club was to protect and promote this type of short-haired Belgian Shepherd.

The Groenendael has a profuse double coat that is similar in length and texture to the Tervuren's. The colour is solid black, but a small amount of white is allowed on the chin, chest and the tips of the toes. The lips, nose and eye rims are black. Eyes are brown and almond-shaped. This is currently the most popular of the four types of Belgian Shepherd.

The Laekenois can be red, mahogany, fawn, red sable or fawn sable in colour. Black hairs may be mixed in with the underlying colour. The coat is medium in length, and rough and wiry. Facial fringing gives the head a rather shaggy look. The tail is thick and bushy. This is the rarest of the four Belgian Shepherd breeds. Originally bred to herd sheep, the Laekenois was also used to guard linen when it was put outside to dry after washing.

Belgian Shepherds are herding dogs that require a good deal of exercise. The herding instinct is still strong, and they may try to herd up family members or chase cars and cyclists. With early socializing and obedience training, this can be corrected.

It is a very loyal dog, forming a strong bond with its human family. It does not like being left alone for long periods, and can develop separation anxiety. If bored, it may become destructive. A trainable and very intelligent dog that needs mental as well as physical exercise, it can be trained for canine sports, including herding trials, competition obedience, agility, working trials and the breed show ring. It is used as a therapy or assistance dog, and by military, police and service personnel for a range of activities, such as search and rescue.

Breed box
Size: 56–66cm (22–26in),
   20–30kg (44–66lb)
Grooming: Variable, depending
   on coat type
Feeding: Moderate
Exercise: High
Temperament: Loyal and intelligent

Bergamasco

The Bergamasco, or Cane da Pastore Bergamasco, is an ancient breed of herding dog that originated from the Italian Alps. It is still used by farmers in this region to herd cattle and sheep. It works independently, and can be sent out from the farm to collect and herd stock back home without any human intervention. It is such a good herding dog that shepherds kept the bloodlines a secret for many years.

Puppies are born with short hair that grows as the dog matures. The coat is very distinctive, consisting of three types of hair that mat or felt together over time to provide a thick, insulated covering. The mats start to form from the spine and grow longer each year until they reach the ground.

Breed box
Size: 54–62cm (21–24in); male 32–38kg (70–84lb); female 26–32kg (57½–71lb)
Grooming: Medium
Feeding: Moderate
Exercise: High
Temperament: Patient, protective

▲ *The Bergamasco's coat, described as greasy to the touch, makes it appear unkempt, but also keeps the dog warm and dry. It tends to form loose mats, which are not brushed out.*

▶ *Grooming may be a problem with this breed.*

▶ *Coming from a cold and mountainous region, this dog is not suitable for hot countries.*

This can take up to six years. Long hair on the face falls over the eyes; this provides protection from the bright glare of snow.

This dog is heavy-boned and looks very chunky, but underneath the felted coat is an agile dog that requires exercise and a job to do. The breed is very good with children, with whom it forms a special bond. It accepts other dogs and, if introduced at a young age, tolerates cats and domestic pets. Like all herding dogs, it is happiest if it has a job to do.

▲ *Under all that hair, bright eyes watch its owner constantly.*

Bernese Mountain Dog

The Bernese Mountain Dog is a handsome, affable animal. At its tallest, it reaches a height of 70cm (27½in) and it is built on sturdy lines. Its laid-back temperament allied to a great love of its food means that it tends to be overweight.

Its coat is soft and wavy, and responds to vigorous brushing by producing a real sheen. The colour is mainly black with patches of reddish brown, with a striking white blaze on the head and a white cross on the chest.

▶ *The massiveness of the leg bones and the power of the shoulders show why the Bernese is a favourite for pulling dog-carts.*

▶ *The white blaze and cross on the head and chest are characteristic of this handsome Swiss dog.*

The Bernese Mountain Dog is an intelligent and trainable dog, full of *bonhomie* and courtesy, making it a very suitable member of a country household. This is not a dog for the town dweller, however. It was originally a draught dog, and will pull a light cart with evident enjoyment.

◀ *The cheerful nature of this ancient breed comes over clearly as this dog gazes attentively upwards at its owner.*

Breed box
Size: 40–44kg (88–97lb); male
   64–70cm (25–27½in); female
   58–66cm (23–26in)
Grooming: Medium
Feeding: Medium to large
Exercise: Medium
Temperament: Good-natured

Border Collie

The Border Collie is the classic farm dog. It is neat and agile, it thinks on its feet, and if its owner does not occupy its mind with useful training, it will get into mischief because its brain is always active.

Ideally, it stands some 53cm (21in) at its withers, although it may look lower to ground because when it travels at speed it takes on the posture of a permanent crouch. Its eyes show keen intelligence, and this type is the favourite for those who wish to compete at top-level obedience or agility competitions.

Breed box
Size: Male 53cm (21in), 23.5kg
    (52lb); female 51cm (20in),
    19kg (42lb)
Grooming: Medium
Feeding: Medium
Exercise: Demanding
Temperament: Very alert and
    trainable

▲ *The low-slung body of the Border Collie is essential for its super-agile performance at work.*

The Border Collie's coat is usually moderately long, but it is relatively easy to groom as long as the tangles are dealt with on a regular basis. The coat comes in all kinds of colours together with white, but the most common base colour is black.

▲ *This is the sharp expression of what is, by common consent, the most trainable breed of them all.*

◄ *A working dog from the Scottish borders, this breed needs to be occupied constantly if destructive behaviour is to be avoided.*

This breed demands exercise for its muscles just as much as for its brain. It makes an ideal family dog for the grown family, but it is not best suited to be a nursemaid to the very young – although no doubt such heresy will raise a few protests. To put it bluntly, it does not suffer fools gladly, and it is not averse to taking a swift nip at those who do not understand its point, in the same way that it will liven the reactions of the sheep or cattle that are its natural flock.

Bouvier des Flandres

The Bouvier des Flandres is a powerful and rugged-looking dog. Its basic role in life is herding both cattle and sheep, but over the years it has adapted to town life to a surprising degree. It has found favour with police forces not only in its native Belgium, but also in the UK and several other countries around the world.

It stands up to 68cm (27in) and weighs solidly to match. It sports a coat that is coarse both to touch and to view. It also carries a beard and moustache, which add to its fairly fearsome appearance. Coupled with a colour that ranges from fawn through brindle to black, the Bouvier des Flandres might be thought forbidding, but, in fact, it is a trustworthy character and fully deserves its increasing popularity as a house companion for those who enjoy a strong dog.

Breed box
Size: Male 62–68cm (24½–27in), 35–40kg (77–88lb); female 59–65cm (23½–25½in), 27–35kg (60–77lb)
Grooming: Fairly demanding
Feeding: Medium
Exercise: Medium
Temperament: Calm and sensible

▲ The Bouvier des Flandres is a solid and stable dog. That, combined with its size and forbidding expression, has encouraged several police forces to train it for service.

▲ Despite its expression, this dog is an amiable breed unless provoked.

▲ Ears are small and high-set. Show dogs are trimmed every 3–5 weeks.

◄ The Bouvier was once a cattle dog in its native Belgium, and was also used to pull carts. It is balanced in body and limb – a true power-pack.

Boxer

The Boxer is one of the canine world's most popular characters. It is rightly recognized by its vast army of devotees as an extrovert. It is intelligent, but still needs to be convinced that its owner knows best – any other relationship is liable to be a disaster.

It stands up to 63cm (25in) high, and its supple limbs and body are well covered with muscle. It is full of stamina and considers its purpose in life to be to guard its family household – and woe betide anyone who does not recognize this fact.

▲ *Nothing gets past those flashing eyes. The Boxer is one of the very best of all the guarding breeds.*

◄ *Originating in Germany, the Boxer's ancestors were used for hunting wild boar and deer. Today, it has one of the most distinctive shapes of all dog breeds.*

Its coat is simple to keep clean and neat; its colour ranges from red-fawn through various shades of brindle, with degrees of white. Some Boxers are born entirely white; a percentage of these are deaf from birth, and as a result many breeders put them down.

The Boxer is not a particularly greedy dog, but its appetite needs control if it is not to become overweight. Its concept of exercise is that life is to be lived at speed. It can be trained to be obedient, but anyone who sets out to harness this canine power-pack needs to realize what they are facing.

Its pugnacious, upturned chin gives it the appearance of a pugilist; it does not start fights frequently, but it will never back down if challenged.

◄ *A relaxed Boxer is a rare sight, but this breed will still react in a flash if it needs to.*

Breed box
Size: Male 57–63cm (22½–25in), 30–32kg (66–70lb); female 57–59cm (21–23½in), 25–27kg (55–59½lb)
Grooming: Easy
Feeding: Medium
Exercise: Demanding
Temperament: Biddable and fearless

Briard

The Briard is a farm dog from France with a Gallic charm about it, making it very captivating. It has a rugged appearance subtly combined with a slightly dapper look. At up to 68cm (27in) tall, it is a big dog, but underneath the long, wavy coat it is not a heavyweight.

The coat comes in black, slate grey or varying shades of fawn. It needs regular grooming, especially as the breed thoroughly enjoys exercise in town or country, and can bring the great outdoors back indoors on returning home. The Briard is one of a mere handful of breeds that is not only born with double hind dewclaws, but it should also retain them. This gives its feet a very hairy appearance, which adds to its tendency to act rather like a floor brush.

A Briard is trainable; all that is needed is determination and patience. The dog must have total confidence in its owner. When it plays, it plays rough. It is good with children but perhaps not with toddlers – they may get knocked over. This, of course, is true of many breeds, but it would be wise to remember that this dog started off as a guard dog for flocks of nomadic sheep.

▲ *This breed takes up a fair amount of space and needs a considerable degree of effort to keep it tidy.*

▼ *The Briard is a very impressive animal with a kindly disposition, but is also capable of being an effective guard dog. It is intelligent, loyal and faithful. In some countries, the breed is used by the police and military.*

▲ *In spite of all the hair around its eyes, a Briard is extremely sharp-eyed, making it a good watch dog.*

Breed box
Size: Male 62–68cm (24½–27in), 38.5kg (85lb); female 56–64cm (22–25in), 34kg (75lb)
Grooming: Demanding
Feeding: Demanding
Exercise: Demanding
Temperament: Lively and intelligent

Bullmastiff

The Bullmastiff evolved from crossing the Old English Mastiff with the Bulldog, to produce a very effective guard dog. In an age in which several large guarding breeds have been imported into the UK from mainland Europe, the original role of the Bullmastiff as a gamekeeper's assistant has tended to be forgotten.

This dog stands as much as 69cm (27in) high and weighs up to 59kg (130lb), which means it is both big and powerful. It is not to be trifled with and it does not suffer fools gladly, so it merits ownership by those who

▶ *This original gamekeeper's dog can achieve a truly awesome turn of speed, in spite of its size.*

appreciate its cardinal virtue and utter faithfulness, and can handle a dog of independent nature.

It has a close-fitting, hard coat that can be brindle, fawn or red. It does not take much effort to keep clean

and neat. It is muscular all over, and its head is reminiscent of the old-fashioned Bulldog of the 19th century, which had a longer nose than the modern Bulldog. It does not therefore suffer the breathing problems that beset some brachycephalic breeds, and it enjoys exercise without being over-demanding. The Bullmastiff enjoys obedience, tracking and carting.

▲ *The power of the Boxer's jaws is obvious. Note the short muzzle.*

◀ *As befits a reliable guard dog, the Bullmastiff is noted for its alertness.*

Breed box
Size: Male 63.5–69cm (25–27in), 50–59kg (110–130lb); female 61–66cm (24–26in), 41–50kg (90–110lb)
Grooming: Easy
Feeding: Demanding
Exercise: Medium
Temperament: Reserved, faithful

▶ *This is an extremely strong dog that may be stubborn and over-protective; it is not one for the novice owner.*

Rough Collie

The Collie originates from Scotland. The name is thought to have come from the Anglo-Saxon word *coll* meaning 'black', and could be a reference to the Scottish black-faced sheep which this breed herded. Nowadays, this dog is bred more for looks and as a companion than for its working ability, although some lines

▶ *This is the breed known to the world as the* Lassie *dog of film fame.*

Breed box
Size: 53–66cm (22–26in); some breed standards stipulate larger dogs; 25–47kg (55–105lb), depending on size
Grooming: Extensive
Feeding: Medium
Exercise: Medium
Temperament: Calm and loyal

retain their herding instinct. The long double coat can be sable and white, tricolour or blue merle. The AKC also accepts predominately white dogs. All Rough Collies should have white on parts of the collar and legs, plus a white tip to the tail. The head is similar to that of the Shetland Sheepdog. Ears are semi-erect and tip forwards.

This dog does not require as much exercise as most other herding breeds. It can be a little shy if it is not socialized early. As it is good with children, it makes an ideal family companion. It will alarm-bark and does not always know when to stop unless trained to quieten. It will adapt to town or country living, and is calm within the home.

Smooth Collie

In some countries, the Rough Collie and Smooth Collie are considered as two separate breeds, while in others they are regarded as variants of the same breed.

This breed has a short double coat. Outer guard hairs are harsh and cover a dense, soft undercoat. Colours are similar to those of a Rough Collie. Merle dogs may have blue, merled or odd-coloured eyes. The head is wedge-shaped with a chiselled face. Both the Rough Collie and Smooth Collie should have a 'sweet expression'.

This dog is a non-aggressive breed that is good with children and is loving towards its family, however it will bark and needs to be trained as to when this is appropriate. It needs regular exercise but not as much as most of the herding breeds. The

◀ *Rough and Smooth Collies used to be considered as one breed, and were called Scotch Collies.*

Smooth Collie is intelligent, sensitive and easily trained, including being quick to house-train. As well as taking part in many dog sports, the breed is used as a therapy dog and as an assistance dog for the disabled.

Breed box
Size: 53–66cm (22–26in); some breed standards stipulate larger dogs; 25–47kg (55–105lb)
Grooming: Easy
Feeding: Medium
Exercise: Medium
Temperament: Faithful and intelligent

Dobermann

The Dobermann, still known as the Doberman Pinscher in the United States, originates from Germany and is a tough, fast-moving guard dog. It was bred selectively by Herr Louis Dobermann as an all-purpose tracking/police dog. It is built on clean, powerful lines and ideally reaches 69cm (27in) at the withers.

Its short, close-lying coat responds well to polishing, giving a true gleam. It is most commonly seen as black, with tan colouring on the muzzle, forechest, legs and feet, but the black can be replaced by red or blue, or, more rarely, with fawn. The tail is raised when moving or standing.

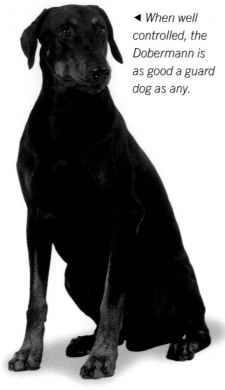

◄ *When well controlled, the Dobermann is as good a guard dog as any.*

This breed is energy personified, and at one time it had a reputation for being bad-tempered. Careful, sensible selection and training has altered this to a very large extent, but the Dobermann is still a dog that needs to know who is going to be the boss in any family or work place. As a house dog, it ranks with any breed for faithful performance. It demands exercise as a right, and needs to be provided with a sizeable amount of food as a result.

▲ *The Dobermann's soft expression is the result of leaving the ears uncropped, which is done in the UK.*

◄ *This elegant and powerful breed has an enormous following throughout the world, but frightens some people.*

Breed box
Size: Male 69cm (27½in),
   37.5kg (83lb); female 65cm
   (25½in), 33kg (73lb)
Grooming: Simple
Feeding: Medium to demanding
Exercise: Demanding
Temperament: Alert and biddable

Canadian Eskimo Dog

The Canadian Eskimo Dog, also called Canadian Husky, is one of a group of husky types. It is smaller than the Alaskan Malamute, but thicker-set than the Siberian Husky. It was bred to haul fairly weighty sleighs over snow for the Inuit people; its temperament was not important, and it had to fight for its very existence. It is the classic dog portrayed in books about polar exploration.

This dog stands 68cm (27in) high and weighs up to 47kg (104lb), and when it decides to pull on lead or harness it does just that – it pulls. It has a thick double coat of any known dog colour, and grooming it is hard work. It eats well and voraciously, and training it takes time and patience. It requires a lot of exercise, so think carefully before choosing this breed.

▲ *The Canadian Eskimo Dog follows very much in the tradition of the polar-exploration dogs; it is willing to lie for hours waiting for the next task.*

▲ *This breed displays a watchful eye and has a somewhat reserved attitude towards people.*

◄ *The coat protects against the rawest of cold weather, but this means the dog is prone to heatstroke in summer.*

Breed box
Size: Male 58–68cm (23–27in), 34–47kg (75–104lb); female 51–61cm (20–24in), 27–41kg (59½–90lb)
Grooming: Demanding
Feeding: Demanding
Exercise: Demanding
Temperament: Wary and alert

Estrela Mountain Dog

The Estrela Mountain Dog is a sturdy, sizeable dog of the mastiff type, which comes from the mountainous regions of Portugal.

It is a well-mannered breed with a delightfully shambling way of going about. It regards people as friends and enjoys living with a family. It also enjoys exercise as befits its size, at a top level of 72cm (28½in) at its withers. It eats well but is not greedy.

Its coat is usually fairly long, and comes in fawn, brindle or wolf grey, but the general impression is of a large, benign dog with a dark muzzle. It has a moderate double coat that can be yellow, grey, fawn or brindle, and the mask should be dark. It is amenable to training but will seldom retrieve objects. It is a good watch dog and enjoys the company of children. The Estrela is becoming increasingly popular as a companion dog.

▲ The Estrela Mountain Dog looks what it is – massive and yet kindly. It requires a spacious home and a large garden or yard.

▲ The benign expression of eye is the key to this dog's personality.

Breed box
Size: 30–50kg (66–110lb);
　　　male 65–72cm (25½–28½in);
　　　female 62–68cm (24½–27in)
Grooming: Medium
Feeding: Medium
Exercise: Medium
Temperament: Loyal but stubborn

◀ The Estrela is not a dog to delight in cramped accommodation; it needs a good amount of space.

Finnish Lapphund

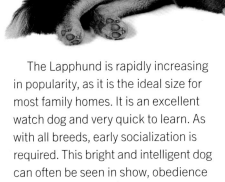

The Finnish Lapphund has herded reindeer for centuries, working in sub-zero temperatures on snow-covered tundra. Its survival was in doubt during World War II, when many dogs in this region were killed. Fortunately, dedicated breeders worked hard to conserve the breed.

The coat is thick and double, with a coarse outer layer of hair. This protection is needed to withstand extreme cold. All colours are permitted, as long as the main colour is dominant. Many Lapphunds have distinctive 'spectacle' markings around their eyes. The tail is carried over the back when the dog is moving, but may hang down when at rest.

The Lapphund is rapidly increasing in popularity, as it is the ideal size for most family homes. It is an excellent watch dog and very quick to learn. As with all breeds, early socialization is required. This bright and intelligent dog can often be seen in show, obedience and agility rings around the world.

▲ *The Finnish Lapphund is a typical spitz-type dog, and was originally used to herd reindeer in the snow.*

▼ *This breed has become increasingly popular in recent years. It requires regular and thorough grooming to keep its thick coat neat and tidy.*

Breed box
Size: 46–52cm (18–20½in),
    20–21kg (44–46lb)
Grooming: Fairly demanding
Feeding: Medium
Exercise: Medium
Temperament: Calm and
    intelligent

◄ *The sharp, intense look on this dog's face befits the breed's character exactly.*

German Shepherd Dog

The German Shepherd used to be known by some as an Alsatian; with either name, it is a very well-known breed. Its breeding and training have led to its renown as a herding sheepdog, a leader of the blind and a police dog. Police forces, the armed services, prison officers, drug officers and private protection agencies all over the world employ the GSD.

There are considerable variations in what is regarded as the ideal shape for this multi-purpose dog. Traditionally,

Breed box

Size: Male 60–66cm (24–26in), 36.5kg (80½lb); female 55–60cm (22–24in), 29.5kg (65lb)
Grooming: Medium
Feeding: Medium
Exercise: Demanding
Temperament: Steady and highly trainable

▶ *This is a handsome all-purpose dog that enjoys walking.*

▲ *The eyes show this breed's intelligence – the German Shepherd Dog does not miss a trick.*

the dog is a proud, powerful creature, standing an average of 63cm (25in) tall, with a body length slightly greater than its height. Coat lengths vary; some enthusiasts state that a medium-length coat is the only acceptable version, while others accept a long-haired type. Colours include black, black and tan, and sable. White and cream dogs do occur, but raise horrified protests from

many aficionados – something to bear in mind if your ultimate intention is to show your dog.

All such matters of taste aside, the fact remains that, at its best, the GSD is an intelligent, trainable dog with a pleasant and loyal disposition, and makes a first-class household member. It needs exercise and, on occasion, may need to be stimulated in that direction as it can be wilfully idle. On the other hand, most need to have their energies directed into useful pursuits, as the GSD, in common with many other breeds that were bred to work, originated as a shepherd dog and stock protector.

Giant Schnauzer

The Giant Schnauzer is the largest of the three Schnauzer varieties (the other two being the Standard and Miniature, covered in the Utility Group chapter in this book). This big dog is very similar in shape to its smaller cousins, being a clean-cut, square-built dog that can stand as high as 70cm (27½in) at its withers. It is found in the same colours – black or pepper and salt – as the smaller ones, but naturally it is a more imposing-looking animal.

▲ *This dog has a distinctively moulded head and huge eyebrows.*

▼ *The Giant Schnauzer will defend its territory very keenly. It is not a breed to be treated casually.*

At one time employed as a cattle-droving dog, it has become popular as a household guard dog in Germany and the UK. It also has a role as a police dog in Europe, because it is highly trainable and loyal.

This breed needs regular trimming, it enjoys family life, it does not eat a vast amount considering its size, and its beard and moustache give it the sort of expression that will impress those with felonious intent.

▲ *This is a no-nonsense breed that is used in Europe for police work. It is not aggressive unless provoked.*

▼ *In some countries, the Giant Schnauzer's ears are cropped.*

Breed box

Size: Male 65–70cm (25½–27½in), 45.5kg (100lb); female 60–65cm (23½–25½in), 41kg (90lb)
Grooming: Medium
Feeding: Medium
Exercise: Medium
Temperament: Bold and good-natured

Great Dane

The Great Dane is a true giant among dogs; it stands an absolute minimum of 76cm (30in), but the adult male should be considerably taller. Its coat is short and dense, and therefore relatively easy to keep neat and sleek.

It has five official colours, which are jealously guarded by the breed enthusiasts: brindle, fawn, blue, black and harlequin, this last one being a basic white with all-black or all-blue patches that give the appearance of being torn at the edges. Any other colour is incorrect, and it is unwise to pay extra money on the suggestion that 'this unusual colour is very rare and therefore more valuable'.

◄ *The Great Dane is remarkably gentle for such a huge creature.*

Breed box
Size: Male minimum 76cm (30in), 54kg (119lb); female minimum 71cm (28in), 46kg (101½lb)
Grooming: Simple
Feeding: Demanding
Exercise: Medium
Temperament: Kindly but dignified

This breed is a strong, deep-chested dog. It is used for chasing wild boar in its native country of Germany (not Denmark, despite its name). As it is intelligent, it can be trained to be reasonably obedient. It likes both exercise and creature comforts, recognizing the pleasure of occupying the major part of the hearth in front of a roaring fire. For those who see it as the dog of all dogs and can afford its large appetite, it is a must. However, like all giant dogs, it has a regrettable tendency to have a shortish life span.

▲ *This breed's large head is carried high, giving the impression of great strength.*

◄ *This brindle bitch takes up a lot of space – she won't curl up easily in a small house or apartment.*

Hovawart

This German watch dog was bred by wealthy landowners in the Black Mountain region to guard their property and livestock. Their numbers have varied, and the breed almost died out in World War II, but

▶ *The Hovawart needs a job to do; it excels at search and rescue work.*

enthusiasts have worked hard to form a breeding programme, and numbers and popularity are increasing again.

This is a very handsome medium-sized breed. There is a clear difference in both the size and appearance of dogs and bitches. The coat of both is long and water-resistant. Three colours are permitted: black, blonde, or black

and blonde. The long tail hangs down when the dog is standing, but is raised over the back when moving or alert.

This a confident breed that has a strong working drive. It can be rather independent and learns better with the use of positive motivation.

Breed box
Size: 30–50kg (66–110lb); male 63–73cm (25–29in); female 58–65cm (23–25½in)
Grooming: Medium
Feeding: Medium
Exercise: High
Temperament: Confident and courageous

Hungarian Kuvasz

Predominantly a flock guardian, the Hungarian Kuvasz's ancestors are believed to have come from Tibet. From medieval times, these dogs would accompany herdsman with their flocks. Like many breeds, the Kuvasz almost became extinct during World War II

Breed box
Size: Male 70–76cm (28–30in), 45–52kg (100–115lb); female 65–70cm (25½in–28in), 32–41kg (70–90lb)
Grooming: Medium
Feeding: Demanding
Exercise: High
Temperament: Independent and protective

when kennels stopped breeding due to food shortages.

The Kuvasz has a dense white, water-resistant coat that is odourless and repels dirt. The hair can grow to 15cm (6in) in length. Some breed standards call for the coat to be straight, while others state that it should be wavy. Despite the white coat, skin pigmentation is dark and the nose leather is black. Eyes are almond-shaped and dark brown. This is a large, sturdy and muscular breed that is said to move in a wolf-like manner. It is a fit dog that can trot for 24km (15 miles) without ill effects.

Although loyal and patient, it can be challenging to train because it is very independent. It is not recommended for a first-time dog owner, but requires

▲ *The Kuvasz comes from a cold climate, hence its thick coat.*

a person who understands and can enforce pack leadership. It will instinctively protect its owner and will bark at anything that is considered a threat, including visiting children.

Hungarian Puli

The distinctive and eye-catching Hungarian Puli is a herding and livestock guardian dog similar in type to the Komondor. Its coat varies from black through grey and fawn to apricot. It grows massively into the

▶ This breed has an unusual corded coat that swings like a loose rug as it goes on its energetic way.

weather-resistant equivalent of an Eskimo's parka, withstanding both cold and wet.

As the dog matures, the coat tends to form into cords. These cords are not to be confused with the mats that are the sign of an idle owner. The coat takes a great deal of hard work to keep in order. The cords cover the dog completely from head to toe, including the face and tail. There is, indeed, very little visible of the dog beneath the coat. When the dog moves, the cords swing *en masse* rather like a curtain. The Hungarian Puli is a fast-moving and energetic creature that loves exercise and people. It is a great barker and therefore an effective burglar alarm. This is a dog for the devotee.

Breed box
Size: Male 40–44cm (16–17½in),
 13–15kg (28½–33lb);
 female 37–41cm (14½–
 16½in), 10–13kg (22–28½lb)
Grooming: Very demanding
Feeding: Undemanding
Exercise: Medium
Temperament: Lively but reserved
 with strangers

Komondor

The Komondor is another dog from Hungary, where it guards flocks and farms. It has a huge corded coat that reaches the ground in the adult. It is white immediately after the dog has

▶ This is a dog for the wide, open spaces and an owner with plenty of time to maintain it.

been bathed and dried; drying it is a long, drawn-out process. Its whiteness tends to be rapidly compromised by contact with the countryside.

Its ancestry is as a farm dog; bringing such a dog into a town atmosphere would be totally misguided. Its basic instinct is to guard, and to trifle with a dog of such dimensions is risky, to put it mildly. This is definitely a breed that is only for those who understand what they are taking on, and certainly not one for the first-time owner.

▲ In spite of the thick coat over its eyes, the Komondor misses nothing.

Breed box
Size: Male minimum 65cm (25½in),
 50–51kg (110–112½lb);
 female minimum 60cm (23½in),
 36–50kg (79–110lb)
Grooming: Very demanding
Feeding: Medium
Exercise: Medium
Temperament: Wary and protective

Lancashire Heeler

The Lancashire Heeler is a stylish little dog. It stands a mere 30cm (12in) high, and is slightly longer than it is tall. Its forelegs tend to be slightly bowed, but this should not be excessive. As its name implies, this breed was used on farms to herd cattle by nipping at their heels, and it still does when required.

Its coat is not truly short, but it does not grow to any great length. It is always black and tan in colour, and a thorough, brisk grooming will have it shining in no time. It enjoys exercise, but does not make an issue of it. It makes a terrific household companion, and loves children and joining in games. It has a sharp bark, which is louder than one might expect from such a small package, it eats well and is highly biddable.

▼ *Short legs carry a powerful little body; this breed of dog will clear the house of rats as a bonus.*

Breed box
Size: 6.5kg (14lb); male 30cm (12in); female 25cm (10in)
Grooming: Easy
Feeding: Undemanding
Exercise: Medium
Temperament: Happy and affectionate

◄ *This is a small and active dog that adapts easily from droving to being part of a household. The original Lancashire Heeler was used to drive cattle, much like the Welsh Corgi.*

▲ *The prick ears are a sign of the dog's readiness to join in any form of fun.*

Maremma Sheepdog

The Maremma Sheepdog is Italy's version of the nomadic flock guardian. As such, this is a breed that has been derived from generations of working guard dogs. It stands as high as 73cm (29in), but it is not heavily built.

Originating from Italy, the popularity of this breed now sees it recognized by most of the world's major kennel clubs. It is used as a livestock guardian by farmers in Europe, Australia, the USA and Canada. The breed is renowned for bonding with the animals that it is required to guard, if introduced to them when it is a puppy.

▼ *The expression on this breed's face suggests that it is not a fawning animal. It will take its time to admit strangers to the heart of its family.*

◄ ▼ *This dog's ancestry means that it requires plenty of exercise as well as discipline from its owner.*

It is an intelligent dog that requires calm constancy in training.

It carries a medium-length coat that fits it closely. The colour is white with a slight touch of fawn. The dog has an alert expression that denotes the watchfulness of its ancestry. It is a worker and requires regular exercise to maintain it as the fit, muscular creature that its breeding has made it.

Breed box
Size: Male 65–73cm (25½–29in), 35–45kg (77–99lb); female 60–68cm (24–27in), 30–40kg (66–88lb)
Grooming: Medium
Feeding: Medium
Exercise: Demanding
Temperament: Lively and active

Leonberger

Originally bred for use as a farm, watch and carting dog, the Leonberger has a strong work ethic. It derives from the town of Leonberg in Germany, and has traces of several large breeds in its ancestry. As could be expected from its bulk, it needs a great deal of feeding to sustain it.

▶ *These are powerful, self-confident dogs, but entirely good-natured.*

much of it. The colours range from reddish-brown through golden to a lighter yellow, but most specimens have a black mask on their cheerful face.

This dog's attitude to exercise reflects its attitude to life and people – it is accommodating and easy-going. It does not see much point in hurrying anywhere, preferring to amble amiably. It is also a good swimmer in any weather and, given its size, is best suited to country life. It is first and foremost an easy and genial companion.

▲ *The large size of this breed means that it is not suited to living in a small dwelling. Grooming is lengthy.*

It is a friendly dog, but it can give a good account of itself if asked to guard its home. Its coat is of medium length and is not difficult to groom, except for the fact that there is so

▲ *The closer you get to a Leonberger, the more you can see the kind expression in its face and dark eyes.*

▼ *Leonbergers move deliberately with a long-striding gait, and a great deal faster than their size might suggest.*

Breed box
Size: Male 72–80cm (28–32in),
54–77kg (120–170lb); female
65–75cm (25½–29½in),
45–61kg (100–135lb)
Grooming: Fairly demanding
Feeding: Demanding
Exercise: Medium
Temperament: Kindly

Mastiff

The Mastiff, also known as the English or Old English Mastiff, stands up to 76cm (30in) and is built on massive lines. Giant dogs such as this grow remarkably quickly and require care in feeding; they do eat a lot and can be expensive to rear. In addition, a dog that weighs as much as its

▶ *The Mastiff's hindlegs are not always well formed, so care has to be taken in selecting a sound puppy.*

Breed box
Size: 70–76cm (27½–30in);
male 68–113kg (150–250lb);
female 54–82kg (120–181lb)
Grooming: Simple
Feeding: Demanding
Exercise: Medium
Temperament: Steady

owner requires determination as well as ability to control it. Although the Mastiff is not demanding in its exercise requirements, it still needs an adequate amount of freedom.

This dog has a short-lying coat that is reasonably easy to keep in order.

The colour varies from apricot-fawn to a dark brindle-fawn, always combined with a black mask and ears. Fortunately, this breed has a calm temperament despite its massive jaws in a very solid head – if not, it would be a dangerous animal.

Neapolitan Mastiff

The Neapolitan Mastiff, aka the Italian Mastiff or Mastino Neapolitano, has a square-shaped head and muzzle with loose skin around the jowls, lips and under the neck. The body is powerful and has strong limbs. The coat is short and can be black, blue-grey, mahogany, tawny or brindle. Skin on the body is tight-fitting.

This dog is courageous and protective of people and property. It can be stubborn and a little challenging to train. A prospective owner needs to be prepared for the fact that the Neapolitan, as with most mastiffs, eats a lot, snores and dribbles, all of which may prove off-putting.

Breed box
Size: 65–75cm (25½–29in),
50–70kg (110–154lb)
Grooming: Undemanding
Feeding: Fairly demanding
Exercise: Medium
Temperament: Devoted guard dog

▶ *The skin folds down this breed's neck protect its vital structures from attack.*

Newfoundland

▼ *The Newfoundland has immense charm and a sense of humour.*

The Newfoundland is a massive, cuddly bear of a dog, its large face radiating *bonhomie*. It is a water dog *par excellence*, to the extent that its fanciers warn purchasers that if they do not want to be forcibly rescued from water, they should not go swimming with a Newfoundland! It is known colloquially as the 'Newfie'.

This breed can stand up to 71cm (28in) high, which is not particularly tall by some standards, but its body is built on generous lines, as are its legs. Its feet have webs between the toes, which help the dog to swim strongly at speed. It weighs up to 69kg (152lb) and eats to match.

Breed box
Size: Male 71cm (28in), 64–69kg (141–152lb); female 66cm (26in), 50–54.5kg (110–120lb)
Grooming: Fairly demanding
Feeding: Demanding
Exercise: Aquatically demanding
Temperament: Delightfully docile

It has an all-embracing coat that has a slightly oily feel to it. Not surprisingly, this renders the animal totally waterproof. The colour can be black, brown, or white with black markings, which is generally known as 'Landseer' (because Sir Edwin Landseer included Newfoundlands of this marking in many of his paintings).

In spite of being an aquatic dog, the Newfoundland has its own style of movement on the ground – it tends to roll in a charming, nautical fashion. It expects exercise, but prefers it to be in water. Then, when it gets back home, it has an engaging habit of shaking vigorously. This is a dog for the whole family, but not for the house-proud or the apartment-dweller.

▲ *The rather deep-set eyes give an expression of benign relaxation.*

◄ *The lung space is evident even in a front view of this master swimmer among dogs.*

▼ *A house needs plenty of room to accommodate a Newfie.*

Norwegian Buhund

The Norwegian Buhund is a neatly shaped spitz. It has erect ears on an intelligent head and a lively attitude to life. It measures around 46cm (18in), so it is not an imposing dog, but it has an air of alertness about it that makes people pay attention.

Its coat is close and harsh. The most common colour is a wheaten

Breed box
Size: 41–46cm (16–18in),
24–26kg (53–57½lb)
Grooming: Undemanding
Feeding: Undemanding
Exercise: Medium
Temperament: Energetic and
fearless

◄ *This dog's shape is the archetypal outline of a spitz – all neatness and expectancy. This breed was once used as a sled dog in its native country.*

▲ *The Norwegian Buhund is an easy dog to keep clean; it actually seems to dislike getting muddy.*

◄ *This is a breed of energetic dog that may initially be wary of strangers, but it fits family life well.*

gold, but dogs with black and wolf-sable coats are seen. The coat is short enough to require no great skill or time to keep it well groomed.

This breed is a herder in its native Norway, and its good hearing allows it to react swiftly as a guard dog. It gets on well with its family, but is somewhat reserved with those it does not know. It thoroughly enjoys exercise and is relatively biddable, so its bustling style can be kept under control when let loose in field or park.

Old English Sheepdog

The Old English Sheepdog is instantly recognizable by those of a certain age as being the dog from the paint advertisement. It is one of those breeds that could be classified as distinctive the world over. It has evolved from a practical, working-style sheepdog into a stylized show dog; its use in commercial advertising has led to a growth in its popularity, sadly to the breed's overall detriment.

It stands around 61cm (24in) high, but its huge fluffed-up coat makes it look somewhat taller. The owners who exhibit their dogs have to put in hours of work in order to maintain them in

▶ *The Old English Sheepdog was previously known as the Bobtail, since its tail used to be customarily docked.*

show-ring style. Left ungroomed for any length of time, the harsh-textured coat can become matted to a degree that leaves little alternative but to clip.

This is a cheerful extrovert and makes a good family companion, provided the family is committed to

the dog's exercise and can cope with its occasionally explosive nature. It will join in every possible activity with enthusiasm. It is capable of being a first-class guard of its owner's property, with a highly distinctive bark to emphasize its presence.

▲ *This breed goes back at least 150 years, and possibly longer.*

Breed box

Size: Male minimum 61cm (24in), 36.5kg (80½lb); female minimum 56cm (22in), 29.5kg (65lb)

Grooming: Very demanding

Feeding: Medium

Exercise: Medium

Temperament: Friendly and outgoing

▶ *The higher rump end is the result of grooming the hair upwards.*

Pinscher

The Pinscher, originally from Germany, is best described as a midway stage between the Dobermann and the tiny Miniature Pinscher. It wears the same short, dense coat in the same basic black-and-tan colour combination of the Dobermann, with the same alternatives of red, blue and fawn with tan.

It is a sharp-outlined dog with an alert-looking head and expression, and a neat, muscled body. It moves with nimble, athletic strides. As it stands up to 48cm (19in) tall, it is capable of accepting plenty of exercise and can make a splendid member of either a town or country family. It can be possessive.

▶ The Pinscher is a very bright breed with clean-cut features and bright eyes.

This breed needs minimal grooming to polish it into a glossy shine. It does not ask for excessive food, and it possesses a sharp voice and an intelligent mind, which make it a handy watch dog. It is territorial and not above following up a warning bark with a sharp nip. Owners need to ensure that they are the alpha member of this partnership. One breed club describes the Pinscher as 'energetic, watchful, agile, fearless and determined' — a good summary of this sharp, medium-sized dog that retains strong terrier-type characteristics.

Breed box
Size: 43–48cm (17–19in), 11–20kg (24–44lb)
Grooming: Easy
Feeding: Undemanding
Exercise: Medium
Temperament: Active and confident

▲ This red-coated version positively shines, indicating the dog's good health. Salt and pepper and harlequin-coloured dogs became extinct due to the decline in breeding and loss of dogs during World War I and II.

◀ Although the Pinscher can be distrustful of strangers, it is responsive to training and makes a good family member. The breed originated as the German farmer's terrier and was recognized by the German Kennel Club in 1879. Popularity has been increasing in the United States due to its recognition by the AKC in 2003.

Portuguese Water Dog

Also known as the Algarvian Water Dog or Portuguese Fishing Dog, this breed was used to herd fish into nets and carry messages from one boat to another or back to the shore. It was also trained to find and retrieve lost or damaged fishing tackle.

Not widely known outside its country of origin, the Portuguese Water Dog gained media attention when it was revealed that the former US president Barack Obama owned two.

Although similar in type to a Standard Poodle, the Portuguese Water Dog is more solidly built, with stouter legs and heavier bone. It has webbed toes to assist it when swimming. The non-shedding coat is curly or wavy, or a combination of these two types. The colour can be solid black, brown and white, or mixtures of these. This breed is slow to mature, both physically and mentally.

Active and intelligent, this dog makes a fine companion. It is good with children and other pets if brought up with them. It is very affectionate, but can be reserved towards strangers. It loves water and requires vigorous daily exercise. It can be destructive if bored, or if it does not

▲ *This dog is similar to the Poodle, but without such a refined head.*

have sufficient exercise. It excels in a range of canine sports. As this breed is non-shedding, it requires frequent clipping in addition to daily grooming. The coat is high-maintenance and can be costly to keep in good order.

Breed box
Size: Male 50–57cm (20–22½in), 19–25kg (42–55lb); female 43–52cm (17–20½in), 16–22kg (36–48½lb)
Grooming: Demanding
Feeding: Medium
Exercise: Demanding
Temperament: Tireless and amenable

Polish Lowland Sheepdog

The Polish name for this dog is Polski Owczarek Nizinny, and this is shortened to PON, a term used for the breed worldwide. It is believed to be the result of breeding the Hungarian Puli with various other breeds, including the Tibetan Mastiff, Tibetan Terrier and the Lhasa Apso.

With a long and dense, shaggy, wire-haired topcoat plus a very thick, soft undercoat, the dog requires extensive grooming. Colours range from white or grey with black, grey, chocolate or sand patches, to solid white or black and black and tan.

Colours fade as the dog matures. This is a muscular, medium-sized dog with facial hair that forms a beard.

It is an independent breed that has a very good memory. It is easy to train but can be wilful.

▶ *Some dogs have blue eyes, but this is not acceptable with most kennel clubs for the show ring.*

Breed box
Size: 42–50cm (17–20in); male 18–22kg (39½–48½lb); female 13.5–18kg (30–40lb)
Grooming: Extensive
Feeding: Medium to high
Exercise: High
Temperament: Lively and clever

Pyrenean Mountain Dog

The Pyrenean Mountain Dog, also known as the Great Pyrenees, is a solidly built animal measuring as much as 70cm (27½in) and weighing up to 60kg (132lb). It is one of the flock-guarding dogs of the European

Breed box
Size: Male 70cm (27½in),
  50–60kg (119–132lb);
  female minimum 65cm (25½in),
  40kg (88lb)
Grooming: Demanding
Feeding: Demanding
Exercise: Medium
Temperament: Confident and
  genial

▶ *The Pyrenean Mountain Dog is massive and requires a firm handler. A steady-moving dog with very considerable dignity, it can be quite reserved with strangers.*

nomad shepherd; with its coarse-textured white coat, it merges into the flock. As a domestic house dog, it requires regular grooming, and bathing it is no easy task.

The modern Pyrenean has more of the permitted badger coloration, especially on the head and ears, than it did during the 1960s. It is a breed that grows large double hind dewclaws, which help it in snow-covered terrain. It does not require excessive exercise, and normally moves at a dignified amble in a park or pasture. It makes a good household member, its basic temperament having become more gentle as a result of generations of selective breeding.

Pyrenean Sheepdog

Still relatively unknown by many people, this dog is beginning to be seen more frequently. There are two varieties: rough-faced and smooth-faced. The former has long hair all over the body, while the latter has a short coat with a ruff around the neck and some feathering on the tail, legs and belly. Coat colours include fawn, with or without a black mask, brindle, grey, black and merle. Solid colours are preferred, but some white is permitted on the head, feet and chest.

This breed is very energetic, and this characteristic, combined with its intelligence, makes it ideal for dog sports, including agility, flyball, tracking and obedience, as well as the breed show ring. It is ideal for an active family.

◀ ▲ *This second breed from the Pyrenees is totally different in looks. Both breeds work with sheep, but they perform in contrasting styles.*

Breed box
Size: 38–48cm (15–19in),
  8–15kg (18–33lb)
Grooming: Medium
Feeding: Undemanding
Exercise: Medium
Temperament: Alert and wary

Rottweiler

The Rottweiler comes from Germany, and is a handsome and striking breed. The male can stand as tall as 69cm (27in) and is solidly built of hard muscle, giving it immense strength.

Bred as a droving and carting dog, the Rottweiler's usefulness has evolved to encompass search and rescue work and use as a guide dog and police dog. Lack of socializing and training can turn this incredibly strong dog into a potentially dangerous animal. It is a breed that can be territorial and reactive, but with the correct care and in the right hands, the Rottweiler is calm and confident. It currently ranks in the top-ten pedigree breeds within the USA, but is not recommended for the first-time dog owner.

The coat is invariably of medium-short length, and black and tan in colour. Grooming is rewarding; the coat produces a magnificent shine very easily. Exercise is essential because of the muscular nature of the breed. It likes its food and expects plenty of it.

This is a breed for an experienced dog owner who will devote time and attention to the dog. The Rottweiler merits much of the enthusiasm it engenders, but needs good control.

▼ *An average-sized, strong and agile dog, the Rottweiler is not a suitable breed for the nervous owner or for a newcomer to dogs.*

Breed box
Size: Male 63–69cm (25–27½in), 50kg (110lb); female 58–63.5cm (23–25in), 38.5kg (85lb)
Grooming: Simple
Feeding: Demanding
Exercise: Medium to demanding
Temperament: Courageous and trainable

▲ *The powerful muzzle shows why the breed has earned respect as a guard.*

◄ *The Rottweiler will respect the authority of an owner who merits it – both handler and dog need training.*

St Bernard

The enormous St Bernard is an instantly recognizable breed. It stands tall, but it is its massive frame that makes it so remarkable. It originated in the mountains of Switzerland, and is traditionally depicted with a miniature brandy barrel attached to its collar as it locates a traveller who has been stranded in deep snow.

▶ This breed was first taken by monks to the famous hospice in the Swiss Alps, where it was used as a guard dog and companion in the 17th century.

Breed box
Size: Maximum 91.5cm (36in);
    male 75kg (165½lb);
    female 68kg (150lb)
Grooming: Medium to demanding
Feeding: Demanding
Exercise: Medium
Temperament: Steady and
    benevolent

Everything about the modern St Bernard is huge, right down to its feet. It has a great breadth of skull and huge jaws. Its lower lip tends to droop at the outside corner, which means that it drools a fair amount.

Its limbs are big-boned, so rearing the young is expensive and needs to be well understood. Exercise in the puppy should be increased very slowly as it grows, to ensure that the minimum strain is put on tender tissues. Exercise in the adult is usually a gentle progression; a St Bernard pulling on its lead can be a struggle for the handler.

◀ The St Bernards is a massive dog with truly powerful bones in the forelegs.

▶ It is all too easy to fall for the charms of these dogs when they are still youngsters.

Grooming is not a problem, except there is a lot of coat to be dealt with. The coat is normally medium in length, but there is a short-coated St Bernard. The colour can be orange, red brindle or mahogany brindle with white markings, or white with any of the above as coloured patches.

Temperamentally, the breed is trustworthy and benign, which is just as well since the rare occasion when a St Bernard does erupt is awesome to behold. This is an attractive breed, but those who fall for it should consider carefully how well they can cope.

Samoyed

The Samoyed is the 'Laughing Cavalier' of dogdom, with its brilliant white colour and its typical spitz expression. It stands up to 56cm (22in) high, and it is very slightly

longer than it is tall. Its coat is harsh and stand-off in a basic white, but many of the breed carry varying amounts of biscuit, which is a light reddish-fawn.

Grooming is hard work, but the Samoyed is tolerant and will submit for hours, if necessary, to lying on its side while the owner brushes and combs it. The breed has a history as a sled dog, and has hairy, flat feet to enable it to cope with the surface ice that would otherwise pack into the spaces between its pads.

It enjoys exercise but needs human company; it is a super member of a family household, but still manages to be a great companion to those who live alone. In spite of its energetic

▲ *This is a happy-go-lucky breed with never a nasty or negative thought – but plenty of mischievous ones.*

lifestyle, it is not a huge eater. Its only real drawback is its tendency to bark noisily, especially when it is enjoying itself – which is most of the time.

▲ *The Samoyed has a smiling and cheerful expression. The nose leather can be black or brown, but the lips must be black.*

▶ *Under this dog's coat there is usually a muscular frame that fits well into a sled harness, given the opportunity. The breed originated with the Samoyeds, a nomadic tribe of northern Asia who roamed Siberia.*

Breed box
Size: Male 51–56cm (20–22in),
    23kg (50½lb); female 46–51cm
    (18–20in), 18kg (39½lb)
Grooming: Very demanding
Feeding: Medium
Exercise: Medium
Temperament: Alert and smiling

Shetland Sheepdog

The Shetland Sheepdog is a diminutive version of the Rough Collie, although few companion dogs are genuinely as small as the official maximum height permitted for show dogs, which is around 37cm (14½in). In fact, this very attractive little dog has all the instincts that its name implies and, although today it tends to be very much a family dog, it is still quite capable of reacting as a worker.

It carries a long, straight topcoat that can be coloured sable, tricolour, blue merle, black and white, or even black and tan. The undercoat is thick, so it requires thorough grooming fairly frequently if it is not to become matted and impossible to cope with.

This is an alert dog and will take a great deal of exercise if it is offered, but can just as easily make a first-class companion for an elderly person. It is watchful and capable of following a scent when the occasion demands.

▶ *The slight tilt of the head, as if asking a question, is typical of the 'Sheltie'.*

▲ *This miniature version of the Rough Collie is a worker in its own right.*

Breed box
Size: 9kg (20lb); male 37cm
 (14½in); female 35.5cm (14in)
Grooming: Demanding
Feeding: Undemanding
Exercise: Medium
Temperament: Affectionate and
 responsive

▼ *Shelties are sturdy, cheerful and easy to train. They are also photogenic!*

Siberian Husky

The Siberian Husky is the racer of the sled-dog world. It may seem a harsh thing to say about what, in many ways, is a very charming dog indeed, but it lives only to pull a sled! It stands up to 60cm (23½in) tall at the withers, it is lean at its muscular best, and it has a head that is distinctly reminiscent of a wolf, but with a kinder look.

Its coat is fairly long and will keep the animal warm in the most bitter cold. It can come in virtually any colour or pattern of colours. Its eyes are the most remarkable feature of its face, as they too can vary in colour, even

Breed box
Size: Male 60cm (23½in), 23.5kg (52lb); female 53.5cm (21in), 19.5kg (43lb)
Grooming: Medium
Feeding: Demanding
Exercise: Very demanding
Temperament: Friendly but reserved

to the extent of one being brown and the other blue. If that were not odd enough, some dogs are found whose individual irises can show two halves of different hues.

This dog's attitude to people is of extreme tolerance, but to its own kind it can be very domineering, and there is a distinct pecking order in a

racing pack. It is possible to persuade the odd one to walk on a loose lead and even obey basic commands, but it simply is not its idea of how a dog should behave. People who keep Siberian Huskies usually exercise them in front of a sled if snow is available, or by having them pull a wheeled rig on forest tracks. Husky racing events take place all over the UK, USA and Europe. You should think carefully before choosing this as a companion animal.

◀ This breed can jump a good height from a standstill.

▲ The Siberian Husky rarely lowers its pricked ears.

◀ The legs are very strong, keeping racing Huskies on the move. The front legs are parallel and straight.

▶ Siberian Huskies were originally draught dogs with the Inuit people. Half a dozen dogs attached to a racing sled will give an exciting ride.

Swedish Lapphund

The Swedish Lapphund is built on very similar lines to the Finnish Lapphund. It may stand up to 51cm (20in) tall and is of typical spitz construction. Its coat is weather-resistant and of medium length; it is a mixture of black and brown, with an occasional touch of white on its chest or feet. It is not difficult to groom.

▶ This stout-framed dog has a coat that is fit to withstand Scandinavian weather.

▼ The Swedish Lapphund has a gentle character.

This breed is a friendly and intelligent dog, and its temperament would appeal to a family household, as it enjoys exercise and is not greedy. Good training is required to control its tendency to bark continuously.

Breed box
Size: 44–51cm (20in),
  19.5–20.5kg (43–45lb)
Grooming: Medium
Feeding: Medium
Exercise: Medium
Temperament: Active and friendly

Swedish Vallhund

The Swedish Vallhund looks and acts very much like a grey or yellowish Corgi. It is built on similar lines, standing a mere 35cm (14in) tall, but is somewhat longer in body than height. Its coat is reasonably short, harsh and easy to keep in shape.

It comes in grey, greyish-brown and varying shades of yellow with reddish-brown thrown in.

Its job is to herd, and it does this, as do the Corgis, by nipping at the heels of cattle that are not as quick to move as required. It has sharply erect ears and is cheerful. The breed is steadily gaining in popularity, although it is not registered in the USA. It makes an excellent family pet, as it delights in exercise and human friendship.

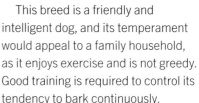

▲ If you are looking for real intelligence in a dog's expression, it is to be found in this charmer.

◀ The Swedish Vallhund is a low-to-ground heeler type – agile, nimble and very biddable.

Breed box
Size: 11.5–13kg (25–28½lb);
  male 33–35cm (13–14in);
  female 31–33cm (12½–13in)
Grooming: Undemanding
Feeding: Undemanding
Exercise: Medium
Temperament: Friendly and eager

Tibetan Mastiff

The Tibetan Mastiff is an unusual member of the mastiff world because it has a longish coat. It has a genial expression, but odd specimens can be touchy. On the whole, they are likeable creatures with coats of varying colours, ranging from black, through black and tan, to gold and grey.

It stands up to 66cm (26in) tall, which means it is not a giant, but its body is solidly made. It is also unusual for a mastiff in that it carries its tail high and over its back. It is a useful guard dog and enjoys its exercise, but those who choose it need to be prepared to handle a powerful dog.

◀ *Well suited to the rugged countries of Asia, this breed has a thick protective coat that requires regular grooming.*

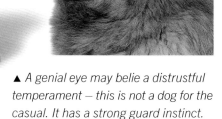

▲ *A genial eye may belie a distrustful temperament – this is not a dog for the casual. It has a strong guard instinct.*

▶ *Originating from areas of Tibet, Syria and Arabia, this is a real mountain dog. It was used by nomadic tribes to protect livestock from leopards, tigers, bears and wolves. The Tibetan Mastiff guarded monasteries, palaces and villages, too.*

Breed box
Size: 66cm (26in), 64–82kg
　(141–181lb)
Grooming: Fairly demanding
Feeding: Demanding
Exercise: Medium
Temperament: Aloof and
　protective

Welsh Corgi – Cardigan

The Welsh Corgi comes in two separate versions: the Cardigan and the Pembroke. The Cardigan Corgi stands ideally 30cm (12in) at the withers; it is relatively long-cast on sturdy, short legs. It is unlike its Pembroke cousin in that it carries a full tail, which is long and very well coated. This breed is not hard work to groom, nor is it greedy for food.

Colour-wise it can be almost any dog colour, although white should not predominate. It has large, erect ears and intelligent eyes. It does not bustle about very rapidly and is prepared to take life as it comes, but when working with cattle it has to be nimble enough to nip at their heels and avoid retaliatory kicks.

▲ *This practical and adaptable breed is friendly and full of stamina.*

As a member of a household, it has a curiously benign attitude, but can raise the alarm vociferously if its territory is invaded.

Breed box
Size: 30cm (12in); male 11kg (24lb); female 10kg (22lb)
Grooming: Medium
Feeding: Undemanding
Exercise: Medium
Temperament: Alert and steady

Welsh Corgi – Pembroke

The Pembroke is the better-known version of the Welsh Corgi. The breed is favoured by the British royal family – Queen Elizabeth II famously owned over 30 of them during her reign. The dog stands 30cm (12in) at the withers, and has a longish body. It is

▶ *The most common colour of the Pembroke Corgi is red and white.*

sturdily built with a sharp, bright expression and prick ears.

It has a straight, dense coat of medium length and is not difficult to groom once it has dried off after a country walk. Its colour is usually red with white markings, but it does come in sable, fawn, or even black and tan.

It is traditionally a cattle-drover, hence its occasional tendency to nip the heels of humans rather than cattle. The slightly doubtful temperament it may have had in past decades has improved since the 1980s.

It is a popular household dog with families who enjoy its brisk, energetic attitude to life, but it has a slight tendency to over-eat, and therefore needs rationing on occasion.

▲ *The fox-like head should show an intelligent and alert expression.*

Breed box
Size: 25.5–30.5cm (10–12in); male 10–12kg (22–26½lb); female 10–11kg (22–24lb)
Grooming: Medium
Feeding: Medium
Exercise: Medium
Temperament: Workman-like and active

THE TOY
GROUP

This group is made up of breeds that are among the smallest of all. The largest of these are the ever-popular Cavalier King Charles Spaniel, Chinese Crested and Löwchen, while at the other end of the scale are the Chihuahua and Pomeranian. Height measurements are not given in many of the Kennel Club's official breed standards; rather, these tend to give ideal weights or weight ranges. The name 'Toy' is in some ways misleading; admittedly some of the breeds tend to appear to be animated playthings, but their temperaments suggest that they are anything but. The breeds included here have some common factors, such as the ability to be picked up and carried easily, but they vary widely in size, type and behaviour. The misconception to be avoided is that they are all dear little creatures that behave impeccably and do not take any effort to look after. Many are feisty characters that are not afraid to nip.

◀ *Many dogs within the Toy Group will need extensive grooming and styling. This is so with the Löwchen, which has a very distinctive clip.*

Affenpinscher

The Affenpinscher, originally from Germany, is a dog that often makes people laugh. It is said to resemble a monkey facially, and certainly its twinkling eyes give its expression a thoroughly mischievous glint.

It has a coat that is harsh in texture and generally looks pretty untidy, so grooming it is not an over-serious business. This breed is game for fun, and is capable of taking part in family activities since its muzzle is not so exaggeratedly short as to interfere with its breathing to any real extent.

It is normally black all over, although a grey coloration does sometimes appear. As a house companion, it is one of the best choices because it is fearless and delights in confronting any intruder.

◀ *A sense of mischief prevails whenever two or more Affenpinschers are gathered together. You can see why they are also known as Monkey Terriers.*

Breed box
Size: 24–28cm (9½–11in), 3–4kg (6½–9lb)
Grooming: Medium
Feeding: Undemanding
Exercise: Medium
Temperament: Lively and self-confident

▼ *The coat is rough and of uneven length over the body – it is shaggy in some places and shorter in others. This example is a truly hairy specimen. Bred as ratters, the coat offers protection.*

▲ *The tail curls gently over the back when the dog is moving, and hangs relaxed at rest. This dog can be excitable.*

▲ *The greying effect produces a remarkable facial study. The Affen is a mischievous and loyal companion.*

Australian Silky Terrier

The Australian Silky Terrier, known variously as the Sydney Silky or just the Silky, is a mixture produced from cross-breeding the Australian Terrier and the Yorkshire Terrier. The result is a sharp-featured, silky-coated dog that stands some 23cm (9in) high at the withers and weighs 4kg (9lb).

◄ A compact dog, the Australian Silky Terrier may have been bred primarily as a household companion, but it is also a pretty good rat-catcher.

◄ At times, the Silky can put on quite a serious expression, but this is not accurate evidence of its true temperament.

▶ Silkies should have small, cat-like feet, with no long hair on their legs.

Breed box
Size: 23cm (9in), 4kg (9lb)
Grooming: Medium
Feeding: Undemanding
Exercise: Medium
Temperament: Alert and friendly

One would expect any animal produced by mating one from Australia with one from Yorkshire to be only too capable of holding its own, so the term 'silky' should never mislead anyone into thinking it denotes anything soft. Not a bit of it – this dog is full of character!

Its coat, which is fairly long and straight, comes in blue and tan, or greyish blue and tan, and it can become glossy with minimal brushing. This dog is intended as a household companion and does the job splendidly, but with a strong prey drive.

▶ In silhouette, the essential sharpness of this dog's outline and its fixed gaze become obvious – it is a good mixture of toy and terrier.

Bichon Frise

Believed to be a cross between Barbet Water Dogs and Poodles, there are many stories about the Bichon Frise, or Bichon Tenerife. It is known that this dog came from the Mediterranean area, and that they were admired by sailors who took them back to their home countries. Paintings and documents show that the breed was present in the court of Henry III, and was much loved by 15th-century Spanish Infantas. Its intelligence together with its good nature has gained it worldwide recognition.

This happy little dog has an arched neck and slightly rounded skull. Ears are dropped and covered with long hair. The nose is black, and eyes are dark in colour. Tails are well plumed and carried in a graceful curve over the back. The white, cream, apricot or grey coat is curly and dense, with minimal shedding. Daily grooming and monthly trimming and bathing are needed to prevent matting and to keep the coat in good condition. Movement is balanced and effortless.

Breed box
Size: 23–28cm (9–11in),
    3–6kg (6½–13lb)
Grooming: Demanding
Feeding: Medium
Exercise: Medium
Temperament: Friendly and
    extroverted

▲ *A Bichon will enjoy learning tricks and taking part in canine sports.*

Bred as a companion dog, the Bichon is good with children and animals. It loves human company and is playful and affectionate. This dog can be difficult to house-train, so owners need to be diligent in this task.

Bolognese

The Bolognese is a bichon type, and is closely related to the Bichon Frise, Havanese and Maltese. It is named after the Italian city of Bologna. This breed is known to have been in existence in the 1200s, and was favoured by the Italian nobility. Bolognese dogs feature in paintings by Goya and Titian. They have been owned by many famous personalities, including Catherine the Great of Russia and Marilyn Monroe.

The Bolognese is a small dog that has a square, compact and stocky body. It is white, with dark eyes and black eye rims, lips and nose. Apricot shading is acceptable on the ears. It is a single long-coated breed and does not seasonally moult, but eventually loses and replaces individual hairs.

▶ *This happy breed is a real home-lover.*

The coat is woolly in texture and falls in loose, open ringlets. This dog is not normally trimmed, but requires daily brushing and monthly bathing.

More reserved than a Bichon Frise, the Bolognese is easy-going and intelligent. It is very responsive to obedience training but does not like repetitive tasks. This breed can be very stubborn if it does not get its own way. It is a non-aggressive family dog that is good with other dogs and children. It makes a good watch dog, barking only when there is good reason. It is not a high-energy breed, but still requires a daily walk.

Breed box
Size: 25–30cm (10–12in),
    2.5–4kg (5½–9lb)
Grooming: Intensive
Feeding: Undemanding
Exercise: Low to medium
Temperament: Intelligent and
    easy-going

Cavalier King Charles Spaniel

The Cavalier King Charles Spaniel, or Cavalier, is a very popular toy dog and a true favourite. Built on the lines of a small gundog, it has a charm for the elderly as well as the young family. It loves people, and it does not find fault with other dogs.

Its weight is 5.5–8kg (12–18lb), which is a wide enough range, but as a breed it does tend to get even heavier. The Cavalier's placid nature

▶ This is a neat breed that is ideal for anyone who wants an active and cheerful companion. Like other spaniels, the Cavalier is a hunter. It will chase birds, small mammals and even butterflies if given the opportunity.

and friendliness often prompts people to give it injudicious titbits, but unfortunately this encourages obesity.

This breed has a good-looking head and a well-balanced body. It can appear in a series of colours, ranging

from ruby (red), black and tan, and tricolour (black and white with tan markings) to Blenheim, which is a mixture of rich chestnut and white, often with a lozenge of chestnut in the centre of a white patch down the middle of the head.

It enjoys exercise and is built on elegant, athletic lines; indeed, it needs good exercise in view of its hearty appetite. It is not difficult to groom, as its coat can be kept tidy with normal brush-and-comb techniques.

▲ The charm and affability of the Cavalier's expression is beautifully caught in this head study.

◀ The Cavalier is in fact a miniature spaniel, combining all the qualities of dogs in the Toy and Gundog Groups.

Breed box
Size: 32cm (13in), 5.5–8kg (12–18lb)
Grooming: Medium
Feeding: Medium
Exercise: Medium
Temperament: Very friendly

King Charles Spaniel

The King Charles Spaniel, also known as the English Toy Spaniel, is similar to the Cavalier King Charles Spaniel, but has a shorter nose and a more domed head. It has a long, silky coat, which comes in the same colour range as the Cavalier – black and tan, ruby, Blenheim and tricolour – and it is equally rewarding to groom.

This breed is more reserved than the Cavalier, but has the same kindly and intelligent disposition. It makes a devoted companion, and does not need much exercise or food.

Breed box
Size: 3.6–6.3kg (8–14lb); male 25.5cm (10in); female 20.5cm (8in)
Grooming: Medium
Feeding: Medium
Exercise: Undemanding
Temperament: Gentle and affectionate

◀ This breed is easily mistaken for the better-known Cavalier King Charles Spaniel, but it has a slightly more snubbed nose. The Cavalier was developed from this breed.

English Toy Terrier

Formally called the Miniature Black and Tan Terrier, the English Toy Terrier is on the United Kennel Club's list of vulnerable native breeds. In an attempt to increase numbers, the UKC is allowing North America's Toy Manchester Terrier to be re-registered as an English Toy Terrier. Very popular in Victorian times, this dog was used as a ratter working in towns, on farms and on ships, controlling rodents. Competitions were held in taverns when dogs were put into rat pits to see which could kill the most rats in a given time. When this sport was made illegal, this dog's popularity continued in early dog shows, but numbers have since declined dramatically.

This elegant dog has a sleek and compact body. The head is long and narrow, with almond-shaped dark eyes. Pointed ears are set high on the skull and they face forwards. The ears are referred to as 'candle-flame' in shape. The coat is ebony black with tan markings on the face, chest and legs. There should be a clear division between the colours. Movement is similar to that of an extended trot in horses.

This breed is alert but should not be nervous. Like many of the toy breeds, it does not like being left alone for long. It is good with children, but due to its fine bones it could get injured in rough play, so supervision is required. The short, shiny coat needs little attention. This dog can be slow to house-train, so its owner needs to be diligent and patient. This breed is not keen on going out in the rain.

Breed box
Size: 25–30cm (10–12in), 2.7–3.6kg (6–8lb)
Grooming: Easy
Feeding: Undemanding
Exercise: Low to medium
Temperament: Charming

◀ This remarkably tiny dog makes up for its lack of size by possessing a mighty yap.

Chihuahua

The Chihuahua probably originated in South America, and is indeed named after a Mexican state. It comes in two versions, one of which is smooth-coated, the other long-coated. Apart from their coat, they are identical, tiny dogs of tremendous spirit. They weigh up to 3kg (6½lb), but lighter specimens are generally preferred in the show ring. The Smooth Coat has a soft, glossy covering of a coat, while the Long Coat is never coarse and is relatively easy to keep neat. The Chihuahua is very proud of its tail, which it carries high like a flag. This typifies the breed's personality. All colours are accepted, but fawn to red with white is the most frequently seen.

This is a brave dog, putting up with pain remarkably stoically, but not accepting cheek or insult from any dog that is vastly larger than itself.

◄ Three of a kind with two Smooths and a Long. This is an alert breed with a loud bark that can sound rather like a duck quacking.

It does not appreciate humans who invade its home without permission, yelling defiance and threatening mayhem as it races to defend its home and family.

Rearing a young Chihuahua puppy requires care in moving about; a high-stepping human can very easily trample on such a tiny creature, so Chihuahua breeders soon learn to use a shuffling method of walking. The breed, however, is not a weak or delicate one; in fact, the opposite is true. Both versions enjoy exercise and are extremely game, but families with young children must supervise all interaction between puppy and child carefully and constantly.

Breed box
Size: 15–23cm (6–9in), 1–3kg (4–6½lb)
Grooming: Medium
Feeding: Undemanding
Exercise: Undemanding
Temperament: Spirited and intelligent

◄ The Chihuahua is a well-proportioned little dog ready to take on anything.

▲ The large, round, bright eyes set wide apart are a hallmark of this spritely breed. Eye colour varies.

Chinese Crested

Despite its name, it is very unlikely that the Chinese Crested originated from China. The breed is believed to have come from Africa, and was originally called the African Hairless Terrier. Chinese traders brought these dogs home and the name was subsequently changed to Chinese Crested. There are two varieties, Hairless and Powderpuff, with both being produced in the same litter. Each type has equal recognition with most major kennel clubs.

The Hairless variety has long, single-coated hair on the head, extending down the neck and socks, and a plumed tail. The Powderpuff is covered in a long, silky double coat all over the body. Hair and skin can be any colour – solid, mixed or spotted. Both have almond-shaped eyes and

▶ The Hairless version has a crest on the head and neck, a plume on the end of the tail, and thick hair on the feet and lower legs.

▼ The Chinese Crested Powderpuff, once seen as an outcast by breeders, is now recognized as essential to the future of a very unusual breed.

elongated toes or 'hare feet'. The Hairless has primitive dentition with pointed teeth, and may have forward-pointing canines or 'tusks'. It suffers from tooth decay and tooth loss, while the Powderpuff does not. In both, the head is wedge-shaped and topped with large, erect ears.

These agile and alert dogs are very loving and do not do well in a kennel situation, as they need to be part of the family. They are suitable for town living but, despite their size and looks, need an active lifestyle. They are quite happy to go for long hikes and to

▲ The Powderpuff has an undercoat topped with long, silky hair.

take part in a range of canine sports. The Hairless needs a coat or jumper for warmth in colder climates, the Powderpuff requires daily grooming, and both types need regular baths. Hairless dogs also need to be given sunscreen and skin moisturizers.

Breed box
Size: 30cm (12in), 4.5kg (10lb)
Grooming: Moderate
Feeding: Undemanding
Exercise: Medium
Temperament: Loving and agile

Griffon Bruxellois

Named after the capital of Belgium, the Griffon Bruxellois, or Brussels Griffon, is one of the most delightful characters of the Toy Group. It is truly bright and cheerful. With a monkey-like expression and its usual harsh coat of red, it displays the equivalent of canine cheekiness. As well as the harsh-coated version, there is also a smooth-coated type, and this is an equally pert animal. Both kinds can come in other colours besides red.

It weighs anything from 2.2–4.9kg (5–11lb), but the middle of that range is the most common. It has a bit of the terrier about it, so it thoroughly enjoys exercising with a boisterous family, but it also makes a cheerful and fearless companion for those who live alone. It does not take much grooming, but occasional professional stripping in the rough-coated form is not a bad idea.

◀ Originally bred as a street ratter, this dog still retains a prey drive. The rough-coated version sports a splendid walrus moustache and beard.

▶ Two of a kind, both harsh in coat, with the less common black colour in front.

Breed box
Size: 18–20cm (7–8in),
2.2–4.9kg (5–11lb)
Grooming: Medium
Feeding: Undemanding
Exercise: Undemanding
Temperament: Lively and alert

▲ This is the typical smooth-coated head, with a bright and observant eye.

◀ The coat of the rough-coated Griffon Bruxellois is comprised of wiry, harsh hairs that stand away from the body. This breed featured in the 2001 British Academy Award-winning film Gosford Park.

▶ The smooth-coated type has a solid body on neat legs, and is not too difficult to keep clean and tidy. Both types are very affectionate and loving.

Italian Greyhound

This breed has been in existence for at least 2,000 years. Mummified dogs of similar type have been found in Egypt and Pompeii. The name comes from a surge in its popularity in Italy in the Renaissance. It is the smallest of the gazehound dogs, and is classified in the Toy Group by the UK and US kennel clubs, but in the Sighthound Group by European kennel clubs.

Breed box
Size: 33–38cm (13–15in),
    3.6–8.2kg (8–18lb)
Grooming: Easy
Feeding: Undemanding
Exercise: Medium
Temperament: Elegant, sensitive

▶ *The Italian Greyhound shows balanced musculature in the hindquarters.*

The Italian Greyhound is very fast and agile, and has a high stepping gait when trotting. At the gallop, it is able to move with all four feet off the ground at the same time; this is called 'double suspension'. It can reach speeds of 40km/h (25mph), and with its strong prey drive, exercise should be on lead unless in a safe, enclosed area. The very short, smooth coat comes in a range of solid or parti colours.

This is a beautiful companion animal that requires more exercise and entertainment than most of the other breeds in the Toy Group. Its slender build makes it rather fragile, and therefore it is unsuited to rough play with children. It is suitable for either town or country living, but does like to run and is active in the home.

Japanese Chin

The Japanese Chin, or Japanese Spaniel, likely originated from either China or Korea, but it is known that the Chin was in Japan around AD1000. Bred as a companion, ownership

▶ *The oversized eyes are a recognizable feature of the Chin.*

was restricted to Japanese royalty or high-ranking nobility. In part, this may account for differences in the breed, as each noble house bred these dogs to suit their own requirements. A pair was given to Queen Victoria in 1853, and the AKC recognized the breed in the late 19th century.

It has a large, broad head, wide and slightly protruding eyes, a short, broad muzzle and feathered ears. It has a bouncy gait and charming expression, and the single coat is white, with patches of either black, red, lemon, orange or sable, or tricolour markings. The coat can take up to two years to grow to completion.

This is a happy, lively, devoted breed that likes to be the centre of attention. Early socialization is needed. Although generally quiet, it will alarm-bark to warn of approaching strangers or unusual events. It does not thrive in extremes of temperature, and is not suitable for outdoor living.

Breed box
Size: 18–28cm (7–11in),
    2–7kg (4½–15½lb)
Grooming: Moderate
Feeding: Undemanding
Exercise: Low to medium
Temperament: Devoted and
    intelligent

Löwchen

It is unclear how the Löwchen, also known as the Petit Chien Dog or Little Lion Dog, originated. Bichon or Tibetan Terrier may be in its distant ancestry, but this cannot be proven.

The coat is long, flowing and slightly wavy, and is made up of a mix of thick and fine hair. All colours or combinations are acceptable. Most dogs are presented in a 'lion clip', with the coat shaved over the haunches, back legs and front legs (retaining a bracelet of hair around the ankles), and part of the tail. The rest of the coat remains long, giving the impression of a little lion.

This breed is an ideal companion and family dog but it needs early socialization to prevent nervousness. It is happy to live in town or country, but is unsuited to kennel living. It does not like being left alone. It can walk long distances, but is content with two short walks and a garden to play in.

▶ *A somewhat grave expression belies the fact that this dog can be a real live wire.*

Breed box
Size: Male 30–35.6cm (12–14in), 5.4–8.1kg (12–18lb); female 28–33cm (11–13in), 4.5–6.8kg (10–15lb)
Grooming: Moderate
Feeding: Undemanding
Exercise: Low to medium
Temperament: Active and playful

Maltese

This companion breed has been in existence since Roman times. It was once called the 'Roman Ladies' Dog'. The breed was introduced to the UK in the reign of Henry VIII, and most stock in the USA can trace its British heritage. It nearly died out in the 17th and 18th centuries, but enough healthy stock was found to build numbers and size back.

▶ *The Maltese often sports a 'top-knot', to keep hair out of its eyes.*

This enchanting, long-coated, pure white dog has a rounded skull with a black nose and dark eyes. The compact body is square in shape, and the face is framed by pendulant ears. A jaunty flowing gait makes the Maltese look as if it is moving through a soft white cloud of hair. A dog in full show coat needs extensive grooming to prevent tangles and knots.

This dog remains active and playful into old age. It is a good watch dog, but may bark excessively if untrained or lacking in socialization. If allowed to be dominant or spoilt, it can become snappy, but as it is easily trained, this trait can be overcome with time.

Breed box
Size: 18–30cm (7–12in), 1.4–4.5kg (3–10lb)
Grooming: Extensive
Feeding: Undemanding
Exercise: Moderate
Temperament: Energetic and playful

Miniature Pinscher

The Miniature Pinscher, abbreviated to 'Min Pin', is the smallest version of the pinscher breeds. It stands up to 30cm (12in) high at its withers, and wears a hard, short coat that is easily groomed to shine. It comes in black, blue or chocolate with tan, and also various solid shades of red.

It carries its neat ears either pricked or half-dropped on a stylish head. It is sturdy in body and definite in its way of going, which is like that of a Hackney pony. It gives the impression that it loves being loose in a garden or park; it has quick reactions and makes a useful household watch dog.

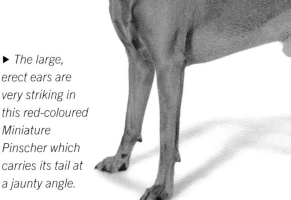

▶ The large, erect ears are very striking in this red-coloured Miniature Pinscher which carries its tail at a jaunty angle.

◀ The black and tan coat is the one most often seen in this toy breed.

Breed box
Size: 25.5–30cm (10–12in), 3.5kg (7½lb)
Grooming: Easy
Feeding: Undemanding
Exercise: Medium
Temperament: Alert and courageous

▲ The front view of the dog shows the neat, straight legs. It may be toy in stature, but it is very athletic in style.

◀ This ancient breed can trace its origins back to the 17th century.

Papillon

The Papillon, or Butterfly Dog, is a
very attractive animal. It stands up to
28cm (11in) tall on neat, trim legs, and
underneath its easily brushed long,
silky coat it has a surprisingly strong
body and fleet feet.

▲ *The tall, fringed ears represent
the butterfly's wings. Puppies are
born with folded ears, but these are
normally erect by 8–12 weeks of age.
Teething can affect ear carriage.*

Breed box
Size: 20–28cm (8–11in),
2–2.5kg (4½–5½lb)
Grooming: Medium
Feeding: Undemanding
Exercise: Medium
Temperament: Lively and
very intelligent

▲ *The white line down the forehead
is said to represent the body of a
butterfly, from which the Papillon
derives its name.*

The coat is a basic white with
patches of a variety of colours,
except liver. The traditional markings
on its head and large, erect ears, with
a neat white stripe down the centre of
its skull and on to its nose, produce a
combined effect resembling the body
and open wings of a butterfly, which
is how it was given its name.

It can be trained to a high level of
obedience and delights in exercise
with the members of its household,
but is not suited to live with very young
children in case it gets trodden on.

▶ *The whole dog is neatly covered
with long, silky hair, but beneath all
the glamour is a highly intelligent and
trainable animal.*

Pekingese

The Pekingese has its roots in ancient China. Tradition tells us that it derives from the palaces of the Tang Dynasty, and this seems to be firmly engrained in its character, although it does show glimpses of a humorous nature on occasion. With a huge personality inside a relatively small body, it is a dog for the devotee.

It has an ideal weight of around 5kg (11lb), with the bitches tending to be heavier than the dogs. Inside an apparently small framework are heavily boned legs. The dog has a broad head and a very short muzzle, which can lead to severe breathing problems; careful selection is necessary to breed healthy 'Pekes', and there are no shortcuts to getting this right.

Exercise is a matter over which a Peke is not ecstatic. It tends to move with a dignified and leisurely roll; consequently, country walks are not a good idea. The coat, which can be of virtually any hue except albino and liver, is long and profuse. It needs regular and dedicated attention to achieve a creditable result.

▶ *Modern Pekes have very pretty heads, and this photograph shows the true beauty of the Peke's expression with its lustrous, soft eyes.*

▼ *Pekingese dogs were at one time carried by ladies of the Chinese court, and were referred to as 'sleeve dogs'. Modern Pekes seem to be aware of their illustrious heritage!*

▲ *Many Pekes have huge coats, but no matter what the dog looks like, it is essential that it can walk freely.*

Breed box
Size: 18cm (7in); male
    maximum 5kg (11lb);
    female maximum 5.5kg (12lb)
Grooming: Demanding
Feeding: Demanding
Exercise: Undemanding
Temperament: Loyal and aloof

Pomeranian

The Pomeranian, or Zwergspitz, is the smallest of all the spitz-type dogs. It weighs up to a mere 2kg (4½lb), with the bitches being slightly heavier. Its abundant stand-off coat is normally a whole colour such as orange, black or cream, through to white. Regular grooming is necessary to achieve the overall look of a ball of fluff.

The margin between sturdiness, which even this tiny breed should possess, and a shell-like delicateness is a fine one, and some breeders find this difficult to achieve. A 'Pom' exhibits a tremendous amount of energy, pirouetting gaily on the end of its lead. It is capable of producing a barrage of fairly shrill yapping, which may deter burglars – and interrupt conversation and gain attention!

▲ The Pomeranian can charm the hardest heart. This tiny character has all the courage of a lion in its eyes.

▼ This family trio is in the best of coats – but do not buy a Pom until you have tried grooming one yourself.

▲ A Pomeranian should have an expression of intelligence and complete confidence in its eyes.

Breed box
Size: 22–28cm (8½–11in), 1.8–2kg (4–4½lb)
Grooming: Demanding
Feeding: Undemanding
Exercise: Undemanding
Temperament: Intelligent and extroverted

Pug

The Pug is a robust aimal weighing up to 8kg (18lb) and packed tightly into a sturdy, compact frame. It wears a short and smoothly glossy coat, which most commonly comes in fawn, but can also appear in apricot, silver or black. It traditionally has a black mask. It is easily kept tidy.

The dog carries its tail tightly curled into a roll on the top of its back, and when it is in its most perky state of alertness, it gives the impression that

it is leaning forward towards whatever its large, lustrous eyes are gazing at.

It is a dog who tends to make people smile when they see it, because it is so convinced of its own importance. For such a stocky dog it can move fast. Its slightly short nose sometimes causes it problems in hot weather as it restricts its breathing, but breeders tend to select for the wide nostrils, which will enable it to exercise as freely as it wishes.

Breed box
Size: 25–28cm (10–11in), 6.5–8kg (14–18lb)
Grooming: Undemanding
Feeding: Medium
Exercise: Medium
Temperament: Lively and cheerful

◀ An ancient breed of miniaturized mastiffs, Pugs were once the companions of Buddhist monks. They arrived in Europe with the Dutch East India Company, and became favoured dogs of the House of Orange.

▲ The stern expression of the Pug belies its real sense of fun.

▶ The tightly curled tail balances the snub nose exactly, to produce a very tidy little dog.

▲ The Pug is adaptable, sociable and good-natured, and makes a good family dog. It is a real charmer.

Yorkshire Terrier

The Yorkshire Terrier is a breed of two distinct types. The tiny version, seen immaculately groomed in the show ring, weighs up to 3.1kg (7lb), while the jaunty dog seen on a lead in the street or racing joyfully around the park is the same dog but often twice the size. The fact is that the long steel-blue and bright tan hair that bedecks the glamour star of the shows would break off and become short if the dog were to run loose. But the spirit of the true 'Yorkie' is the same inside, whatever the outward appearance.

Grooming the household companion — a dog that is immensely popular throughout the world — is easily accomplished with ordinary brushing skills. As a home-loving animal, the Yorkie is tough, ready to play with children, or able to dispatch any rat unwise enough to invade its owner's dwelling.

Breed box
Size: Maximum 3.1kg (7lb); male 20.5cm (8in); female 18cm (7in)
Grooming: Demanding
Feeding: Undemanding
Exercise: Medium
Temperament: Alert and intelligent

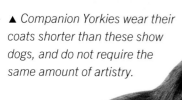

▲ *Companion Yorkies wear their coats shorter than these show dogs, and do not require the same amount of artistry.*

◀ *This elegant display shows canine grooming at its most spectacular. Pet dogs are usually clipped to make coat care easier. This stops the hair falling into the dog's eyes and getting covered with food when eating. A dog coat may be required in cold weather.*

Useful addresses

KENNEL CLUBS

UK
The Kennel Club (KC)
10 Clarges Street
Piccadilly, London W1J 8AB
www.thekennelclub.org.uk

USA
American Kennel Club (AKC)
260 Madison Avenue
New York, NY 10016
www.akc.org

United Kennel Club (UKC)
100 E Kilgore Road
Kalamazoo
MI 49002-5584
www.ukcdogs.com

Canada
Canadian Kennel Club (CKC)
200 Ronson Drive
Suite 400, Etobicoke,
ON, M9W 5Z9
www.ckc.ca

Australia
Dogs Australia
dogsaustralia.org.au

South Africa
Kennel Union of Southern
Africa (KUSA)
PO Box 2659
Cape Town 8000
www.kusa.co.za

India
The Kennel Club of India
(KCI)
No.28/89 AA Block
First Street
Anna Nagar
Chennai 600040
www.kennelclubofindia.org

Japan
Japan Kennel Club (JKC)
www.jkc.or.jp

Worldwide
Fédération Cynologique
Internationale (FCI)
Place Albert 1er,
13. B-6530 Thuin
Belgium
www.fci.be

CHARITABLE ORGANIZATIONS

UK
Blue Cross
Shilton Road, Burford
Oxon OX18 4PF
www.bluecross.org.uk

Dogs Trust
17 Wakley Street
London EC1V 7RQ
www.dogstrust.org.uk

RSPCA
Wilberforce Way
Southwater, Horsham
West Sussex RH13 9RS
www.rspca.org.uk

USA
ASPCA
424 E 92nd Street
New York
NY 10128-6804
www.aspca.org

Canada
Peoples Animal Welfare
Society (PAWS)
23000 Lawrence Avenue East
Box 73039
Toronto, ON, M1P 2R2
www.pawscanada.org

CANINE HEALTH

UK
British Veterinary
Association (BVA)
7 Mansfield Street
London W1G 9NQ
www.bva.co.uk

USA
The Academy of Veterinary
Homeopathy (AVH)
PO Box 232282
Leucadia
CA 92023-2282
theavh.org

Canada
Canadian Veterinary Medical
Association (CVMA)
339 Booth Street
Ottawa
ON, K1R 7K1
www.canadianveterinarians.
net

Worldwide
The World Small Animal
Veterinary Association
(WSAVA)
www.wsava.org

World Veterinary Association
(WVA)
Avenue de Tervueren,
12, B-1040 Brussels
Belgium
www.worldvet.org

DOG TRAINING

UK
Association of Pet Dog
Trainers (APDT)
PO Box 2629
Henfield BN5 0FT
www.apdt.co.uk

USA
Association of Professional
Dog Trainers (APDT)
2365 Harrodsburg Road,
Suite A325, Lexington,
KY 40504
apdt.com

Canada
Canadian Association of
Professional Pet Dog Trainers
(CAPPDT)
3226 Cambourne Crescent
Mississauga, ON L5N 5G2
www.cappdt.ca

Australia
Australian Association of
Professional Dog Trainers
www.aapdt.org

National Dog Trainers
Federation
20 Havelock Road
Bayswater
VIC 3153
ndtf.net.au

Worldwide
COAPE Association of Applied
Pet Behaviourists & Trainers
www.capbt.org

NUTRITION
European Society of
Veterinary & Comparative
Nutrition (ESVCN)
www.esvcn.com

FEDIAF European Pet Food
www.fediaf.org

American College of
Veterinary Nutrition
www.acvn.org

Index

Acknowledgements

This edition is published by Lorenz Books
an imprint of Anness Publishing Ltd
info@anness.com; www.annesspublishing.com
© Anness Publishing Ltd 2023

Publisher: Joanna Lorenz
Editor and layout: Lucy Doncaster
Editorial: Helen Sudell and Felicity Forster
Text: Dr Peter Larkin, Rosie Pilbeam, Mike Stockman (breeds), Patsy Parry (training) and John Hoare (holistic care)
Photography: Robert and Justine Pickett
Additional photography: Jane Burton and John Daniels
Jacket designer: Nigel Partridge
Index: Marie Lorimer
Production: Ben Worley

Although the advice and information in this book are believed to be accurate and true at the time of going to press, neither the authors nor the publisher can accept any legal responsibility or liability for any errors or omissions that may have been made nor for any inaccuracies nor for any loss, harm or injury that comes about from following instructions or advice in this book.

The reader should not regard the recommendations, ideas and techniques expressed and described in this book as substitutes for the advice of a qualified vet or dog training professional. Any use to which the recommendations, ideas and techniques are put is at the reader's sole discretion and risk.

The publishers would like to thank the many dogs who agreed to be photographed for the book and the help of their owners and breeders.

Some material in this book also features in a larger volume, *The Complete Book of Dogs* by Rosie Pilbeam.

All images (c) Anness Publishing Ltd, except as noted. We would also like to thank the following for allowing their photographs to be reproduced in this book (l=left, r=right, t=top, m=middle, b=bottom). Alamy: 102tr, 111t. Ardea: 7br, 150, 181t, 237b. DK Images: 124b, 131bl. Fotolia: 131br. Lucy Doncaster: 60b. SuperStock: 103b. Tracy Morgan Animal Photography: 163br.